"A Soldier's Story"

By

John S. Roberts Jr

CPT, USA, (ret)

Prologue:

"I've always figured the Lord smiles on Soldiers and fools, and my entire life I have been in one set of boots or the other..." John S. Roberts CPT, USA (ret)

I don't know where the above quote came from, it just popped into my head one time, most likely after doing something stupid, but I truly believe it is true and have made it one of the many "mantras" of my life thus far. You are certain to be subjected to many more like this in this book.

Enough philosophy for the moment though, a little more about me personally. I am a nobody, and yet a unique individual. I am one of probably 4 billion others just like me who also feel they are unique. That leads to the question "Why are you writing a book?", that is a fairly easy question to answer because while I do have many similarities to those 4 billion others, I still have some very unique travels, acquaintances, and experiences that make me "stand out" at least a little bit from the masses. These facts along with the few dozen people over the years who have said "you should write a book" made me realize that I may truly have a story to share.

I am under no illusion that I am the next Stephen King or Dean Koontz, or that the New York Bestselling list will be clamoring to get the correct spelling to my name. My only goal in this work is to leave a little part of the so many beautiful, breathtaking, terrifying, frustrating, satisfying experiences to posterity.

I have no doubt that many times throughout this book, the reader will (like some of the great sitcoms like "Roseanne" or "All in the Family") be able to think "Why I've done that" or "I know exactly what that is like." I am sure that for some, there will be some educational parts in this text as well, working to either help, or prevent others from journeying down the same path in their journeys. I would like to say this will be an entire work of non-fiction, but alas my memory (like everyone else's) "fills in the blanks" where the big gaping holes left by a few too many scotch on the rocks, purple mescaline and sinsemilla are now.

If nothing else good comes of this "literary gem", at least my children and their children's children with have some insight on what "Dad's" (referred too frequently by the kids as "Boomer" "John Juan" or "Grandpa") life was like during his allocated time slot in history.

So, sit back, enjoy and daydream away!

For my son:

Jonathan Sidney Roberts, 1988-2020

I love and miss you so

Table of Contents

Chapter 1: "It all begins"

My earliest memories are in the back seat of a car, very early in the morning. Always had a great feeling, the city was quiet, the streets were empty, mom and dad were quiet as well as we moved quickly down the dark, empty streets. The radio was always on, albeit at very low volume, playing the greatest AM hits of the day. This morning's memory has me thinking of Petula Clark singing "Downtown" Despite being very young, I still remember thinking "How appropriate" it was for this song to be ringing out helping Baltimore "wake up" on what for most, like my parents at the time, was just another workday.

It was a new decade, the 70's and what I didn't realize then was how difficult the economy was for young families, like the one I was a member of, to make ends meet and not literally go hungry. Both my parents were at a particular disadvantage as neither of them had so much as a complete High School education. My mother had a difficult childhood. Her biological father, an alcoholic womanizer walked out on his wife and 4 kids when they were all very young. My Grandmother Edna, being a divorcee (which was extremely stigmatized during that era), could only secure work as a waitress in one of the local diners. Despite repeated court attempts to bring her deadbeat husband to court to obtain some form of support to raise those children, none were successful. This left my Grandmother Edna with as difficult a decision as any young mother could ever face. As there was no way she could feed or cloth her children on a waitress salary and tips she was forced to give mom, my aunts, and uncle up for foster care. My mother and Aunt Pat were kept together in one foster home, while my Aunt Shirley and Uncle Steve were sent to another. No doubt this situation influenced my mother's next course of action in life. Probably because of this, at age 21, she had already dropped out of school after the 9th grade, became pregnant and subsequently married at age 16. Naturally, this marriage ended in divorce after only two years due to her "husbands" alcohol abuse and subsequent physical abuse. It's funny how they say women will inadvertently be attracted to male figures resembling their father. It was not so funny in regard to my mother's choice of her first husband. My father, despite being intelligent, did not like the structured environment of high school and small-town life in Reed City. So, once he turned 17 (and completed the 10th Grade) he dropped out of high school to begin a career in the Navy as his father before him had. A few years later, his time in the service ended. With his honorable discharge in his hand, he was a civilian again. Unfortunately, he was also a civilian with only a 10th grade education. The opportunities for people in this situation were limited. At least not having a high school diploma did not carry the social stigma in the 60's that it started to carry the very next decade and beyond.

I always remembered Dad and Mom working very hard. Mom was working the early shift at Metropolitan Box Company assembling shipping boxes and Dad was working some other fairly menial job in the area as well. We were, by any standards, poor. Not as poor as many others though. I never went hungry, and I always had clothing that was in good repair. I do remember eating a lot of food that came out of black and white boxes and cans from someplace called the 'Department of Agriculture" whatever that place was. I also remember mom and dad waiting until we were finished eating before they would sit down to eat. They always said, "Were busy at the moment, you kids eat and we'll be there in a few minutes." Although I did not realize it then, I know now it was because there was only limited food and they wanted to make sure us kids had all we wanted to eat before they sat down to what was left. We lived in a type of housing referred to as "row housing" or "townhouses" in what was known to all as a "checkerboard" area. We were surrounded by Pollacks, Niggers, WOP's, Jews and "those Catholic families" with ten and eleven kids or so. Although this reads incredibly racist by today's standards, it never felt that was back then. All of "us" were pretty much in the same boat of struggle, too busy worrying about how any of us were paying the next month's rent of keep ourselves fed. The good part about townhouse living is you tend to be close and know a lot about your neighbors, whether you wanted to or not. There were rows of double and triple level structures, all attached to each other, going down entire blocks in a row. In the fronts were nice little entryways, two or three steps with a wrought iron railing. In the back a little fence divided each little yard. At the back of each little yard ran the alley. Across from that alley was the long fence that was the back of the next row of townhouses on the next street.

These front porches and alleys were where the entire "social life" of tenement dwellers occurred. We had a great Catholic family on one side of us, who had more kids than I remember being able to count. They were nice folks though. They would sit on their front porch and drink coffee. This was very strange to me as EVERYONE in Maryland drank tea. Of course, the tea they drank was the “hot” version, the habit carried over from ol’ England so many years ago. This was the very beginning of my obsession sf drinking tea the rest of my life. I switched from the hot version to the iced tea version which helped me became more “Michiganized” in the years down the road. Two cups of black coffee in the morning, shortly thereafter followed by keeping a glass of iced tea in my hand the rest of the day. But I digress, which I will do frequently throughout this text. Memories are funny that way. It was from these nice Catholic folks, right there on their front porch, I tasted my first “cup of coffee”. I remember not being that impressed with it. Little did I know at the time that it wouldn’t be too many years and tea would go out the window and that bitter, bitter coffee would become my morning drink of choice for the rest of my life! There was always a great smell coming from their house as one of their “side gigs” was making candles! I remember looking in awe at the many different colors, shapes, number of wicks, and scents of candles that frequently covered their entire kitchen table. Despite their home being elbow-to-elbow people, I honestly never remember hearing a coarse word or tone coming through their wall. I wish I could say the same about the black couple who lived on the ”other wall” of our house. The only time there wasn’t screaming or yelling was when there was just simple arguing going on. This was entertainment sometimes though, because the walls between these homes were sufficiently thin, that you didn’t have to wonder what people were talking or arguing about as you could truly make the words out through the wall. I wonder now what memories our family left those folks with so many years ago. The backyards and alleys were where everyday life really played out though. Everything happened back there. The little back porches facing the yards always had folks sitting on them. Smoking, drinking, barbecuing and usually laughing. Everyone was at least acquainted with their neighbors for two or three houses on either side of yours. The alleys were the arteries for these townhomes as well. Your trash was picked up there, anything good that came delivered in the back of a truck was solicited back there as well. My favorites were on the rare occasion there was a little extra money to stop the ice cream truck for a treat, or maybe even the "Crab truck" for dinner. You could get a dozen or two of the best steamed blue channel crabs right off the back of the truck in the alley. There were usually a lot of parked cars back there as well, some that would never move again until the wrecker hauled them to the salvage yard. We always had loads of fun playing in the alleys. Those alleys never felt dangerous as during the day everyone on either side could see clearly into them. It was common knowledge to all kids though, once the street lights went out, it was time to go home and leave the alleys to the drunks, junkies, prostitutes and other miscreants of the night. Occasionally, in the middle of the night you would see the police car lights back there, or the occasional whine of the ambulance siren, but when the sun came out, all was swept away, clean and ready for another day of play.

My mother's family was all living in the local area, and we always had a lot of great visits and spent quality time with them while we called Baltimore our home. Most times Dad was always at work, but Mom was usually between jobs and had more free time, so it was her that would take us to visit. We would spend time with my great-grandmother Swann who had this awesome tri-level townhouse that was only one room wide but went up 3 floors and had a basement for a total of 4 levels to play “hide and seek” on. My Aunt Pat and Grandmother Edna were always there as well. I remember Grandma Swann’s townhouse being so fascinating as each “level” was like its own antique store on to itself. The best part of these visits was that my mother’s entire family used to coordinate these visits so everyone could catch up at the same time. This meant getting to catch up with my cousins as well. While the ladies were at the table, cackling over tea and Tareyton cigarettes, we kids would just roam free between the floors and have a grand old time. The most important thing about these “meetings” was that they ended by 1 or 2 pm in the afternoon prompt. This was so the wives had time to get home and ensure the houses were cleaned and the dinner was on the table by the time my father got home. I never recall spending a tremendous amount of time with my father during these years as he worked literally every waking hour to make sure my mom, sister, brothers and I never went without at least the bare necessities. Even so, I never recall ever hearing a word of complaint, and it instilled in me a work ethic I carried my entire adult life. When he was home, he was usually exhausted and just caught up on some sleep. I always remember looking up to him in awe, love, respect and fear. Yes, you read correctly fear. These were long before the days of man buns, feelings, warm fuzzies and interventions. You either “towed the line” or your father would clean your clock. The most frightening thing of all was that one tool your mother wielded over you. That terrifying phrase “You wait till I tell your father when he gets home what you did” I remember being asked many times in various counseling or mental health sessions “Did your father ever hit you?” I am always like

"Are you kidding me? My father would whip my ass!" BUT, and key point here, I never, ever received an ass-whipping I didn't ask for, EVER. And praise the Lord, my mother, God rest her soul, never told my father more than 2% of the time she had actually said "You wait till I tell your father…."

My father's life wasn't entirely work though. We had some of the best family friends that anyone in life could ask for. Almost all of the friends my folks made in Baltimore they kept for the rest of all of their lives. Many a Saturday night was spent either at these friends' houses or at ours. Cards, beer, cigarettes and enough "bullshit" to fill a semi-truck were always a part of these social events. Rob and Trudy were one the couples who I always enjoyed these visits with. The things I remember of them most in those days was they had two daughters who were a little older than the rest of us and always seemed so streetwise to me. They also had an entire basement full of fish tanks. Miss Trudy LOVED her pet fish and had every size, color, shape and type of them in the 20 or so tanks she maintained in her basement. Interesting point to note here as well, notice in the previous sentence I refer to "Miss Trudy"? In those days children NEVER referred to adults by their first name alone. Adults that you had little or no acquaintance with you referred simple to as "Sir" or "ma'am", but that group of adults who you may be more acquainted with in a friendly manner you could use their first names, but ALWAYS with 'Mister" or "Miss" in front of. This covered your bases as far as showing the respect that was required while remaining less personal than "Sir or ma'am". This was the East Coast solution to "Mr……" or "Mrs…… While on the same topic it is important to note that aunts and uncles were always referred to as "Aunt" or "Uncle", to not do so was the equivalent of uttering an obscenity. I only went partly though kindergarten while we were in Baltimore and I remember it being a long walk. I remember some particular things about that walk as well. There were a lot of alleys and two or three storm and sewer streams that ran along side the alleys I had to walk down. I remember jumping into a couple of those “streams” on a couple of those walks when it was particularly hot. When I think of how polluted those little waterways was that I was flopping around in with my friends it’s a miracle that none of us didn’t contract some raging infection, but I guess kids are resilient right? Another fun thing I remember was pretending to be a “miner” there were a lot of areas where sulfur was naturally right near the surface and my friends and I would use regular spoons and “mine” the yellow, stinky, flaky stuff. It was really fun when you could sneak off with a match because it burned a really neat color and smelled like brimstone. The things that amuse children vary widely depending on where they are located.

This was an interesting time historically as well. Vietnam was still raging away, and Nixon and Vice-President Spiro T Agnew were occupying the White House. Now normally a child would have no real recollection of who the President was or give two shits what was going on outside of the small microcosm of their existence. My experience was a little different for a couple of reasons. My father had just gotten out of the Navy about the time Vietnam really started becoming an “American issue”. As such, he never had to worry about being drafted as being an honorably discharged Veteran and having three little kids put him about as far down the list as you could get for the draft. Unfortunately, the same could not be said for a lot of his friends and acquaintances. His older brother was still serving in the United States Marine Corps and went for his first of what would become three combat tours there. My uncle was drafted and sent abroad as well, he returned as so many others did, killed over there and didn't even know it. He turned to cocaine and alcohol to keep his demons at bay. It didn't take too long before my aunt had had enough of this and divorced him, despite having to then bring up two kids on her own. I heard seven or eight years later, his heart just exploded from cocaine abuse. I guess he put his demons to rest for the last time by age 35. I do remember, despite how history might judge him in later years, everyone loved President Nixon and applauded his efforts to get America out of the shitstorm of Vietnam he had inherited from his predecessor L.B.J. And Nixon's Vice-President Spiro T Agnew, who history would truly exposed and being a complete crook a few years later, was loved by everyone in the area, as his job before the White House was as Governor of Maryland. My greatest memory of this White House administration was an elementary school class project. The teacher instructed all of us to write a letter to President Nixon, just to cheer the guy up I guess. My little brain started turning, thinking "why he's going to get so many letters he'll never even read mine!", Then it occurred to me, "Why I'll write to the VICE-PRESIDENT, that will get my letter read!". So away I go, and penned a little script to old "Spiro T." I got it approved by the teacher and addressed it to "Vice President of America, Washington DC.." Sure enough, a month or so later while the rest of my class had long forgotten their class project, a letter arrived from Washington DC TO ME! I can't remember exactly what the letter said, except that Spiro was glad to hear from me, and hoped I was doing well. The thing I remember most was the fact it had a REAL signature from him on it! Not stamped, not by a secretary, but by Spiro T himself! I had no way of knowing that was probably one of the last letters he would ever write on White House stationary as shortly thereafter he was fired and subsequently charged with racketeering, extortion and a host of other charges from his tenure in Maryland. None of that mattered to me then, or now. I would saw my left leg off to get my hands on that letter today but it, like so many things in my past are long, long gone.

There was always a newspaper in the house and my parents were glued to Walter Cronkite every evening on channel 3 at 530 pm. Walter Cronkite WAS the "news" to America and if he said it, you believed it. Watched him till the day he finally, officially went off the air. Probably good for him that he is in the "great newsroom in the sky" as he would roll in his grave seeing how "news" has been transformed into "pure propaganda" anymore, but I digress (again)... Even in "hometown" America it was troubled times. The race riots in many of the inner cities were still fresh in everyone's mind, and poverty and unchecked pollution were the prevailing current of the day. My Uncle Fred finished his tours in Vietnam and came home as emotionally fucked up as everyone else I suppose. One thing a military training does make you good at was becoming a cop. Uncle Fred went from the U.S.M.C. to the Los Angeles Police Department. He was thrown from one combat zone right into another as the riots were in full swing in L.A. He did well though and would spend his entire career as a police officer in the California area. My father also tried his luck, being a veteran, at a career in law enforcement. He was fast tracked through the Baltimore police academy and earned his badge. These were the days before patrol cars I suppose in the inner cities and officers like my father “walked the beat.” It scared my mother to death everytime he went to work at night. Apparently one evening walking his beat he comes across an individual walking with two bags of groceries in his hands. This might not seem peculiar if it hadn’t been 2 a.m and every grocery store in town had closed hours before. Naturally my father stopped him to ask what was going on. Immediately the guy drops the groceries and makes a grab for dad’s service revolver on his hip. Apparently around 15 seconds and 30 or 40 baton strikes to this guys head and he was down in a pool of blood waiting for the patrol car to haul him off to jail. For years afterwards, compliments of this incident, the only thing I would hear from my father about people of African descent was “how thick those nigger’s skull were.” My father wasn’t really a bigot per se’ as he held no hatred of anyone simply based on the color of their skin. It was simply a different era and those were terms everyone used. Fortunately for me, I would be personally exposed to persons of color once I went into the military and able to shake all the premonitions I had been raised with. Of course, by the time dad got home his shirt was covered with blood and when my mother saw it she almost passed out. She had no way of knowing it wasn’t his blood on it when she first saw it. My brother and I were younger than 4 years old and my mother sat each night on pins and needles wondering if that night she was to become a widow with two babies. She pleaded with my father to change careers for her mental health. As much as he enjoyed that line of work, he sympathized with her and turned his resignation in to the Baltimore P.D. It was in this environment that my father, finally realizing he probably was not going to realize his fortunes in the big city decided to return “home”. Home, for him, was a small town in West Central Michigan (Lower peninsula, important to note if you know anything about Michigan) called Reed City.

Reed City is a small town, good or bad, that I will always end up and refer to as 'where I'm from" or "home" as well. This is the place where my real childhood memories are made. Baltimore was wonderful and planted the proverbial seed as to many of my thoughts and opinions about people and life but is still just a side note of my childhood. I felt like it was important to include because a lot of the opinions and attitudes I developed in the "big city" were at the very least problematic for life in the small town, and at the most made me socially exclusive. My mother really struggled on our move to Michigan. She was a big city girl through and through. Considering that she had convinced my father to leave the Baltimore P.D. she really couldn't argue too much about her husband wanting to return "home" to his family area. But before that time, I don't believe she had ever really spent significant time in a small town let alone lived in one. To say she experienced some culture shock would be the understatement of the year. I have no doubt my mother did not want to leave Baltimore or her family then, or ever. But again, times were different, the phrase "Father knows Best" wasn't just a TV sitcom, it was a mantra and as such there really was never any debate of whether we were moving once my father's mind was made up. My mother had said many, many times throughout her life, "Where my husband goes, I follow" and Lord knows she did. Despite the next 52 years she would live in Michigan, she kept that Maryland accent to the day she died. It was toned down a lot when surrounded by Michigan folks with their "accent", but it was always there. It was particularly humorous that when we would visit friends from Maryland, or I would hear her talking on the telephone to someone "back home" (to her anyway) that accent would step right to the forefront just like she was speaking at the market downtown. The one remaining contact I would love from Maryland was a little gift my grandmother "Nan" would send me from time to time. A Lipton tea bag box filled with Crab shells! I do not to this day know why they fascinated me so much, but they did, and in addition always truly amazed all my new childhood Michigan friends who had never seen such a strange thing in their life! They still had that glorious smell of the Old Bay seasoning they had been tenderly steamed and ultimately devoured in.

Reed City was a wonderful place to be a kid. It would become for me, the place that everyone has, that they fondly recall their "childhood" in. It wasn't a bad place to be a grown up either. Much like every other small town, there are 5 or 6 last names there, that pretty much comprise 80% of the entire population. The other 20% could usually be counted to on even be "related" to one of those last names through lineage that sometimes grew very thin. Long story short, everyone there knows, or knows of, everyone else. The Roberts family had been a part of the fabric of Reed City virtually since its founding in the 1860's. My great-great grandfather Mertz (on my great grandmothers side) collected his 80 acres just north of the town, as grateful payment for his service to the "Grand Army of the Republic" Shortly thereafter, he found a widow woman whose husband had received his 80 acres for service as well. Unfortunately for him, and fortunately for great, great grandpappy he didn't live long enough to enjoy it. So, Great, Great Grandpappy decided he would kill the proverbial 'two birds with one stone" and married this widow. This made their combined farm a respectable 160 acres. This sounds like a great tract of land by today's standards, but it was the bare minimum in those days to scratch out enough to keep you and your family fed. Unbeknownst to many, Michigan isn't the greatest farmland in the country by any standard. In fact, the term "Hillbilly" is defined in Websters dictionary as "A Michigan Farmer". My new pioneering ancestor's family did well for themselves and had two fine boys, my Grandfather Fred and his brother Henry. Once Fred was 17 years old or so, his father told him "Why don't you go down the road and talk to that farmer and ask him for one of his 8 daughters for a wife". Fred did just that and in his own words "I looked at the youngest one, whom I thought was the prettiest and asked that farmer if I could take her to the altar" He said "yes" and away Fred and Lillian went to get married. These were long before the days of love, devotion and choice were essential to the institution of marriage. Marriage was an absolute necessity because without a spouse, you could not have children and without children it's hard to tend a poorly soiled160 acres of farm! This was assuming you were still either young or healthy enough to even try. No children also meant that you had a 50/50 chance of going hungry in your old age as this was also long before the days of "social programs". But a good wife, a few great kids and you could be assured of being surrounded by and cared for by loving family members until the Lord decided you would draw your last breath. Once Fred had married though, he decided the farming life was not for him and since his brother could help "ma and pa" tend the farm, he pursued a different career path. He was not only the main auto mechanic in Reed City, but he also served as a deputy sheriff for Osceola County for many years. I would hear many stories about great grandpa's time in a uniform from his son, my grandfather. It was that crazy time in American history when all alcohol was considered "vice" and a constitutional amendment made alcohol illegal in these United States. That time was called "Prohibition." It was well known that EVERYONE continued to drink alcohol during prohibition. This alcohol was generally manufactured locally by some enterprising folks who would set up a "still" out in the woods somewhere. Naturally these stills were all illegal and if discovered by law enforcement, promptly destroyed. This destruction was usually performed by the local sheriff departments, my great grandfather included. Since everyone drank and you had to buy you're your booze from the local manufacturer, it would be considered a "conflict of interest" if a person was to buy booze from a guy and then have to destroy his still the following week if anyone found out about it. All the local sheriffs found a simple solution to this dilemma. You would never buy your booze from within the county your law enforcement jurisdiction was in. You would simply drive to the next county to purchase your "medicine." I guess more than a few times, my great grandfather Fred and the deputy sheriff from Lake County would pass each other on (what was to become in a few years) US-10 and wave at each other. Both smiled knowing exactly what they were on the road to do. Another incident involved old Ernie Finkbeiner up on the hill just outside of town. Apparently ol' Ernie got drunker than shit one Saturday night and beat the shit out of his wife. Great Grandpappy was dispatched to go out and pick him up and haul him to jail. Since the other deputy was on another run, Grandpappy told his son (my then 14 year old grandfather Sidney) to drive him in the squad car out there to get this done. Once they arrived ol' Ernie thought he might not want to go to jail and put up a little scuffle. It didn't take a moment and grandpappy had him face down in the dirt with his hands behind his back. He told Sidney "Bring them handcuffs over here and put them on him." Well, when Sidney went to put the cuffs on him, ol' Ernie turned his head to the side and bared his teeth a little bit. Grandpappy said with the slightest of breath "you don't even want to think about biting my boy" and I guess ol' Ernie turned white as a sheet, put his head quietly back down in the dirt and was hauled off to jail. At any given time most of the occupants of the county jails were there with alcohol related offenses, mostly just drunk and disorderly. They would get a 3-day sentence and be set loose to repeat the cycle over and over. Of course the hardest of the alcoholics would begin to suffer with delirium tremors in a day or so, and rather than have them screaming, hollering and suffering the jailer had a remedy for them too. It wasn't alcohol, remember that was illegal, but they did keep a bottle of formaldehyde compliments of the local undertaker. The jailer would just give the old drunk a tablespoon of formaldehyde and that would keep their demons away until they were set loose to find that next bottle. Fred and Lillian would go on to be blessed with 4 kids, two boys (my Grandfather Sidney and his brother "Butch") and two girls (Marjorie and Vita). He worked his entire career in Reed City and once retired stayed as well. He and my great grandmother Lillian were one of the "Grand Marshalls" for the Reed City Centennial parade in 1975. Great, great grandpappy Mertz was long deceased by the time we arrived in Reed City, but my Great Grandfather Fred and wife Lillian still happily lived in the same house on Stimson Street next to the church that they had by then occupied for the last 60 years. In Reed City, "Roberts" was one of the last names that occupied 3 or 4 pages of the 15 page "Reed City, Leroy, Evart, Hersey and Ashton" telephone book. In 1940, my grandfather Sidney would marry into one of those 6 most prevalent last names in the local phone book, by the name of "Preston." I always considered it a blessing to have a grandfather (Sidney, who would become Osceola Counties longest living resident before his death at age 100) who was a walking Osceola County historian and more than a few great stories. One of grandpappy's favorites was the time when the rail spur had just moved into Reed City and his grandfather (the GAR Veteran and gentlemen with the wife and 4 kids mentioned above) decided that old train was no match for his great mare "Marge" and decided he would show that conductor which one was faster! Needless to say ol' "Marge" took a commanding lead early on, but the one thing that can be said about trains that you cannot say about horses is that they "run out of steam" My great-great grandfather and "Marge" are long gone, (I can show you where they lay up on R.C's Boot hill with the other 6 generations of my family) but the railroad would remain a vital part of Reed City for the next 70 years or so. This is my first knowledge of the extensive military lineage my family (and soon enough myself) would be a part of. In addition to having a service member as part of the G.A.R., my grandfather would serve in World War II in the Navy, his brother Butch in the Army. I know that service to our great Nation was on both the paternal and maternal side of my family. I was told (and shown the marker in the cemetery of) that my grandmother Leyvonne's father was a member of the Calvary and was with good old Teddy Roosevelt during the historic charge up San Juan Hill in Puerto Rico. Of the 4 sons my grandfather Sidney had (Fred, John, Bruce and Kirk) three would end up spending time in the Armed Forces. It was apparent early on that I too would become a part of this proud heritage. My personal experiences will be shared in the chapters ahead. I still have an entire childhood experience to share in these pages. I believe this background is important though because for everyone it's "Where you've been makes you who you are."

Now despite the fact we had never lived in Reed City, once we arrived, we "knew" everyone there and everyone "knew" us. This had some real advantages for my family. Another thing all small-town American locations shared was that there was always one (two sometimes if a town was prosperous and strategically located) factory, or workplaces that provided employment for virtually every person in town. Reed City was fortunate that it was located at the intersection of the two main throughfares of West Central Michigan and as such had two great employment locations. My father, by the nature of his last name, landed a position in one of these locations, the Gardner-Denver corporation. We moved into a great little house in town right on the corner of Upton Street and Osceola Avenue. There were kids in virtually every other house located on this block and I rapidly developed friendships with them. I believe this was as close to being financially comfortable as my parents would ever be in their entire lives. Reed City really was a bustling little town back then. It was the Osceola County seat and had all the establishments that made small town life enjoyable. For a while Reed City even had its own fully functioning hospital right in town. My brother Chris was born in that old original building. Reed City had some of the great stores as well. It had A & P and an IGA for grocery shopping, Ben Franklins and a 5 & 10 Store for all kinds of little things. There were two hardware stores and two fine drinking establishments where every man would congregate after a hard week (or days in some men's case) work. There was the "Buckboard Bar" which was where the rougher crowd congregated, and then there was "Henry's". Henrys was the "working man's" place. It was very much like the TV sitcom "Cheer's." The main exception being it was only about a third of the size. I remember it having a large antique wooden bar with the bend in it. This bar was of the size to maybe seat 10 to 15 patrons at any given time, and each of these seats was guaranteed to be full by 7pm on any given Friday night. There were maybe 3 or 4 little tables in the room as well with seating for 4 folks at each. As I recall, there was also a pool hall across the street from Henry's with rows of pool tables and they charged "by the ½ hr and hour" rates. The sidewalks of town were usually full on the weekends and everything in town was well within walking distance. Michigan's US-131 was a major throughout fare and ran right through the center of town. Reed City did have one unique item (well, 6 actually) that I never saw anywhere else in America or the world for that matter. Located on Upton Avenue, (the name for Main Street in RC) on each side of the road, one on each end of the block and one in the center, there were 3 cement artesian drinking fountains. These were roughly 2' around and 3' high, with one 3/8" diameter copper pipe that ran right up the center. There were no valves or handles required to operate these, the water just flowed from the top of the pipe and then ran back into the drains inside the fountains. These ran 24/7 for many, many years and on the quietest of mornings in addition to the streetlight changing, you could also hear these fountains just bubbling away. Although Reed City was no stranger to the bitterest of Michigan Winters, these fountains never froze over as I recall but would have the most beautiful "ice statues" along the sides of them. The train ran through town twice a day like clockwork, but after living in town about a week or so, (Unless you lived on 5th Avenue which ran directly adjacent to the tracks) you never even noticed the whistle of it anymore. Of course, us kids did the same as the past 3 generations of the kids before us and created some incredible "works of art" with these railroad tracks This was accomplished by placing pennies or nickels on the tracks and being amazed when we returned the next day to find them completely flattened.

As I had stated earlier the best part about Reed City as a kid was you could walk anywhere and everywhere. Naturally during all this walking kids will migrate towards each other and soon become friends, or enemies, but acquaintances regardless! My childhood was no exception. My best friends in the whole world lived about half a block up the street on Upton Avenue, the Carvers. There were seven kids in this family and naturally two of them were approximately the same age as I was. Even as a child you knew enough just by observation how good or not so well a family was fairing. The Carvers gave a new definition to being poor. You see, their father had walked out on the mother and seven kids a few years earlier leaving Mother Violet alone to raise, support and attempt to maintain order over the entire gang. The one glimmer of hope she had was that she did have a good job, as she was a registered nurse. She worked right in town at the Reed City hospital. I never saw this poor woman looking anything but utterly exhausted the few times she was actually able to be home. I truly believed she ran on nothing but coffee, Pall Mall cigarettes and pure necessity. The house was always a disaster, filled with clutter, clothes, toys and dirty dishes as the poor woman literally worked every waking moment of her life. This was certainly exhausting and excruciating for her, but it was GREAT for us kids! Why is that you might ask? What is better than having a whole house to just run roughshod in with no adult supervision to do or play or go anywhere you wanted to! Somewhere during all this play time, I took my first taste of a cigarette compliments of her Pall Mall's that were pretty much lying everywhere. With my new friends I also got my first real exposure to the style of music I would come to love the rest of my life. The two oldest girls in the house were in their late teens and on the few rare occasions they left their bedrooms, their albums and portable record player could be absconded to add a "soundtrack" to our play. Elton John's "Yellow Brick Road" and Alice Coopers "Billion Dollar Babies" were still on the hit list then and we played them repeatedly. Both these albums are in my iPhone this very day and I enjoy not only the music still, but these great childhood memories every time I listen to them. We, like all kids of the era, were never inside the house anyway when it was daylight and not raining outside. There was way too much to explore in town, and we knew every backyard path, alleyway, and shortcut to get to any and every place fun. Many of our favorite adventures involved water. Reed City, in addition to being ideally located at that intersection, was also blessed by having the Hersey River, a state recognized trout river, running right through it. In the Summertime, swimming and fishing were always the order of the day. I was told that the river was horribly polluted, compliments of a creosote factory that was in Reed City 90 years earlier manufacturing railroad ties. The state of Michigan had recommended that you didn't eat too much of the fish or swim in the water but as I stated above, we paid no mind to either warning and are none the worse for wear because of it. Another favorite adventure of ours was little pond we referred to as "Pecos Pond."

Now how it got that name I have no idea and I'm not even sure I could find it if it still existed today, but I have great memories of it. I do remember it was probably a mile outside of town and you could follow the railroad tracks west of town to take you almost right to it. A mile is a long way when you're a little kid and it seemed to be almost an hour walk to get there. It was always worth it though because "Pecos Pond" was full of as many bluegills as you could care to catch. In fact, they were so overpopulated that you didn't even require bait to catch them as these small fish would strike on a shiny hook or even a small piece of tin foil attached to a hook once it caught the sun just a little to sparkle. We caught many of these as well as more trout, and the occasional pike or bass, out of the Hersey River than I could ever count.

The Reed City public schools were only a couple of blocks walk away from my house and had a huge playground to enjoy. There were no fences around anything, and we could go and play anytime we liked for as long as we liked. It was important to watch your step though or where you rode your bike across the playground though. Marbles was the big elementary school game at the time and your social status was completely dependent on how many "Boulders", "Pearlies" or "Steelies" you had in the little bag you carried with you everywhere at school. Playing this game required digging a small "cup" or hole in the ground (Think roughly one-third of a golf course hole) around which a circle was drawn in the sand around 6" out and each opponent would take a turn trying to "flick" a marble into the depression you just created in the earth. The first player to get the marble in there, got to keep both marbles. When 50 to 100 kids have this set up in the school yard for play every recess, the playground took the appearance of a miniature World War I French battlefield. Each day was filled with the fun and wonder of an eternal youth, and those days ended only when the automatic street lights came on in town. This was the unspoken rule for generations of kids. When those lights came on, your little ass better be in the house or in the yard where your parents could see you.

It was during these wonderful years I recall taking my first interest in members of the "fairer sex". My buddy Chuck and I had a couple of girls, Pam and Tracy, that we decided to ask (via the small, folded paper with the "yes" or "no" boxes written on it) to be our "girlfriends". They said "yes" and all four of us got our first initiations into the world of love, lust and sex. Of course, none of the three ever actually occurred to speak of. One of the girls had a garage with a loft, and up there all four of us would climb, retreat to two different corners to perform clumsy attempts at doing what we had heard was "sex". It was just a lot of kissing, I did learn about French kissing there, and a less than innocent hand slipped up a shirt or down a pair of pants was as far as that ever went. A short time later, the novelty of all this wore off and the focus shifted to getting back over to the playground to score big on some marbles. More than a few times we would "spend the night" over at a friend's house, and it was always the recipe for a great time when I stayed at Chucks. We usually always stayed at his place since his mother worked midnights at her second (or third) job and we could stay up all night, sneak a pall mall or two and listen to music. At my house we were NEVER left unsupervised, and this translated into a boring evening of a little television and early bedtime. One of these grand evenings, Chuck and I decided around 3 am we would like to go for a bicycle ride, and away we went! We had a blast, riding down the middle of main street, not a car in sight, nothing but the sound of the traffic lights and water fountains. It was so invigorating and exciting on a warm Summer night. That was until it turned to terror, you see, Reed City, (also like every other small town) had its own police force and it wasn't long until we saw Chief Warsteiner's headlights coming down the street. We did not stick around to see what he would have had to say about this "adventure." Reed City had a youth curfew (10 pm every night for anyone under 16 signaled by a tone from the fire station) that we were clearly in violation of. We bolted down the back streets and paths to get our asses back to Chucks place and quietly got back in the house, Scot free! Another day, one of our great adventures involved the brand-new Catholic Church built right next to the 5th grade school building. We just so happened to be playing "hooky" from that day so we were not in class but instead trying to find places where we would not be seen or noticed. A short 50 or 60 yards from the main sanctuary building and rectory there was a small building, more like a walled-up closet, just out there by itself. Of course, being curious youth, we were wondering "What in the hell is that?" Immediately we knew we would have to more closely investigate. Once we arrived at the little enclosure, we pulled the side door open and slipped in. Why all that was inside of that building was a bell. I guess that's different than most Church's which place them high up inside a steeple. While under examination a small noise began to emanate from the circuitry and the bell started to move. We went tearing out of there and back across the field as the bell rang and rang away behind us. We knew we were in trouble, how was the Priest going to explain to the flock why they had been called to mass in the middle of a weekday? One thing we did realize, which was surprising for our age at the time, was that facing up to the issue rather than trying to duck it may be the only way to keep us in good graces with the Lord and the Catholic Church. We headed back towards the rectory and located the door marked "Priest Office." With heavy hearts, guilty consciouses, and shaking knees we knocked on the door. Naturally the Priest invited us in and with all the honesty we could muster we admitted that it was us, fooling around with the bell and causing it to go off to signal the beginning of mass. The Priest, with the strangest expression on his face, could not keep himself from bursting into laughter. He went on to explain, "Boys, while I admire your courage and your honesty, you had nothing to do with that bell going off, it does that EVERY DAY at noon"; of course our reply was "Why?", to which the Priest got a great big smile on his face and replied ""I'm not sure boys, to scare the hell out of the birds I suppose" We both were shocked to actually hear a Priest say what we thought was a "swear" word. Oh, the innocence of youth. I was also a very active member of the Boy Scouts for a few years there. Troop 74 of Reed City was blessed to have a few of the greatest scoutmasters any group could ask for, we had Mr. Knauf, who reminded us of Elmer Fudd with his short, rotund stature and the ever-present cigar, Mr. Weinrich, another older gentleman with his long, "handlebar" mustache, and Mr. Ruggert. Mr. Ruggert had a speech impediment which seemed strange to us as children. What we did not know is that impediment was due to the fact he was deaf and communicated fully with us, by his ability to read lips. These three gentlemen were the kindest, most patient men with us boys and were very wise in all things Scouting and outdoors. I probably spent at least as much time with these men (or more) and my fellow scouts than I spent with my father at the time. This was because he always worked long hours to keep us all fed. Many wonderful weekends were spent scouting, camping and exploring. Mr. Knauf had a wonderful piece of property in the woods with a cabin on it. It also had an outdoor sauna building as well. This was where we went to perform our winter scouting skills and I got to experience the joys of going from sitting in a balmy 180 degrees, then jumping into a 30-degree snowbank. A very short 3 seconds later you would run back into the 180 degrees. Surprisingly, when you first jump into the snowbank you do not feel cold as the snow that stuck to you immediately melted and turned you into a large cloud of steam. It was at precisely that moment that the sensation of cold hit you. If you you can repeat this pattern two or three times, you are as sparkly clean and refreshed as the Good Lord can make you and will sleep like a stone that night. Another great memory I had from my scouting years was the week I spent at camp and Camp Greilick (most certainly not to be confused with the Army's Camp Grayling) in Northern Michigan. It was a wonderful, fun filled week. Each day had a schedule of activities and the opportunity to obtain many merit badges was available. Many of those badges, like "Sailing" or "Archery" I would have had no way of getting back home as I had no access to the required devices used. I think I ended up getting the better part of 10 merit badges that week which was phenomenal. I still vividly remember the beautiful, massive lodge building where we all would have our meals, and I learned the meaning and taste of "Bug juice.' It was fortunate that the Boy Scouts did have financial assistance for Scouts in regards to the cost of camp or I would have never been able to attend. It was also because of this financial assistance that I was able to attend one of the largest events Scouting hosts every year, the "National

Jamboree." This is usually a lifetime event for a scout, and I had the good fortune that the year I was in Scouting it was being hosted in Mackinaw City in Northern Michigan. I will never forget the sights, sounds and smell of hundreds of small campfires on the beach, with the "Mighty Mac" bridge as the lighted backdrop for the whole scene. It was truly breathtaking, and I remember the vision as vividly today as I did over 40 years ago. I advanced rapidly through the ranks of scouting achieving the rank of "Life". Now "Life" is only one step below "Eagle" and I had obtained all the merit badges, and appropriate time required to achieve the rank of "Eagle". There was only one thing holding my back, to become an "Eagle Scout" a scout must develop, present and execute a final "Eagle Project". This project must be something profound, lasting and beneficial to the community for years to come. This was a stumbling block I could not overcome as I could not think of a project that fit all those requirements. Had I done this, I would have become Troop 74, Reed City's youngest Eagle Scout at age 14. This missed opportunity would become one of the few regrets I would carry the rest of my life. Despite this, these were still the greatest childhood years of my life. My family remained in Reed City until I started the 8th grade. I truly thought that this was the place that I would graduate high school with my friends from and live, like my grandfather and his father, the rest of my life it. Despite this all so many years ago, I still have my group of Reed City school friends that I stay in touch with and have been invited to the High School reunions over the years.

This all came crashing down as my father had another touch of wanderlust and thought that he wanted to "live in the country". As our little house in town sold much more quickly than we could find "just the right place" in the country we moved in with another family we were friends with. While living in Reed City and working at the Gardner-Denver Company my father found a friend with a hard-working gentleman by the name of Phil Grout. Phil and my father had a lot in common having both grown up in large, poor, hardworking families. They then grew up to have and become the same things, the heads of large, poor hardworking families. Phil also had previously lived in a small house in town, but had gotten the "itch" to move to the country a year or so earlier than my dad did. He found a great, huge old farmhouse on Cedar Road to rent. Huge was a necessity as he and his wife had seven kids across the entire age spectrum. Naturally, over many Saturday nights while the parents played cards, drank and smoked cigarettes, our friendships grew close since we were all pretty much the same age. I have no doubt that working side by side with my father, his tales of the joys of country living helped my father decide that it too, was the life for us. So, the nine of them and the five of us all moved into this great farm. Living with another family is fun when you're a kid. It's like having an "overnight" social event every night of the week. I never remember it as being particularly crowded as it was a huge house and of course if it wasn't raining or dark, we were outside anyway. There are advantages to having ten kids under the same roof in the country. The games you could play were limitless. This house had a large barn with a couple of cows or pigs the folks had invested in to keep us all fed through the wintertime, but the animals occupied the bottom of the barn and the hay, farm implements and usually all of us kids occupied the top. "Hide and seek" played in a barn is the best ever, as the hiding places were literally 3 dimensional and we used all of them. The very best memories I have of this house are of the great front yard it had. You really couldn't call it a yard as much as a field since the house sat roughly a quarter a mile of the road with a winding two track which led to the main road. This was good and bad. The bad parts were, first and foremost, the snow shoveling in the wintertime. A few inches of snow easily translated into hours of hard work even for seven boys. That long drive was also a pain in the ass during the school year as it was almost a ten-minute walk to the road where the school bus would pick us up. Ten minutes, added to whatever time you had to wait for the school bus to arrive, seemed like forever when it was ten degrees below zero or pouring rain outside. None of these minor inconveniences mattered to us though. This "field" was heaven sent to us kids for two reasons, In the Winter, despite having to shovel that snow, there was a bright side to its arrival. The Grout's had one of the old original seven-foot toboggans. This field had just the right slope and distance on it to really get a great ride on this wonderful seven-foot piece of birch with the bent up front. All six to nine of us kids, all the family dogs, with our hats, snowmobile suits and mittens would climb on this thing at the top of the slope and away we'd go. Ever so slowly at first, sometimes you even had to give the sled a little "boost" or two. But once that sled started moving you could count on having the ride of your life (again). You always had to be situationally aware (I had no idea what that term meant then but would become very aware of it in a few short years) because at the end of the toboggan run was the barbed wire fence which separated the field from the paved Cedar Road. baseball. If we really had a great run to the bottom, it would end with a cacophony of yelling and screaming "Jump!". No matter how fun that field was in the Wintertime it really had one true purpose and that was baseball. Our summer days, when we were not in school, or on the weekends, were spent from the minute it was bright and warm enough to start, until it was too dark to see the baseball flying at you. We were always all out there playing. The distances to home plate and each of the bases was carefully paced out. These were usually a paper plate nailed in the dirt to be used as the bases and our outfield went out as far as the best hitter among us could drive the ball. More than a few times the "grown-ups" would join us on our makeshift diamond for a few games. On a great Saturday or Sunday my uncle "Ick", (his name was Lynn, but I never even knew that until I was probably 15 years old, he was just "Uncle Ick") would pile his six kids in the car for a day in the country and most importantly on the baseball diamond. If you've done the math here, there were the four of us kids, the seven Grout kids, and the 6 Preston children giving us a total of seventeen kids to play baseball. If the adults came out to play, always the dad's, I don't ever remember mom or the other ladies playing, (I imagine they just enjoyed the quiet time to be without kids and housework) it gave us a lineup of twenty players in total. This was more than a complete lineup for two teams. When the fathers came out to join us, they always took the easy positions, like pitching, catching, or first base so they could play and keep their beer cans handy. Some of the displays of athleticism on occasion were truly remarkable. If Uncle Ick played he always pitched because he was usually too damn drunk to do much else on a ball diamond. Even though we all figured he could never move fast, I do remember one particular game when the oldest boy Rob smacked a 400-mph line drive right at Ick's balls. Uncle Ick can thank the good Lord that your reflexes and that "fight or flight" are the last thing to go in a man. His gloved hand snapped down within the millisecond to snatch that ball which would have most certainly ended his gender identity. All game play stopped as we all stood shocked after seeing such a sight and once the collective sigh of relief was exhaled the laughter could have been heard a mile away. Even as a child then, I remember wishing those days would never end. I've often thought that if there is a personalized heaven for me, this little baseball field will be on it. Another hobby, or habit you may say, I acquired out there was my love for motorcycles. The Grout boys came across an old 70cc Honda. It had one-cylinder, one long seat a long frame and set of handlebars. We all would take turns riding the absolute shit out of that thing. It's a miracle that none of us were ever killed on it. Despite it being a small displacement machine, it had a two-cycle engine and was pretty damn powerful. It was easily capable of speeds up to 60 miles an hour. I remember riding on the seat behind one of the Grout boys driving like a bat out of hell. Well, we hit a bump at about 40 mph (pretty much top speed for two passengers) and that bike flipped end over end. My "driver" caught both handlebars in the rib cage in the process. While I had been thrown 20 yards through the air I was otherwise unhurt. When I went to check on him though, he was lying on the ground gasping for breath and we both thought he was going to die. It was my first time seeing "Getting the wind knocked out of you" up close and personal. A minute or two later he was breathing just fine and a few short minutes after that, we were whizzing along just like nothing had happened. That Honda was considered an "Enduro" meaning it was a half-breed between a dirt bike and a street bike. Another of our friends down the road had a yellow Yamaha 400cc. This was also a one-cylinder machine, but this was a 4-cycle engine, built for power, speed and most definitely was a "dirt bike." I never drove that one very often as I recall but I do remember one specific thing about it. Those were the days when anything on two wheels we could afford did not have the luxury of an electric starter. Our "toys" had to be started the old-fashioned way, the infamous "kick starter." That damn Yamaha was finicky and being a 400-cc dirt bike was pure high-compression. Long story short, when you kicked down on the lever one of two things happened. If you got lucky and the choke was right, and you were giving it just enough throttle, the engine would roar to life and away you would go. If you were not lucky the kick starter just lifted YOU back up to the top of the stroke. If you were REALLY unlucky, your foot would slip off that lever and that lever would then hit you in the back of the leg. Right smack in middle of the calf muscle. I learned in college a few years later this is your gastrocnemius muscle. This was excruciatingly painful and I swear that lever was no more forgiving than the wielder of a rattan cane administering punishment in Indonesia. My friend sold that bike shortly thereafter and none of us were too heart broken.

No matter how well our families got along living together, I am sure eventually the lack of privacy and quiet were wearing thin for both Dad, Phil and the wives. Us kids would have kept the arrangement forever, but much like my mother always said, "Where Dad goes, we go" and his search for a place to call his own proceeded with earnest. He first found a small house we could rent across from the Osceola County Rose Lake Park which was right next to a huge dairy farm. The smell and the sound of cows permeated both home and clothes when the wind blew in from the West, which in Michigan is pretty much always. You can ask anyone who has ever stayed in Rose Lake Park, and they can tell you about the dairy farm, but if you ask about the little green house next to it, I promise you 95% of them will reply “what house?” We only stayed in this house for around 5 months approximately from late August until the end of January. The house we were in had no real yard to speak of, but a quick walk across the road and you were in the middle of a great park, complete with a playground. This being the off season, like every other recreational facility in Norther Michigan after Labor Day weekend, it had the “sidewalks rolled up”. This made the exploration of the park that much more fascinating as it was completely empty sans the squirrels and rabbits. It was very surreal, and I always remember how cold, empty and grey both the park and lake seemed without all the campers, barbecues and laughter there. In retrospect, I wish I had had a metal detector. I always found plenty of “treasures” while exploring all the empty campsites even with the naked eye. I can only imagine the things I may have found if I was able to look through a few inches of soil. During that time my father found a suitable ten-acre parcel just 12 miles away with a small mobile home set up on it that he could purchase on a land contract. So, we packed our bags and, on a cold, blustery January day we were off! It always seemed like we, as a family, moved during the shittiest weather days Mother Nature had in store. I mentioned earlier about that day being “cold and blustery.” That was probably the biggest understatement in this entire text to this point. It was a stone cold assed fucking Michigan blizzard at its finest. I remember it distinctly because the wind was blowing hard and cold enough that I remember my eyelashes freezing together every time you had to blink. Now why on earth would anyone move on a day like that? I’ll explain, the house we were moving into had two sources of heat, fuel oil and wood. The prior owner naturally had used up all the fuel oil and was not refilling the tank as they were leaving. And more likely than not, having to come up with the money for the house and move, my father did not have the ready money to buy more fuel oil. This meant the only thing between a wonderful toasty new place to live, and an "ice box" with frozen and broken pipes was the wood stove in the house that required a person to feed its voracious appetite for logs. In that kind of weather, a house can freeze in a matter of hours so once the previous owner told us they were leaving, we had no choice but to get our things in there to keep everything thawed and warm. I remember it as being one of my "day of days." The very next Winter was the infamous "Storm of 1978.

Chapter 2: "Movin to the Country"

Regarding this move, as far as I was concerned, we might as well have been moving to Mars. To say I was devastated was an understatement. While at Reed City, I was popular and excelled both academically and athletically. The only friends I had ever known to that point lived there, and when you're 13 or 14 years old, "uncertainty" is not a great feeling.

This small, insignificant by any travel standard, 12-mile hop placed our family in a different school district. Pine River Junior-Senior Area Schools (P.R.H.S.) was the name of it. The fact that the name has "Junior-Senior Schools" in it is significant for a couple of reasons. Firstly, it shows how small the entire district was. Unlike Reed City High School, which was occupied by grades 9 through 12, Pine River's building was occupied by grades 7 through 12. That also meant that many things, like the "Smoking area" for Students which was right by the gate at Reed City (yes, all high schools had a smoking area at the time where the students could smoke if they chose to) was not legally permitted at Pine River as it was as much a Junior High School as it was a Senior High School. Secondly, being an "Area Schools", it was a consolidated school district. Unlike Reed City High School where every student is a resident of Reed City, Pine River did not have a single "town" to its claim but three. These were Leroy, Luther and Tustin (We were residents of the locale of Ashton who attended Pine River as well, but since Ashton did not have its own zip code, it didn't really count as a "town") Pine River was affectionally referred to everyone in the area as the "Penitentiary". This was due to its location basically in the middle of nowhere. P.R.H.S. was located right alongside the freeway (US-131 between mile markers 166 and 172) on the West side of the highway. It sat up slightly on a hill and was surrounded in its entirety by an 8' stockade fence equipped complete with angled racks on top and three rows of barbed wire. This fencing was placed there to ensure the safety of the students inside. This fence had a main gate at the street entrance. Once all the busses and Students were inside, this gate was closed for the school day. The most interesting part about this fence was the fact that it was the only thing visible to motorists careening down US-131. This is where the school got the nickname "the penitentiary". Of the entire student body (grades 7-12) of around 700 students, not a single student "walked" to school, and we were all bussed in. Once those gates were closed, P.R.H.S. was your entire universe for the next eight hours or so.

To this day I remember the first words spoken to me by a fellow student at Pine River. They were and I quote "You wanna buy a joint?" Despite the year being around 1978 or so, until that point, I had never even really heard of marijuana let alone tried it. I guess now that I think of it, that statement isn't entirely true. The next memory here probably should have been in the prior chapter, but since I really disdain "Cut and Paste" I'll just add it here. As it was a very significant event in my life, I would be wrong to not make mention of it.

A few years before while living in Reed City, at around age 13, I held my first employment. I loved the taste and the joy of having an actual paycheck with my name on it.. Michigan had a work program referred to as the C.E.T.A program, I can't tell you what the initials stand for but in a nutshell it was a work program for young adults whose parents were below a certain financial threshold. These were very limited jobs with stringent hours and daily rules. This made sure this employment would never interfere with school, while at the same time providing some much-needed money into a household, or more importantly a kid's pocket. My first job was at the cemetery on the hill that I would someday have a marker in, even if that was the furthest thing from my mind at the time. This was a great arraignment for me as I could walk to work, it was an easy job, except for the days we had to work digging or refilling a grave or rearranging the sod on it afterwards. Any time there was a funeral or ceremony being held, we were not allowed to perform any work on the premises as this would be considered "disrespectful." I guess those "freebie" days made up for the hard ones. Mostly, we just walked around, kept the trash emptied, clipped the grass closest to the markers that the mower couldn't reach and so on. My "co-worker" was a lovely young lady of 16 named "Lisa". Lisa, little did I know this was the first, but most certainly not the last, huge impression on my life women with that name would have. Well, on a particularly slow and sunny day Lisa asks me "Have you ever and would you like to smoke a joint?", and my reply was (peer pressure at that moment about 9.8 on the Reichter scale) "Of course I have and yes I would love to". So off we go to the little gazebo in the middle of the cemetery (EVERY cemetery has one of these) and proceed to smoke this joint. There has always been a rumor that you don't really get “high” the first time you smoke marijuana. Let me completely dispel that rumor right here right now. Once we finished our “smokey treat” Lisa went on her way to muddle elsewhere in the cemetery. I just laid on my back on the floor of the pavilion and completely tripped balls! I remember it being the most wonderful daydream ever and a joy I would spend many years trying to recapture. My ecstasy was short lived as I soon heard the creaking of footsteps. I looked up only to see the sextant, with his long grey hair, beard and tattoo’s looking down on me. His exact words were “Let’s take a walk”. My ecstasy immediately turned to terror as while we were walking together, he was carefully pointing out all the work that remained to be done. After what seemed like an eternity, wondering if he had any way of knowing I had just imbibed in an illegal substance, he calmly said “Oh, and the next time you want to get high, do it OFF THE CLOCK” to which we both broke out laughing and he went back to his office and I back to work. That was as close as I ever got to Lisa, we’ll call her “Lisa #1” and after we moved. I never saw her again.

Everything about my old lifestyle was all about to change as I guess it does with all young adults at this stage in their lives. Despite my original apprehension about moving to a new school, it wasn’t long before I made new friends. Now with those new friends, and even some of my old friends, I embarked on making the high school memories that each person has in their lives. You see, just after we moved into the mobile home on 12-mile road in Ashton, Phil and his family purchased a home (what was commonly referred to as a “basement home” dug entirely into the side of a hill) just about 3/4th of a mile up the road from where we moved. We on the other hand lived in a mobile home. It was a small 10’ x

50' home with two bedrooms and one bathroom, so I'll you imagine how much room that left for a family of five. My folks had the master bedroom at the end of the hallway and I and my two brothers occupied the small second bedroom with a set of bunkbeds in it. At least I was the oldest, so I got the top bunk while my little brothers shared the bottom one. That top bunk was as close to privacy as I ever had in trailer. Trailers are never built that solidly in the first place and ours, being older and well-used by the time Dad purchased it, was always in a state of disrepair. When you add the hours my father had to spend working on the furnace, floors, drawers, skirting et cetera, to the hours he spent at his employment to keep us fed, it was safe to say that when my father wasn't "working" he was sleeping. This place did have an awesome, huge backyard with the ever-present "fire pit" that every country backyard has in it. Just beyond this yard edge was the "woods". So of these ten acres parcel my father purchased, the front two were where the mobile home was with the small yard. Behind the trailer was that huge back yard and firepit. The other eight acres was a wonderful hardwood stand of maple, cherry and the occasional oak trees. These eight acres of trees provided a great deal for our family. Most of the wood we burned in that little woodstove was acquired from any dead wood in those trees. We did use fuel oil for our main heating source but had a tiny woodstove that was placed inside the 10' x 10' "room" that had been built on the side of the mobile home. That little woodstove would be a God send more than a few times in the dead of Winter when either a) The furnace quit working or b) we ran out of fuel oil with no money to purchase any until the next payday. I remember one particularly "tight" Winter and there was no money for fuel oil to be had and unfortunately, as we would soon find out, we did not have enough firewood cut for what would be the hardest Winter in Northern Michigan in a generation. The winter of 1978 is still a legend remembered by all of us who lived through it." That storm dropped a couple of feet of snow over 24 hours. There was no school, business or activity happening anywhere for the next week or so. I remember having to jump out of a window to get a shovel and shovel the snow away from the front door so it could be opened. So much snow had drifted over it that it was impossible to open. I think school was closed for almost two weeks that winter. Like a lot of things, this just seemed like another adventure at the time. Weather or no weather, people must eat, and since the owner of the Ashton store lived adjacent to the store he was able to keep it open. That was around seven miles from where we were living and there was no car or truck on earth that could have made that trek. Praise the Lord that a few of the guys that lived nearby owned snowmobiles and soon a "grocery caravan" was organized to make sure all the families in the area were able to get food, water and fuel oil. The Ashton store extended credit to all who needed it and none of us froze or went hungry. There were more than a couple times during this period that we had no money for fuel oil, for gasoline, or two-cycle oil for a chainsaw (if we had one at the time or if it even worked, I don't remember now). For those periods life was truly tough for me, each day after school, unless I, everyone and everything in my house, was to freeze overnight, I would have to trudge through the snow, into the woods to find a dead tree or two and cut it up and drag it to the trailer for heat. I could fairly quickly cut up enough for the next day or so. The other limitation to this was I had to find dead timber that was small enough to be reasonably cut by hand with a "bucksaw" which is the tool I had to work with.

In addition to wood the property provided, both back corners of the "forest" were right next to a well-worn deer trail. Venison would become our primary source of meat as it could be obtained for the cost of a shotgun shell and a little elbow grease. In addition to deer, there were rabbits and squirrels that could be had as well, and any of it was "fair game" for the dinner table. I remember clearly the look on my mother's face (remember the "city girl" from Baltimore) the first time my father dragged a deer into the back yard and began to process it. "Process" sounds a lot better than "cut up", "gut", or "Skin". My father taught all us boys how to do the same with all game and I have used these skills many times throughout my life. I still only really felt "cooped" up during the Wintertime there though, as I have mentioned earlier, if it was Summer and daylight I was never inside anyways. All this took place on Osceola Counties 12-mile road. 12-mile road was, and is still, a little quiet, dirt, back country road. It would be safe to say that on an average day only 5 or so vehicles would travel on this road. Unfortunately, of those five vehicles one of them was NOT the School Bus. You see on that road; we were the only residence on that stretch, and because of this the buses did not, and would not make the 1/3-mile trip, one-way, to pick up one family's kids. This meant I had to walk that 1/3 of a mile twice a day during the school year. Another funny thing about the school year is that it occurs during the fall and winter times when walking is least enjoyable. Despite the running joke that every kid likes to say their parents bitched about "Well, I walked 1/2 -mile uphill BOTH WAYS to school" there is nothing fiction about my telling this part of my story. So, while I walked 1/3rd of a mile to the West, and the Grout kids, whose house was ¼th of a mile on the other side of Lakola Road (named that because it was the country boundary line between Lake County and Osceola County), would walk their 1/4th of mile East to the same intersection. I laugh in hindsight how horrible and long that walk seemed on the way to the school bus, but how it was no problem at all when walking over to the Grouts to play or hang out.

The Grouts new home also placed his kids in the Pine River District as well. Although we were new to the district, all seven of us had two advantages that no kids ever get on a move to a new area. First, since P.R.H.S. was a "Junior-Senior High School" and I arrived there in the 9th grade, I was not at the bottom of the proverbial "pecking order". There were two entire grades of Students there who were younger than I was, so I didn't immediately fall into that "victim" class, the new undergraduates in any school automatically fall into. Second, the 5 Grout kids started at the same new school the same year I did, so I automatically had a least a small group of friends to "hang" with.

We "Seven" then proceeded to make our mark in our high school years. It wasn't long and we even gained a group of the "locals" and had our own "clique". One good thing about attending a small class D school was you could pretty much be guaranteed to make any "team" you tried out for. This was simply because of the necessity of having enough athletes to post a squad of could be problematic when a school only had "X" number of kids who were ready, willing, and at least partially able to play in the first place. This ensured I made the junior varsity and varsity football teams in my high school years. I loved playing football, even if I HATED football practice. Practice was a necessary evil if you wanted to stay on the team though. This, at least for me, posed more of a problem than a simple inconvenience. I lived approximately 15 miles from the high school, which required transportation to every practice, game and school function I was required to attend. Transportation was always a difficult hurdle for the Roberts family in those days. That was due to the fact that my parents usually had a vehicle that barely ran, and gasoline, although a lot less expensive then, still cost money which my parents never had enough of. Cars and gasoline had to be apportioned, with priority number one always being getting dad and/or mom back and forth to work. If there was time, and money after that (and the folks weren't too exhausted from work) I could get a ride to practice. Fortunately, with most things in life, where there is a will there is a way. I did find a new, more local friend who lived close by us in our new place. The Pilkens lived around the other side of the section and had a son Rod who was in the same grade as I was. Of all the families who were hardscrabble poor in the area in the 1970's, the Pilkins did pretty well. Their good fortune did come at a cost though. Although the Reed City area did have a few employment places where an individual could earn enough to feed themselves and keep the bills paid, none of these places kept any of their workers very far from living hand to mouth. The real money, much like anywhere else in America, was earned in the greater metropolitan areas. Michigan was better than a lot of other states at the time as it was the center of the auto manufacturing industry of the world. All the "Big Three" Ford, Chrysler and General Motors were based a mere three hours away from West Central Michigan in the Detroit area. A lot of the major subsidiaries of those factories were based in the Grand Rapids area which was only an hour and a half away from us. You see, even though the automobiles rolled off the assembly lines in Detroit, not every piece required to assemble them was manufactured there.

Henry Ford developed this model a hundred years earlier by relying on smaller factories focusing on the more individual parts, starters, alternators, nuts, bolts, pistons to name a few, then these individual parts were shipped to the main assemble locations to be put together to finally make a car. These final assembly jobs were good union jobs and the highest paid of all, and Rod's dad happened to occupy one of them at the Buick factory down there. While this employment provided for the Pilkin family well financially, it cost them the company and guiding hand of the man of the house at least 5 days a week. I only was able to reap the benefits of this arraignment as they always had good transportation, gas money to run it, and since Rod was my age and participated in the same sporting events I did at time (football and wrestling) for the most part I was always able to get a ride to games and practice when I needed to. As a result, I did spend a lot of time with the Pilkin family and was a defacto "adopted son". I grew to love Mr. and Mrs. Pilkin and have kept a relationship with "Mom and Dad" to this very day. Phil Grout had retired by that time and was home a lot of the time, so he was very active in also making sure all us boys got rides to practice and games as he was financially able, and although I rarely remember my parents in attendance at any of my extracurricular events, Phil was always in the stands to cheer us on. Like the Pilkins, Mr. and Mrs. Grout became "adoptive parents" who I maintained a relationship with until the day many years later they passed away. I always felt fortunate to have a group of real men to show me what being a responsible husband, father and provider was supposed to be.

Finally, being involved in sports, social events and feeling a sense of belonging, I finally adjusted to the reality of being a "Pine River Buck" rather than a Reed City school member. I continued to build the best high school memories anybody could ask for. I always had a great deal of fun, and as I grew into my mid-teenage years, start to explore some of the more "adult" life experiences that all teens do. As most of our parents were working most of the time, all us teens had a lot of free unsupervised time on our hands. That time along with acres and miles of countryside to run on led to some entertaining and interesting activities. All our parents, except for the Plinkins, drank and smoked cigarettes. I know now even my father and some of his friends, all being from the Vietnam era, smoked some marijuana as well, but us kids never saw or heard anything about that. For whatever reason, my mother was rabidly "anti-drug." Now whether that was from what she had seen from her brother-in-law so many years before or what activities her ex-husband was up to I'll never know. What I do know is that my mother HATED drugs and to her there was no difference whatsoever between smoking a joint and sticking a needle in your arm. So, any marijuana my father may have imbibed in was carefully hidden from my mother. I do remember one incident where my mother found a tiny little Christmas box in my father's pocket with a big fat joint in it, and hand written "Merry Christmas Johnny, Melvin." Melvin was one of my dad's friends who had served in Vietnam. It was on the table when my dad got home from work and mom laid it out as clear as it could be 'You pick right now, THIS or me." She wasn't kidding, despite her love for him and the 20 years of wedded bliss they had shared to that date, I truly believe she would have packed us kids and left. I am thankful my father made the only obvious choice and I never saw marijuana in our house again. Well, maybe except what I snuck in on occasion but that's a different story for another time. But since our parents did drink and smoke it was only natural that we would follow suit. But unlike our parents, it was the 70's and the drug culture was still going strong and even reached as far as our bucolic universe. My stepsister graduated high school in 1976 and proceeded to become the first in my family to graduate from college. I did not know at that time I would be following suit in a couple of decades at her alma mater, Ferris State College. It would even be Ferris State University by the time I would get there. I knew that she smoked marijuana and used some drugs, but she never exposed us to it when we were young and kept to herself working as a Registered Nurse. Back at P.R.H.S. we smoked a lot of marijuana, hashish, and opium on occasion. Psychedelic mushrooms, peyote and mescaline were readily available. Harder drugs such as acid, cocaine, and crystal meth (soon to become the demon of American society as Methamphetamine) were occasionally available but not in regular circulation. I guess for myself, being essentially poor, kept me from getting into too much trouble with hard drugs as I simply could not afford them. I was an athlete as well and although I never took training that seriously, I did care about my performance so tried to keep myself as healthy as I could considering my current circumstances. I am told in the 50's they had the "greasers" the "poodles" good kids and bad. Well, in our class of "82" at P.R.H.S. we pretty much had two groups, the "Jocks" and the "Stoners", I suppose there was a good percentage of Students who did not fall into either category, but those were the ones who just plugged quietly about their high school days never making too many waves. Getting cigarettes and alcohol was nowhere near as difficult then as it is today for young people. The drinking age was only 18 years old for most of the years when I was a teen, and when it was finally raised, to try to slow the legions of drunk high school students being legally provided for by 18-year-old seniors, it was only raised to 19 anyway. There really was even a lot of debate to raise it that one year as I recall. It was socially felt that if an individual could be drafted, could legally vote, hell they could marry at 16 in most States below the Mason-Dixon line, they should be able to kick back and have some adult refreshments if they chose to do so.

My almost perfect grade point average plummeted from the almost perfect 4.0, to a dismal 2.0 as having fun with my friends, playing in sports and pretty much everything else was a lot more entertaining than studying for grades. Having been raised with the great stories of travel and adventure they military provided to all my older relatives, I had decided very early on that the military was for me, therefore all that time spent working on a grade point average was nothing more than time wasted. While the "jocks" and the silent majority worked steadily for grades, knowing they would be essential to getting into a decent University, those of us that were the "Stoners" had no illusions of what the future held for us. It was either the military, taking your place along the line in one of the local factories, or working in the "family" business of lumber or other ancillary service. I did not like school, I did not like having to get out of bed every morning, I did not like having to sit all day long listening to one string of drivel after another only to be followed at the end of each week with a sheet laid in front of you and an expectation that you would regurgitate the drivel you listened to all week long onto paper.

The only thing that kept me going back day after day was my friends, the extracurricular activity and the knowledge that my father would most certainly put a boot up my ass if I failed at school. As mentioned earlier here, neither of my parents completed high school, and had paid the price for that their entire lives by struggling financially. It was their resolute belief that their children would not suffer the same fate and come to hell or high water; we all WERE going to graduate high school. I clearly remember my mother saying, "You will graduate high school even if you are the only 30-year-old to walk down that aisle", she was not kidding. Of course, my two younger brothers got off the hook from that bullshit, but that is a different story. For what is worth, one of those two, at age 40, went to adult school and obtained a proper high school diploma. Graduate of Evart High School class of 2002. I told him, nothing else he could have done could have made a greater impression on his children in regard to the value of a high school diploma.

It is said that time waits on no man, or boy in my case even if I thought I was a man, and I was no exception. Like the millions of boys and girls before me, something strange began coursing through my bloodstream, hormones that is. Apparently all that activity in athletics insured that I even caught the eye of a member of the fairer sex. And so, woven ever so deeply in the fabric of my memory is another "Lisa". I cannot refer to her as "Lisa #2" in this text because to trivialize the impact she would forever leave in my life by doing this would simply be wrong. She was petite girl, with strawberry blond hair with blue eyes. She was simply beautiful. Just like every other high school kid, we became acquainted partially through the glances in a shared class, but mostly because her little brother Ron participated in wrestling with me although he was a year our junior. Going to school now every day was not only no longer hated, but I remember even looking forward to a Monday morning back in class so I would be able to see her again. Lisa also participated in the wrestling program as a "mat maid", (girls would not be permitted to be "wrestlers" for almost two more decades) I guess you would call the "mat maids" sports assistants by today's standards, they were de facto cheerleaders, janitors, equipment repair folks and more. The most important thing to me though was that this ensured that we would get to spend more time together outside the classroom. She and I did have a lot in common. We both came from middle-sized families neither of which were what would be called financially secure by any measure. We both lived in the country, me by transplant, her the only life she had ever known. Neither one of us were what you would call academic geniuses either. The root cause of this did differ though, my poor grade performance was simply laziness, my college transcripts in later years would prove that I did have academic potential. Her grades were a little better than mine, but she worked and studied hard for what grades she did get. She was always far more blessed than I in that she was gifted with this great thing called "Common Sense". I am now, (although to a much lesser degree) as I was then, generally lacking in that regard. There was one very significant difference in our family lives, my father worked, her father drank, a lot. I struggle to try to find the words to describe how having an alcoholic father really throws a proverbial "wrench" into a family dynamic. Many authors before me have described what family life is like living with an alcoholic, the abuse across all spectrums, the financial and emotional instability, and worse. I'll just leave it at this. This family had to suffer every aspect of this disease. Every day at their home revolved around how "drunk" dad was or wasn't or was on the way to becoming. It was sad also because in what experiences I had with their family was that "dad" could be a very funny and fairly caring guy when halfway sober. Those desirable qualities went rapidly downhill as his B.A.L. (blood alcohol level) went up. When "Dad" was really drunk, I was not allowed to visit, and that was probably a good thing. Regardless, Ron and I have some very good memories of trout fishing in the stream across the road and getting hints, advise and laughs from "Dad" as he was quite the fisherman in his day I was told. Ron and I were more like brothers then and still are to this day.

I only mention all of this because it was a factor in my youth that left a mark. I was struggling in a home which was financially troubled, packed like sardines in a mobile home, with no privacy whatsoever and an absent father due to work. She came from a home and family with the secret "white elephant" in the house and all the terror that came with that. This left us with one thing, each other. We needed each other, we leaned on each other and for teenagers, that translates to love. And also with all teenagers, love soon translates into, well... sex. We were continually "necking" in the hallways and quiet corners at school. Our school bus rides, which were hours back and forth to school and weekend wrestling events were the times when our hands could explore the mysteries of the opposite sex cuddled underneath blankets. The Amish I'm told, even have a special part of their young people's courtship that condones this behavior. In a quiet corner of their home the aspiring couple are sewed together into a blanket, while the rest of the family is in another part of the house. I suppose there is only so much you can accomplish fully dressed and sewed into a small blanket with anyone, but you would think where there is a will there is a way. Far from me to judge what works for anyone else. Lisa and I weren't sewed into a blanket so it was inevitable that we would actually, eventually have sex given the right time and location. That happened to occur one sunny summer day as I was visiting her house. Both her parents were working, and we were under the "supervision" of her older sister. Lisa and I were lying upstairs in her bedroom (she was fortunate enough to have her own bedroom, a luxury I would not know for many years) and her older sister came up the stairs. She looked in the room and I of course said, "Don't worry, I'll keep the door open" to which she replied, "Oh don't worry about it," and closed the door behind her. Well…. A few short moments, with real emphasis on "short", to the awesome guitar riffs of the great new band Van Halen's "Running with the Devil"' neither of us were virgins anymore. I only write of this incident because it was a joking matter that any man should "marry his first piece of ass" but in fact I would do just that in a couple of short years.

Time was whizzing by for me, and it wasn't all bad. I was as complete as I young person could be at age 16. I was getting by in school, I was at the very least a mediocre athlete with the slightest bit of popularity that came with that. I had a pretty, steady girl who fulfilled my needs both physically and emotionally at the time, and in the words of one of my favorite music artists then and now, Tom Petty and the Heartbreakers, "The future was wide open" In fact, the song that I quote from is titled "Rebel without a clue" and as I sit here, that title could not more accurately describe my life at the time. At least while I was bumbling though these years, all my peers at P.R.H.S. were doing exactly the same thing. As I would discover in years to come, it was an advantage to have a smaller population class body. Our P.R.H.S. class of 1982 was around 90 seniors and I knew, or knew of, each and every one of them. I have many, many wonderful memories of all these people from the various school and social functions. Of course, the school sanctioned ones were alright, school dances, prep rallies before sporting events, and of course homecoming and prom each year. The ones we had; I won't necessarily spend a lot of time describing as anyone who has seen such events on a television program knows exactly what they were like. Just change the faces, and if the program was created after 1990 be sure to add LOTS of hair to your imagination. In fact, the hair "pendulum" had just swung in the opposite direction socially from where it had been a decade or so before. In fact, at P.R.H.S, before around 1976 a male student could be expelled from school for having his hair too long. "Too long" was considered any length below the collar for boys. It's almost impossible to imagine such regulations by today's standards but one must remember this was the era when smoking was virtually allowed everywhere as well. I believe, much to their dismay, the teachers had, just a year or so before, been able to smoke at their desks while in the classrooms. Soon enough they were required, in the interest of presenting a more wholesome appearance, to smoke only in the teachers' lounge between classes. And smoke they did, a giant cloud would escape the lounge each time the door world open as a teacher went In or out. Of course, this was not much different than the students in the bathrooms. As there was not time between classes for anyone to walk all the way out to the student smoking area, we resorted to sneaking a puff or two inside the boy's room. Of course, you had to place a guard on the door as smoking in the building was forbidden to students. If a student was caught smoking in the building, they received a three-day suspension from school, which would send your grades into a tailspin. As I recall, suspensions of various lengths were the primary punishments issued for infractions of school rules. The one I always laughed at was the three-day suspension for "skipping" school. In my book, if I played my cards right, I could skip school on Monday, get caught on purpose, return on Tuesday and receive my three-day suspension and then make a great five-day break from school out of it. All I had to do, this era being decades before the days of the "text", was to make sure I intercepted the mail and pull the letter from the school administration informing my parents what had happened. Never really a problem there. My parents looked no further on my report card than the grade letters neatly in a row on the right-hand side of it. Everything else on the card, "Days missed" "Days tardy" "Comments" were simply fine print to them as the letters told them the only thing they wanted to know. Each "D" or "I" was followed by "If you keep bombing these classes you will be in high school until you are 30 years old." That really was one of my parents' favorite phrases for the entire time I was in high school.

Our Class of "82" weekends, and subsequent, "not school sanctioned" activities were always the best though. As I have mentioned earlier, my family never really was in any financial category besides "low.", I never felt embarrassed or apprehensive about this fact, because in North-Central Michigan in the 1970's, every family struggled. There were really no social status symbols like Jordache jeans, Ray-Ban sunglasses, or Nike footwear (for illustration purposes only, Nike tennis shoes would not become the "Rage" for at least another 15 years or so) that I recall anyone in my little class having to impress anyone else. Because of this simple fact, we all resorted to activities that cost no money to participate in. Parties held at one of my classmate's house or the other, depending on whose parents were away, were always fun. There are birthday parties, graduation parties, retirement parties, wedding parties and pretty much a "party" for every happy theme one can think of. Parties in the 70's and 80's meant one thing, loud music, alcohol, pot, some drugs and sex. The entire purpose and goal of our parties was to see who could get the most fucked up and do the most over the top shit to "impress" the rest of your classmates and friends. The music of the day in one manner or the other, extolled the joys of "Sex, drugs, and Rock and Roll" and we did our best to follow their instruction. This could be accomplished pretty much anywhere we as a group could congregate away from the not-so prying eyes of parents. Sometimes this could be a classmate's house, but many times it was alongside of the waterway from which our great school was named the Pine River. These parties were more times than not entire weekend events. This was mostly because we would all just tell our parents that we were going to go camping for the weekend, do some fishing, sit around a campfire and sing some wholesome "kumbaya" songs. We had special names for each of our party locations along a 5- or 6-mile stretch of the river. These places had names like "Meadowbrook", "Silver Creek", "Edgetts", or "Skookum". Those locations carry those names to this very day. None of these places had any amenities such as water, electricity or restrooms. I guess they call that "primitive camping" now and it is considered a bonus. Those facts did not bother us though as none of that stuff was required for us to have the kind of fun we went out there to have. These were the gatherings that forged the friendships with my classmates that I would carry to this very day. I do believe that the memories of these are as fresh in as many of my P.R.H.S classmates' minds as they are in mine. I know this because at each of our reunions, the stories of at least one such memory is bound to come up. What little social strata there was among the 1980-1982 groups of P.R.H.S. classmates always completely crumbled during these extracurricular events as well. Despite the little "cliques" and "groups" that gathered while behind the walls of the "penitentiary", the "Jocks", "Stoners", and everyone else felt completely equal among the trees and campfires and treated each other that way. It was an unspoken understanding though that come Monday morning everyone would fall back into their own little conversation groups. Any discussions, encounters or social faux pas that may have occurred were quickly forgotten, and at the most, discussed only in whispers.

I sit here now as a parent and grandparent simply cringing at the thought of any of my children, when aged approximately 13 to 16 years old, doing even a third of the things I was doing at that age with my friends. Although I am certain that some of them did a few of these things, I was always blessed with the ignorance of not knowing. One might think that the result of these parties would be overdoses, teen pregnancies, and serious injuries up to and including, death. It really was quite the opposite. It truly was for the most part, harmless fun. We did have our share of tragedy among my group, but none occurred during our partying. I guess this was mostly due to the fact once everyone was settled in, unpacked, tents and such set up, everyone pretty stayed put with the others. The worse things I ever recur happening was one or two of us throwing up from drinking too much, an occasional scuffle which ended quickly and I'm certain some sexual activity inside of the tents or parked cars. No one ever died there. The young people we lost before they could walk down the graduation aisle were few, fortunately, but none the less sad. We had one gal who, while getting the complimentary eye exam the local optometrist came to school to give all of us, was discovered to have a particularly lethal form of leukemia and died within 6 months. We also lost 4 classmates due to automobile accidents. In life's list of "Things that don't go together" teens, alcohol (or marijuana), long winding, curving (and icy 6 months out of the year) roads, and fast cars have got to be near the top of the list. This number of 4 may not sound like a large number by an urban or suburban standard, with their student bodies numbered in the hundreds. For us and our mere 90 students, who all lived in the country where there was virtually no traffic, it left a mark. We lost students both on the dirt country roads and on the paved roads as well. The dirt roads in my little universe there were not the best maintained most times and in the sandy loam of Northern Michigan tended to have very soft shoulders. This combined with an intoxicated high school student or two, a heavy vehicle and more than a few ancient maple trees on either side, insured that if one were traveling at a very inappropriate rate of speed, ended up swerving into one sandy side of the roadway or the other, bad results were almost guaranteed. Even if one was not necessarily traveling at an insane rate of speed, whitetail deer (which are populous and everywhere in the countryside) could jump out anywhere, anytime causing an instinctual jerk of the steering wheel resulting in the same, sometimes tragic result. The Village of Luther, which one student group of P.R.H.S hailed from as I mentioned earlier, was serviced by one main throughfare coming into and going out of it. This was a long, 13-mile stretch (From US-131) of a paved secondary road called M-63. The first 8 miles from the expressway was a section referred to as "Woodpecker Flats". As the name implies this was the greatest, and one of the longest, almost flat stretches of paved road in Osceola County. Because of this, it was the perfect location for every "gear head" who thought he had to fastest automobile ever to be produced to attempt to break the sound barrier on. And once you were certain you had the fastest vehicle, the only way you could prove it was to find the next kid who had the same thoughts you did and then side-by-side go screaming down woodpecker flats to see who could be the first to reach Lakola road. As much as you would think this section of M-63 would most certainly be the area that claimed lives it was not. That distinction went to a small ¾ of a mile part, just two miles before the Village of Luther limits. This part consisted of three posted 15 mph curves one right after the other. Despite many curves being posted with a speed that was merely a good suggestion, these curves most certainly were not. That 15-mph limit was a requirement, and that was during perfect road conditions. Once this stretch of road was covered with ice, the top speed safely travelled was around 10 miles an hour. Two of our classmates one Winter evening decided to throw caution to the wind, being the professional drivers, they thought they were, decided (by the sheriff department estimates) they could maneuver these curves at least at 60 miles per hour. They failed and their bodies were extricated from the wreckage the next morning when they were finally discovered 50 yards or so past the roadway lying in the cornfield beyond.

In my recollection, despite the opportunity, we only had one teen pregnancy in our little group. Unlike the glamour MTV seems to have made a TV program out of, teen pregnancies usually result in a lifetime of missed opportunity and hardship for the young family. I can gladly say that this was not the result of this union. This teen pregnancy resulted in the marriage of two very young kids and the birth of a beautiful baby girl. This fine couple ultimately ended up being our (P.R.H.S. Class of 1982) Homecoming King and Queen of that year. They live very well and are still married 41 years later and to my knowledge, still very much in love and happy. I am in awe of their lifelong commitment to one another, and very, very happy to count them among my friends to this very day. It was only by the sheer grace of God; Lisa and I did not end up in the same situation as I have no doubt whatsoever that "our story" would not have had such a happy ending.

Time marched on for us and then the end of my high school years was winding down. My friends and I were beginning to make the decisions which would open the "starting gates" to our lives. Then, as now, I always believed that getting a head start was a good thing and I did not waste the opportunity to get my head start then. The military recruiters frequented high schools at the time and came with tales of success and adventures to be had for the cost of a few short years of committing to work for Uncle Sam. One of these visits must have struck a chord with me, and I remembered one topic discussed was the "Split Option" program offered by the United States Army. Through this program, a young person could enlist in the military and complete basic training between their junior and senior years of high school. I decided this was for me rather than having to walk down the aisle on graduation day wondering (like so many then and now still do) "What in the hell am I going to do with my life?" My sister had chosen higher education and was now successfully working as a Registered Nurse in the big city. I was proud of her and although we always seemed to have a philosophical gap, as well as a 7-year age gap between us, I respected and asked her opinion often. I still was in denial about being in love with school, so college still never even crossed my mind. My mind was made up, I would enlist in the military and know exactly what I job was going to do. The recruiter drove to our house, contract in hand, hoping to gain a signature adding one more notch to the monthly quota I am sure he had to maintain. All was progressing smoothly until my mother stepped into the kitchen. I have mentioned a couple of times in this text my disdain for school as well as my parents absolute resolve that I was going to finish high school. My mother was certain that I would consider my early enlistment was my "ticket" out of high school never to return once I left with this U.S. Army. She was going to ensure, despite the repeated reassurances by the recruiter, that this was not going to happen. Even though an individual was allowed to sign a contract with the military for the early option program, I (and all others who took this option) was still only 16 years old and thus could not engage in any legal contract without the consent and signature of my parents. I believe my contract was the only one in the entire United States Army with a special clause added. My mother insisted that the phrase "Should John S. Roberts Jr not return from basic training to successfully complete high school and graduate, this contract shall be null, and void and he will be immediately discharged from the United States Army" So after ten seconds with an ink pen, this was added to the document, then followed by me and my parents' signatures. If my mother would have known how much ass-kicking in boot camp that little "clause" would cost me she may have reconsidered. Somehow, the Drill Sergeants found out about what was written on my contract and It was an unending source of irritation to them. At least the next six years of my future now had activities planned as part of them.

Chapter 3: "The adventure begins."

Of my group at P.R.H.S. three of us would join the Army as part of the split option program, and our adventure would start at the same place. This place was the Military Entrance Processing Center, or as it was affectionately known as M.E.P.S. You're going to notice throughout this text a great number of acronyms used. The military is the king of acronyms, and many of them I used, I never even know what they stood for. The M.E.P.S station for Michigan was in downtown Detroit. This was about a three-and-a-half-hour drive from where I lived on 12-mile road. This being the case, the Army authorized a hotel room for us the night before, so we could arrive at the M.E.P.S. station at 5 am prompt when all operations began. Ideally by the end of the workday (which was around 2 in the afternoon for the M.E.P.S. crew) the entire group of us from all over Michigan would be in the large room at the very end of the M.E.P.S. building with a giant American flag on the wall, raising our right hand and taking our "Oath of Allegiance". A lot had to be done before that point though. Even on my first official day on the United States Government payroll I had experienced a lot of "firsts." This was in fact the first time I had ever been to what anyone could call a "big city" (Detroit), and the first time I had ever stayed in a motel. The recruiter dropped us off at the "Days Inn" with an ominous tone, "Do NOT get all drunked up because I will be here at 4:30 am prompt to take your asses to the M.E.P.S. station and if you are hungover, sick and or dehydrated you will not pass your physical and this whole trip will be for nothing." He then handed us our $10 government vouchers for our dinner that evening and off he went for the night. Naturally one of our "gangs" at the "Days Inn" was old enough to purchase alcohol. The best part about cheap hotels is that someone is always enterprising enough to know a convivence store offering at least beer and wine would always be successful and our location was no exception. So, after a short walk down the block and back and the small group of us had scored a case of beer. I drank 5 or 6 and after the day on the road, and all that excitement was fast asleep. After what seemed like 8 minutes later, 6 hours had passed, and the recruiter arrived at 4:00 a.m. sharp to take us down to M.E.P.S. for the day's activities. M.E.P.S operates like a well-oiled machine, one you arrive, its "Boys this way and girls that way", followed immediately by "Strip down to your underwear, place your belongings in the lockers and go stand in line #1." After wandering around the entire building from line 1 to line 22 in my underwear I was in a larger room with ten other twelve other "Men?". A very slovenly and obese nurse of oriental decent walked from man to man, grabbed each by the testicles and recited the dreaded "Turn your head and cough." I was a 17-year-old boy and thought that this was the most embarrassing thing I have ever had to do in my life. Little did I know that a few short minutes later, the "bar of humility" was to be dropped all the way to the floor for me. This nurse, once finished grabbing each of us by the family jewels, then proceeded to the front of the room and chortled out "Drop your drawers, turn around, grab your cheeks and spread em'", she then grabbed the cheeks on her fat face with both hands and said, "And I don't mean theeeesssseeee...." We all naturally complied, and I made it through, what was then, and still in the top 5 today, of the most embarrassing moments of my life. As much as I thought I wanted to, I did not die on the spot and a few short minutes later, with smiles on our faces and clothes on our backs again, we were raising our right hands in front of the big American flag. With this I was now officially a member of the United States Army.

It was the Summer of 1981, and I had my whole life ahead of me, Lisa and I were still going steady, but the "honeymoon" period was long gone. We tended to argue a lot and in fact, that year, in the "Wills" of the class of 1981 for us in 1982, Lisa and I were wished a "Trip on the Love Boat." For you readers who may not be aware, the "Love Boat" was a popular TV sitcom of the era, a romantic comedy. We held together though, almost certainly more due to need and stability rather than love and happiness. As someone much smarter than I once wrote "Absence makes the heart grow fonder" and Lisa and I were about to test that theory out. A week or so after my "swearing in" I was headed to the airport for my flight to Fort Leonard Wood Missouri. I did enlist with two female classmates from my class of "82", but at that time military basic training was completely segregated by gender, and after we three successfully completed our physicals and swearing in, they were headed to Fort Jackson South Carolina (the only base that hosted basic training for female Soldiers at the time) and I never crossed paths with them during our military years again. The "firsts" in my life kept on coming along. The TWA flight from Grand Rapids Michigan to St Louis Missouri for basic training was the first time I had ever flown. Although, like everyone else, I was a little apprehensive being packed into a pressurized "cigar tube" the view was breathtaking and awe inspiring. I do remember being especially happy when the "smoking light" came on I'm certain, I quaffed a half pack of Marlboro's in the two-hour flight.

Until that point I had also never been on any commercial bus other than a school bus. It was a two-and-a-half-hour ride on the Greyhound to the gates of Fort "Lost in the Woods." The nickname was well deserved as sitting right in the middle of the Ozarks, land of trees and hills, was the few thousand acres of Ft, Leo Wood. Once dropped at the gate, I would be introduced to a third kind of bus affectionately referred to as the "Cattle car" This was the name for this style because it is exactly what they were, take one of the large livestock trailers you see on the highway, paint it O.D. (Olive Drab for those unfamiliar with this acronym) Stencil "U.S. Army" on the side of it, add some posts in the middle for troops to hang on to while moving and there you have it. We were taken to an area on post with row after row of simple, two story wooden buildings, all white, maybe 20' by 60' in size, with nothing on the inside of them excepts a row of cots on either side, a footlocker at the foot of each cot, a restroom (from this moment forward to ever be referred to as the "Latrine" the ARMY word for restroom) and a flight of stairs going up to the second floor.

The very first matter of business was the fire safety briefing. The Sergeant assigned to my building carefully illustrated where the exit doors were, and how to safely and expeditiously depart the buildings in case of fire. Immediately upon completing that he stated, "Now all that bullshit I just told you? Forget it, go to the nearest door or window and jump out the mother fucker, these building are all wood, were built 75 years ago and burn to the ground in approximately 12 minutes" that was the REAL fire safety briefing. From that moment forward, there was an assigned "fire guard", a Soldier in uniform wearing a spray painted, red helmet who paced back and forth down the halls to sound the alarm should a fire break out. This duty would be rotated every two hours during our authorized hours of sleep. Fire guard, along with "police call" (the Army's term for walking around and picking up everything that wasn't supposed to be there), uniform and equipment issues, and the occasional briefing or two occupied the next 7-10 days or so. The one key part of becoming a Soldier was having an individual forget he was once a civilian. "Civilian" was a term that everyone who was not in the miliary now. The first thing that gives you the impression you are not a civilian anymore is your first trip to the "latrine." You immediately notice the row of toilets 30" or so from one another and there are no dividers between them. Or the urinals for that matter. Long story short, during the "rush hour" for the shitter in the morning you are sitting well within arm's reach to the guys sitting and shitting on the toilets to the left and right of you. The Army "officially" begins this important process by having you pack everything you brought along with you that wasn't O.D. (Olive Drab) green into a box to be shipped to your H.O.R. (that's Home of Record, for all of you who haven't had enough acronyms yet) on Uncle Sam's dime of course. We were then all taken to the P.X. (Post Exchange, you exchange money for goods, to the rest of the civilian world a place like this is called "Walmart") given $18 in cash and told EXACTLY how we were going to spend it, 6 T shirts, 6 pairs men's underwear (we did get to choose boxers or briefs, the only individual choice I would experience for the next 10 weeks), 3 bars of soap, 1 soap dish, et cetera. When I finished my required purchases I had $3.75 to my name. This was to be used for the haircut which was the final stop in our P.X. adventure. Of course, it was the 80's so most of us had long hair, mountains of which was already on the floor of the barber shop when we arrived. I would be leaving my contribution there like everyone else. Some of us left more than others but I do remember who left the most significant contribution of all. We had one kid whose blond hair was the length of the middle of his back drawn neatly into a “pony tail”. He sits down in the chair, and I remember the barber getting a great big smile on his face. At this point he says, “I only get to pull these out once a week or so”. What he was referring to was a huge set of razor-sharp hedge clippers he kept in the bottom drawer of his workstation. 3 seconds and one quick snip later, and the ponytail was no more than a blond topping on the “hair pie” that was lying on the floor. Once we were all finished, I remember having around eighteen cents left to my name. I did get to keep this though because that original $18 in cash was not a “gift” from the government, but an advance on our first paycheck. I would see this $18 deduction on my first L.E.S. Yes, the acronyms are flying, L.E.S. is short for “Leave and Earnings Statement”. The rest of the civilized world just refers to this as a pay stub. I remember thinking “Boy this Basic Training is sure overrated.” I was about to discover how wrong I was.

One afternoon, a large cattle car drove up, we were told to take everything we owned, throw it into the big, green, canvas duffel bag we all now owned and climb aboard. My destination was only a short distance away. This little ride ended with my first introduction to a Drill Instructor. These fine N.C.O’s (Non-Commissioned Officers) were also affectionately known as Drill Instructors or D.I.’s. The D.I.’s were distinguished by large brown derby hats the proudly wore as a testament to their training and commitment to train the next group of fine young Americans to become the defenders of our country. Now, the next few hours were a blur. A loud mass of young people in green, scurrying back and forth surrounded by D. I’s with short wands in their hands. The D.I.’s were screaming, cracking the slower new Soldiers on the backs of the knees, attempting to make an orderly group fall into place. I am certain if you have ever seen the balls of sardines in the ocean being herded in tightly by a group of dolphins preparing for a meal, we would have looked just like the dry land version of this. At the end of it all, while it seemed like an eternity at the time, in 5 or 10 minutes we were assembled in four neat rows in front of a large brick building which was to be our home for the next 10 weeks. I remember very clearly the logo stenciled above the main entrance to the barracks. It was "C-2-4, The more you sweat in peace, the less you bleed in war" this was to be my mantra for the next couple of months. The C-2-4 stood for "Charlie Company, 2nd Battalion, 4th Division" to the left and right of our building, were two identical buildings. To the left was "B-2-4" (Bravo Company) and the right "D-2-4" (Delta Company) A new cycle of basic training had begun on Fort Leonard Wood, Missouri.

Basic Training has one function in the military and one function only, to turn civilians into Soldiers. This is a simple conversion for some, for others not so simple, and for that rare few, impossible. The D.I.'s were tasked with this responsibility and took to it with real zest. The Army in its infinite wisdom, as I was soon to discover, gave me a special "treatment" The D.I.'s were reading aloud the job selections that each recruit in their care had chosen and then would be sent to if they successfully completed basic training. Unbeknownst to me, Ft Leonard Wood Missouri was the home of the Army Engineer Corps and pretty much everyone sent there had some association with that career. 13B is the descriptive (or M.O.S. Military Occupational Specialty) for the Army career field "Combat Engineer". They were reading aloud the M.O.S. indicators; "Phelps 13B,

Phillips 13B, Quincy 13B, Roberts 91B" "WHAT IN THE FUCK IS A 91B?" the D.I. exclaimed. "Combat Medic Drill Sergeant," I smartly replied. The entire cadre of D.I.'s burst out in laughter. 'This is fucking awesome!" The lead D.I. stated, "Usually I must have one of my NCO's carry this cocksucker everywhere, but no more! We got us a medic!" And with a peal of laughter out of nowhere was produced a white metal can around 2 feet, by 2 feet, by 18" deep. It was painted with a huge red cross on the one side and that bitch weighed about 15 pounds. Guess how I know it weighed 15 pounds? Because that damn thing would be on MY back in addition to the rest of the shit I had to carry for the next ten weeks or so. And so basic training "Boot Camp" began. The first two weeks of basic training focus on one main aspect of combat, stress. The Army has methods for creating stress down to a fine science. Stress can almost be achieved single handedly by using its close cousin, fatigue. If those two methods did not work, they always could resort to pain. Now a few short years later the Army made some serious changes in the training of its recruits following some abuse allegations. No longer could the D.I.'s lay a hand on a recruit. Shortly thereafter they could no longer even use foul language. But rest assured neither of those policies were in effect at Ft Leonard Wood in 1981. The D.I.'s would slap the fuck out of you if all other motivational methods failed. Sometimes even just simply because they didn't like you I suppose. I remember what my dad whispered to me the night before I left for basic training. "Just keep your mouth shut and do what you're told and you'll be just fine" his advice served me well. For now, I would be getting (along with everyone else in Charlie Company) between 3 and 4 ½ hours a night of sleep for the next two weeks, the other 20 hours or so were filled with learning how to march, exercise, march some more, Even the most mundane tasks performed in everyday life needed to be forgotten as the Army had its own, unique manner in which to perform the same tasks. New recruits are taught everything (re-taught mostly) they need to remain healthy and somewhat happy, which translates into Army speak as "deployable". I remember classes on how to correctly do; tooth brushing, showering and of course condom use. The last class I remember vividly. The senior drill instructor stepped up on stage, in front of us 120 or so fresh recruits who were sitting at the position of attention (yes you can "sit" at attention, that means back straight, knees together directly in front of you, hands placed straight on top of the thighs, head straight in proportion to the back and eyes straight forward) and proceeded to speak. "We D.I.'s draw straws each rotation to see who gets the honor of teaching this class, it's pretty simple, you visit the whorehouse, you wear a rubber or you get a series of shots AND an article 15 for fucking yourself up and not being able to do your duty" An "Article 15" refers to chapter 15 in the U.C.M.J (Uniform Code of Military Justice, an encyclopedia of law used by the Armed Forces in lieu of the civilian justice system) which describes in great detail, specific punishments and penalties, for specific infractions. "So, to do this correctly" the senior drill instructor says, "you take yourself firmly in hand" at which point he unbuttons his fly, reaches in his pants and presents a massive, full erect penis, the entire front row of Soldiers almost fell over backwards in their chairs. "You then open the wrapper and delicately roll the rubber from the head all the way to the base (he does)" "Now you're ready for action!" At which point he pulls the giant latex prophylactic from his pants, condom covered and all, and throws it out into the audience. Three rows of Soldiers damn near fell over backwards where that damn thing landed. We all burst out in laughter. It was a respite from the stress and rigors of basic training even if only for a few minutes.

By the end of the first week or so, all the individuals who would never be able to handle the rigors of military life were “weeded out” and sent back to their H.O.R.’s, The actual “military training” was about to begin. Besides beginning to get in outstanding physical condition, I began to feel a tremendous sense of pride becoming part of an exclusive club. One with a long and glorious history of the defense of our notion. I also got to start doing some of the cooler stuff one thinks of when they want to “play Army” I would learn how to use any and all of the individual weapon systems the Army provided Soldiers to fight and win our nations wars. In fact, the previous sentence is most of the Army’s “mission statement”. Another misnomer about the military is the food, hell the Army even teases about its own food. My experience was completely the opposite, I never ate so well (or so much) in my entire life. Unfortunately, another method the D.I.’s used to induce stress was by rushing the mealtimes down to the absolute shortest time that they had to. To the instructors, chow times were just an interruption of a very short time frame in which they had to turn “vermin” into Soldiers. It was a necessary evil to them, nonetheless. I developed a few habits from the chow hall that I would carry the rest of my life. The first, and most prominent, was the habit of eating as fast as I can, and although I do eat much slower, it would be safe to say that I do not ever hesitate to “savor every bite”. I also must be careful as to how much food I put on my plate to this day, because I have a psychological hangup of having to “clean my plate” after each meal. At the chow hall, once your allotted 10-12 minutes of "dining" were over, you picked your tray up and proceeded to take it to the steel framed opening at the end of the room. Above that opening was a sign in bold print stating "Take what you want BUT eat what you take" and inside were the dishwashers, who were also the defacto food monitors. If you slid a tray in there that had any real significant portions of food on it, the D.I.'s were notified, and you could count on being singled out and "smoked" right outside the chow hall. Being "smoked" is the term the military uses (at least it's not an acronym) to describe physical punishments. These punishments were generally in the form of a strenuous, repetitive exercise regiment, or being forced to be still in a completely uncomfortable position. Those "positions" go from being uncomfortable, for a few short minutes, to agonizing, usually as soon as 5 minutes or so. Even as terrible as some of this might sound to a civilian it all became what would be called "fun" to me. I was not alone. You must remember that anyone who joins the Army must have at least some desire to become a Soldier or probably played as one as a kid. Well, now we were REALLY becoming Soldiers and starting to have a good time doing it.

Of all the things the United States Military can do, almost the single thing it cannot is stop the clock (Or calendar in this case). My experience was no different. Despite my thinking at the time that basic training would never end, a short two months later, my basic training was almost over. Ten weeks of drill and ceremony, fire watch, exercise (always referred to in the military as P.T. short for physical training), weapons qualification, and being "smoked" Uncle Sam deemed me ready, willing and able to call myself a United States Soldier. It is a title I proudly carry to this day. With that accomplished, Uncle Sam also had to live up to his end of the covenant that he and my mother made and sent my ass right back to Pine River High School to complete my high school education. This would be an interesting transition for me since I was no longer a student, but a Soldier. The rest of my classmates were still young men and women, I was now most certainly and fully, a man. I had started smoking at around age 15 and although my parents always told us if we were going to smoke, to do it in the house and not sneak it from them. I tried to do this, but the dirty looks I got from my father every time I lit up was so annoying I went back to hiding it. When he picked me up from Grand Rapids airport upon completion of basic training, I hopped in the car and through my carton of Marlboro's onto the dash of the car and said, "I'm not expecting to get anymore grief over this am I?" He had a great big smile on his face and never said another word about it. He didn't have to, I had become a man in my father's eyes as well.

If I did not like school before I went into the Army, I would dislike it even more now. It was, in my mind, a complete waste of time as my career path had already begun. I took this displeasure out on every teacher, classmate and associate who crossed my path that final, senior year. I was inconsolable and uncontrollable by most standards. The only good points were that I would be able to spend time with the love of my life, Lisa, again, and the mood of a senior class knowing that high school was coming to an end was very uplifting. I had grown in every way possible a person could grow during that Summer. I had also become somewhat physically intimidating. I went into basic training at approximately 134 pounds or so, but 10 weeks, ample food, plenty of exercise and discipline, I returned at almost 170 pounds. I did have a couple of scores to settle as well. I remember two individuals who had bullied me in previous years because they were much larger than I was. That had also changed, and I think both knew what ass whipping was coming when I came face to face with them that year. Both took their beatings graciously, and I had the satisfaction of knowing that I had "settled the scores". Despite my love for sports in my prior years of high school, and my fair performance even at my smaller size, I did not have a lot of desire to participate once I returned. This is a regret I would carry for the rest of my life as I probably would have been pretty good at my two favorites wrestling and football. I guess I had just endured enough physical stress and discipline over the last couple of months and could not bring myself to voluntarily put anymore of either on my shoulders. All I was focused on that final year was fun, graduation, and getting back into uniform and making some money. My original enlistment, being split option, was in the Army Reserve and having completed basic training, I was able to attend "drill" (the Army Reserve's word for work weekend) with the 1254th Station Hospital in Grand Rapids. This made sure I remained in a state of readiness for the Army and kept some decent spending money in my pocket for my last year of high school. My two original female "battle buddies" also survived their basic training experience in Ft Jackson South Carolina. Since we all had chosen combat medic as our M.O.S all three of us were assigned to the 1254th. As Grand Rapids was 60 or so miles away from where we all lived, we were able to carpool on drill weekends and save us some gas money. All three of us would generally just stay down at the station hospital for the weekend and either sleep in the drill hall (workplace) or more likely head to one of our fellow Soldiers houses for a good Friday and Saturday night party. I think the best part for me about my reserve "hitch" was that I got to take a little two week "vacation" from my Senior year. It was the middle of February 1982, and Northern Michigan was having another of the coldest Winters on record. The Army was about to provide me with a two-week respite though. The 1254th always performed its A.T. (Annual Training, all Army Reserve and National Guard enlistments involved duty requirements of one weekend a month and two full weeks per year, A.T. was that two weeks) at Ft. Sam Houston Texas in San Antonio. It was the first time in my life I had ever been in a location in February and not been standing knee deep in snow outdoors. It was a wonderful two weeks. The weather was a balmy mid-50's and although a little foggy, I did manage to see some sunshine. I worked during the regular workday, Monday through Friday at the post medical facility Brooke Army Medical Center. Since I had not completed my official Army Medical course, there was not a lot of patient care I could do. What I could do was pretty much relegated to dressing changes and bedpan cleaning. I clearly remember this was well before the days of disposable bedpans and urinals. Once those items were "used" it was my job to take them to the latrine, empty them out and run them through the "cleaner". It was like a "dishwasher" of sorts. It was a vertical device faintly resembling what you might call a urinal. You would place the bedpan "business side" forward into the matching and operate 3 levers, the first lever pulled the pan tightly into the machine, the second lever ran a powerful jet of water through the inside, while the third and final lever blasted the inside of the bedpan with a jet of high-pressure steam. At this point you would, carefully or you would burn the shit out of your hands, hang the now clean bedpan up on the rack on the wall and grab a clean one from the other end to take back to the room. Despite my lower echelon duties, I felt like king shit because I was going to work every day and got to drink beer after work. It seemed especially wonderful as I was able to not only purchase my own beer, but I could get Coors beer at a time it was still only a regional drink not available back in Michigan. Sadly, like all good things, this great assignment came to an end. I knew at the end of this assignment that active-duty Army was life for me. Nonetheless, I was on my way back to Pine River to ensure the covenant between my mother and Uncle Sam was fulfilled.

Although I was only 17 at this time I had no problem purchasing any alcohol back in the "World". As a Servicemember there are only two places in your universe, first there was whatever duty station you were located at, performing your duty. Every other location was wistfully referred to as "the world" or "back on the block" depending on the context in which you were discussing it. It was a different era though, and although the drinking age was legally 19, all I had to do was produce the nice, shiny new greed I.D. card I had showing I was a "Member of the US Armed Forces" and the cash register always rang "Sale". Usually the proprietor would simply say "You home on leave son?" to which I would reply "yes" (which was somewhat true) and the result was always the same "Sale". This made me popular among my high school friends as well, as from that moment on dry parties were a thing of the past. It was a good thing that I wasn't much of a marijuana user, because drugs were the things that I could no longer partake in. The Army was a real stickler on that, and routine urine drug testing was now a regular part of my life.

And just like that, all the high school parties, memories, trials and tribulations, were, for me, a thing of the past with a short walk down the gymnasium aisle. I thought that I couldn't be happier, until the next aisle I would walk down followed three months after high school graduation in the fall of 1982 and was the Church aisle. Despite the more than occasional arguments and discord between Lisa and I, we still had the very same reasons of need and dependance on each other that brought us together in the first place. That being said, and the fact now that I was having to depart for a "unaccompanied" (duty stations were, for married folk, "accompanied" meaning your loved one could join you, and "unaccompanied" meaning they could not) training session, we got married. There were a great many benefits for being married in service besides the obvious. Married Soldiers were entitled to B.A.H. and B.A.S. (Basic Allowance for Housing, and Basic Allowance for Subsistence, respectively) which amounted to a 30% or so pay increase. So after a cute little country wedding in the booming metropolis of Leroy, a few days of honeymooning at the Grand Traverse Resort in Traverse City and I was packing my bag for my first assignment as a United States Soldier. Lisa would stay with my parents (as is done in most societies around the world when two people are married and the man must leave) and I was headed for my training as an Army Medic (91B was the nomenclature for the M.O.S. at the time) at Fort Sam Houston Texas.

My extensive official military travel experiences began in San Antonio Texas the location of what was affectionately known as "Ft Sam" or more accurately "The Summer Camp of the Army". This location and training post was a 180 degree turnaround from my Army experiences at basic training. For starters, any courses taught at Ft. Sam were referred to "gentleman's courses". A gentleman's course is one where there is no training after regular working hours, weekends, holidays, and never too early in the morning. Where revile was blown at 4 am sharp at Ft Leo Wood, mornings at Ft Sam did not start until 7 am. This is mid-afternoon by Army standards. Also, unlike Ft. Leo Wood, all the courses taught at Ft Sam were co-ed, and of course all had the most gorgeous girls the Amy had to offer. Almost all the females in the Army at the time wanted to do something medical as a military career. Although Ft Sam had some of the finest, healthy recreational facilities and activities anywhere, most of my spare time was spent either getting sloshed over a barbecue grill or fishing poles with some of my new friends. The most fun to have though was getting really, really sloshed every Friday and Saturday night at Ft Sam's huge NCO club. On rare occasions we as a company group would perform an organized P.T. (Physical Training) morning, but mostly each Soldier was allowed to perform P.T. on their own schedule. As long as you were able to successfully complete the A.P.F.T. (Armed forces Physical Fitness Test) held at the end of the course, nobody really cared about how you got yourself there. During the regular business hours though, the crash course in emergency medicine for field medics was the order of the day. Most everything that could be done to save a fellow Soldiers life, who had been blown or shot to pieces on the battlefield was taught to us there at Ft. Sam. I would have to say on an educational level, our training would have placed us somewhere between to the skills of an L.P.N. (Licensed Practical Nurse) at the low end, and an R.N. (Registered Nurse) at the high end. We could perform all the cleaning, patching, and wound care required of an L.P.N, while in addition we were taught to start I.V.'s, administer subcutaneous and intra-dermal injections and suturing at an R.N. skill level. The primary function of a combat medic was to stabilize and keep a Soldier alive long enough to be evacuated off the battlefield to a facility where much more advanced trauma treatment could be obtained. The Army must have been doing something right since the survival rate of a Soldier who was alive when carried off the battlefield went from around 50-60% during the Civil War to well over 80% after the invention of the medivac helicopter era of Vietnam. The pace of learning was fast as the Army only had 16 weeks to bring everyone in that M.O.S. up to a basic skill set which could be verified. For example, we learned everything you wanted to know about needles during "injection week". I remember at the beginning of that week one of the Soldiers asked, well stated actually, "My recruiter said we practiced on oranges". The cadre burst out in laughter and replied, "You have been misled" If I harbored any fear of needles before, none of that fear remained after those seven days. The fact I had been "stuck", at a MINIMUM, 40-60 times that week probably was the reason for that. At the end of the week though, covered with bruises, we all emerged none the worse for wear. I must have been doing something correct, as I was promoted from E-1 Private, to E-3 Private First Class. There are basically three structural levels of pay, duty assignments and responsibilities in the United States Military. The first, and most basic, the foundation of the Army, as it has always been, is borne by the enlisted Soldier. This level is referred to on paper as "E". This level is the meat, muscle and operational level of the military. At this level an individual could advance via promotion from E-1 Private, to E-9

Sergeant Major. Pay, and subsequently responsibilities all increase along with pay grade. There is a sublevel in the enlisted grades referred to as N.C.O's (Non-Commissioned Officers), always referred to as the "Backbone of the Army". Once an individual reaches the pay grade of E-5 (Sergeant), they are considered an N.C.O. The second structural level of the Army is generally referred to as the Warrant Officer designated with a "W" pay grade. Individuals can advance from W-1 Warrant Officer to CW-5 Chief Warrant Officer. Think of Warrant Officers as the technical guys of the military, maintenance chiefs, helicopter pilots and Army boat captains are usually Warrant Officers. Although a Warrant Officer does not have the official contract (Commission) with the United States Government that a regular officer does, they are considered officers nonetheless and are saluted, allowed entry into the officer's clubs and establishments. This leads us to the final structural level of the military, the "Officer" or "Commissioned Officer" referred naturally to as a "O". Commissioned Officers have a covenant of sorts with the United States government. Once both parties, the individual and the government, arrive at an agreement, the individual is given their Commission and starts at the bottom of the "O" pay scale as O-1 "Second Lieutenant". They can then advance via promotions to the rank of 0-9 "General." Generals are indicated by having 4 stars on each of their collars. Contrary to what Hollywood shows, there are no 5-star Generals in existence anymore. There were only 1 or 2 during WWII I believe, being General of the Armies, Dwight D. Eisenhower, and Douglas MacArthur. Most important to note is that all Warrant Officers "outrank" Enlisted Soldiers, all Commissioned Officers outrank Warrant Officers and so on. That is technically on paper anyway. I had a friend ask me once, while I was describing this to him, “So a 2nd Lieutenant (O-1), can make a Sergeant Major (E-9) do push-ups?”, to which I replied “Yes, only once”. The “once” being because once that Sergeant Major discussed what happened with the Lieutenant Colonel (O-5) or Colonel (O-6) he is certain to work for that 2nd Lieutenant would be immediately called into the office and briefed (the kindest word I can think to use about what is REALLY going to happen) how rank in the military REALLY works. The lieutenants remaining military career, and quite possibly the rest of his or her natural life, could certainly be measured in hours. I felt like I had to include this rank description somewhere in here because it is important for a civilian to understand this basic premise for any realistic discussion of the military to make sense.

It was now the fall of 1982, and I returned home. Home to Lisa, home to Reed City and home to the land of zero opportunity. I took a factory job outside of town at a place called Nartron Corporation. Ironically Nartron was the company that provided all the O.D. green turn signal assemblies for every military vehicle on 4 wheels at the time. Despite that, it was a dismal place to work, and my job was to load machines with different colors of wire for them to be spun together into the various sizes and shapes of wiring harnesses to be used to create their (Nartron's) parts. If there was hell on earth for me, this was it. Life in a factory consists of punching in, to do exactly the same thing for 2 hours or so till the buzzer tells you that you are entitled to a cigarette break. I couldn't tell you what people who didn't smoke did. Then another buzzer and back to work for another 2 hours until the buzzer notifies you that you are allowed to partake in enough nutrition to get you through the next 4 hours of drudgery, in a word "lunch". Then the buzzer again, 2 more hours, another cigarette or 5, 2 more hours and the buzzer finally says you can go home for the evening or at least 10 hours or so till the buzzer starts the next workday. Repeat this ad nauseum for the next 20 to 40 years, and that is the existence of a factory worker. Within 60 days I had my paperwork turned in at the 1254th to change my status from an Army Reserve Soldier to an Active Duty Soldier. I was accepted to active duty with only one caveat. The Army, just like the "world" only has work positions available for so many Soldiers in each job description and since my 91B Medic classification was particularly popular, I had two choices, I could wait the year or two for an opening to happen in that classification or change job classifications. The thought of working around the "buzzer" for even another day was painful, let alone the prospect of over a year. This made my decision to change job classification particularly simple. I had to good fortune of scoring particularly high on the A.S.V.A.B. (yep, acronym for Armed Forces Vocational Aptitude Battery, the test that gives the military the knowledge that prevents floor sweepers from becoming brain surgeons) so I could choose pretty much any vocation I wished to work in. My biggest concern (not exactly the smartest as I look back now) was which vocation would get my back on the road the fastest and back into uniform. It seemed the greatest need the Army had at that time was for mechanics and I chose the M.O.S. of 63D. 63D is known in words as a "Self-Propelled Field Artillery Systems Mechanic", or simply, a "howitzer fixer." That seemed interesting enough so I applied my signature to my new Active-Duty contract and it wasn't a few short weeks and I was back in uniform and on my way to Ft. Knox Kentucky.

Ft Knox is mostly known by everyone for the nation's gold repository which sets upon the property there. I only ever just glanced at the building from over 100 or so yards away which is as close as Joe Q. Public is ever allowed to get to it. To me and everyone else in the Army, Ft. Knox was much more importantly the "Armor Center of the Army". Anything and everything to do with tanks, howitzers and anything that went "boom" on wheels was taught at Ft. Knox. I arrived in the middle of a particularly cold and foggy night. The C.Q. (Charge of Quarters, usually an N.C.O who sat at the desk all night long monitoring all the activity in the building and taking care of all after-hours business) had me just throw my stuff in an empty room down the hall. The only thing that cold, dark room had was a cot on one end and that was fine with me. It had been a long bus ride down (the military was cutting costs, so we were traveling my bus now instead of flying whenever realistically possible), I was exhausted and slept like the dead with dreams of my new adventures filling my head.

Not surprisingly the discord my wife and I had during our high school years did not magically disappear with our marriage vows. Once I returned from Ft. Sam, things were nice for a while but the poverty and drudgery life in the "world" weighed heavily on me, and I drank a lot to alleviate my perceived misery. I had some minor scrapes with the law but nothing that would jeopardize my military career and the fact that I was going back to active duty gave me a lot more leniency in Osceola County than I should have been given. As would happen more often in the future, every time our marriage was really on the rocks with serious consideration of divorce, I would get orders to leave (unaccompanied) again, and just like the adage "Absence makes the heart grow fonder", or at least in our case more tolerant.

One thing I have always enjoyed is education, in any way shape or form, and my courses at Ft. Knox were no exception. Fort Knox introduced me to a new term in America as well, 'dry county." Never would have thought that after 1933 (or whenever the hell else prohibition ended) that there would be places in the good old "U. S. of A" that would still have the sale of alcohol banned. Ft. Know was right smack in the middle of one of these counties so you had to plan accordingly. Every week we could usually find a member of the cadre who was driving on a "booze run" into the next county and score a few cases of beer and liquor for us to get us through the week. The weeks of training weren't bad in Kentucky and went by quickly. Each day we would walk into the open bay which had engines, vehicles and parts in various states of assembly throughout the room. We would go from "workstation" to station and perform repair tasks to insure we could do these things up to a measured standard. On thing I would learn in the future, is there is a world of difference disassembling or re-assembling a vehicle or part in a nice clean bay. Not to mention the fact that literally hundreds of students before you had turned that bolt, or removed that part, before you ensured everything was well worn and loose. At least I would have the memories of how things were supposed to work, even when I would have my doubts performing the same tasks hip deep in mud and freezing temperatures. I would wistfully recall these nice comfortable, heated bays while working on broken shit in the training areas deep in the heart of Grafenwoehr in the Federal Republic of Germany (the official name of West Germany at the time) some years later. A few short weeks later I had successfully completed the 63D course at Ft Knox and was a certified mechanic. Unbeknownst to me, I had also acquired a skill which would earn me a living for years to come. Upon graduation from my course there I was given my first active-duty station and job. I was assigned to A-Battery, T.C.B (Training Command Battalion) at Ft. Sill Oklahoma. I was given two weeks "leave" (that's time off with pay to your civilian types) and headed for home and my wife.

A lot was about to change in both of our lives. We were to embark on a lot of "firsts" for both of us. It's hard to say which would be the most important, but I would have to say it was the fact that Lisa was pregnant with our first child. Another first was this assignment would be my first "accompanied" tour of duty and my wife (and budding new family) would be joining me in Oklahoma. I had also been promoted to Specialist (E-4) so the money was a little better too. I would need it. We said our goodbyes to the only home we had ever known, said our goodbyes and packed everything we owned into a small U-Haul trailer. All our earthly possessions fit neatly into our car, and the smallest 4-6 trailer. There is post housing on every active-duty post in America, but it is never enough to house all of the Soldiers and their families that were assigned there. In order to alleviate some of the shortages, the Army mandated that a Soldier had to be E-5 Sergeant or higher rank in order to qualify for post housing. We were going to do what every other Soldier does who does not meet the requirements for post housing does. We were going to get us a little apartment. The town attached to Ft. Sill was called Lawton, Oklahoma. Pretty much every post in America has a town either attached to it, or in very close proximity. These towns generally have a few things in common. The most common is that they are not affluent by any measure of the term. Most are "inner city" type communities complete with pawn shops, bars, liquor stores and the ubiquitous "Pay-Day Loan" establishments. The only good part about these types of communities was that they had ample, low-income housing that all junior enlisted Soldiers and their families require to survive. We spent our first two weeks on post in the guest house (think Super 8 operated by M.W.R. the Morale, Welfare, and Recreation department), which was nice, but once we found our small apartment we were happy to move in. Lisa's pregnancy progressed superbly, and it was probably the happiest time ever of our married life. My duty assignment was really good as well. It was an easy enough job and was as close to working on nice clean vehicles in nice, heated bays as I would ever come. Training Command Battalion is exactly as the name implies. Ft. Sill is the Artillery Center for the United States Army and ALL things that go "boom" are taught there. It's important to know the difference between "boom" and "bang" since "Boom" is taught at Ft. Sill, and I would consider any projective larger than 1" around a "boom". "Bang" is all handheld weaponry and is taught at the Army's Infantry training center Ft. Benning Georgia. Having never been stationed there, one of the few places, that is about all I can comment on it. My job at A-battery was keeping all the howitzers maintained, serviced and repaired so the "gun bunnies" (a term affectionately used to describe Soldiers whose M.O.S. was 13B "Field Artillery Specialist" can use them to go out and train each day and usually blow the hell out of Mt Scott which was the high ground in the impact area. This reminds me that in addition to rank, there is also a type of caste system in play in the Army. You see in addition to being the highest rank, Officers of all grades were kind of like the highest caste along with professionals such as doctors, lawyers and such. The next caste down was warrant officers and the higher ranked N.C.O's. Then came the caste in which I was mostly a part of at the time, the service caste. This included mechanics, cooks, line medics and so on. Finally, almost regardless of rank was the lowest caste in the Army (much to their argument and disdain justifiably) the line Soldier. This was the cast of 13B's (Gun Bunnies, all graduates from Ft. Lenard Wood), 11B's (Infantrymen, lovingly called "Grunts"), 12B (Combat Engineers), 45D (Tank Crewmembers or D.A.T.'s "dumb assed tankers") and so on. Pretty much any M.O.S. most likely to put an individual in close contact with the enemy during combat (and therefore most likely to get sent home in a box) fell into this caste. So, while the students and lower caste cadre would all do their socializing together, I and my caste would spend out social times together as well. This may all seem insignificant but when you put it all together, hopefully it gives a civilian a basic idea how the day-to-day function of the Army occurs. Despite everything going well in my life, my priorities were nowhere near where they should have been. While chronologically, socially and vocationally I was a man, in reality (as Lisa told me on more than one occasion) I was a "little boy playing at being a man". I did my duty, I went to work every day and managed to stay out of trouble, but when I wasn't working, instead of planning for a new baby, and being a husband, I spent my spare time like the single, young male Soldiers did. That meant drinking, fishing, hanging out with friends and so on. One of the best memories I have of Fort Sill was a weekend when Ron came down to visit. He enlisted in the Army precisely 13 months after I did. He had a few days leave from his first active-duty assignment at Ft

Leo Wood and decided to come down one weekend for a visit. He owned this great "shaggin wagon" (80's term for a van, usually bright exterior color, and shag carpet lined interior) which was a 1972 Dodge van. The outside was pumpkin orange with red trim, and it had a 14" or so oval window on each side in the back. He affectionately named it "The Orange Blossom Special." That Saturday we were together, we decided we would take a small tour of the miles of ranges on Ft Sill. Off to the miles and miles of empty range roads we went. We took a gun and 6 bottles of various flavors of Boones Farm wine and had a grand time. At the end of the day after finishing our refreshments and blasting more than a few road signs, we stumbled back to my apartment and passed out. I am ashamed now of my behavior at the time, and could make all kinds of excuses, such as being only 19 years old, but many young men of that age managed to do the right things and I never seemed to be able to manage it.

Unfortunately, just like the everywhere else in the rest of the universe, I am not able to turn back the hands of time and change the things I did. Time continued to pass for us, and I received the greatest gift of my life at Ft Sill, the birth of my first daughter. It is one of those moments I will never forget. One thing I did actually get right every time was to be present at the birth of my children. Except for my youngest, I was the first human hand to welcome my children onto this earth. When my little girls face first appeared to me, (she was born what they call "sunny side up or facing up instead of down) her little eyes flickered open. Her eyes were the darkest blue and no words can describe what happened in my heart at that moment. I did learn that one more common expression was true. There is such a thing as "Love at first sight" and love is exactly what I was in with that little girl, instantly. I burst into tears and still remember sobbing there telling her how much her daddy already loved her. My eyes still well up a little bit to this day thinking of that moment. I had a similar experience with all my other children as well, and each as emotionally moving as this. A few seconds later, back to reality and once mother and baby were okay, I took that giant sigh of relief each new father feels at that moment. Now operations at a military hospital do differ a little bit from their civilian counterparts and my wife was to learn this first hand. In the civilian world, a woman and her new child are waited on by the staff, for a quiet wonderful birthing experience. In the military hospital, a woman gives birth, is returned to her room, baby goes in nursery and the goal is to get woman and child back into the "world" as expeditiously as possible. The standard to be met for departure was once a woman was able to walk to the restroom, make their own bed and have no major bleeding, mom and new baby are discharged. The very next day I received a call at my workstation from the nurse informing me that my wife and daughter needed to be picked up and taken home. I proceeded to take my lunch break early and drove a deuce and a half (That is truck, O.D. Green, 6x6, canvas covered open back @ 8' tall) to Reynolds Army Hospital, threw a B.D.U. (Battle Dress Uniform) camouflage top over my wife's shoulders and took her and my baby to our apartment in town. It's a laughable moment to this day that despite my new daughter's earliest exposure to the military, and the fact she took her first "car ride" in an Army truck, she never even considered a career in the military. For the record, she has been much more successful, educated and happy as a civilian than I'm certain she ever would have been in the military. The real work as a husband and now father had just begun. I learned one thing quick on, parenting is hard work. This is especially true when you're essentially an overgrown child yourself at age 19. My new baby girl had what the old timers would refer to as "colic", which means essentially that your kid is going to cry and scream their head off no matter what you do. This is nerve wracking even to the most patient person. This is something I have never been for the record. I did finally find a way to get my poor little one to get some rest. That way was to drive her around town in the car. More than a few nights in Lawton Oklahoma, the local police would pull me over at 2 am, naturally assuming I was a drunk driver returning from the bar. In reality I was a young, half-asleep father driving in circles with a sleeping infant in the back seat. It wasn't long and the police didn't even pull me over anymore, but just waved at me as I drove by. I learned a new respect for women throughout this process though, because each weekday, I got an 8–10-hour reprieve from feeding, changing, playing with, occupying and otherwise parenting a new infant. This was something Lisa never got. A real husband and father would have given her a break and let her get away from time to time, I used my free time on the weekends to stay half sloshed with my new Army buddies, watching (by today's standard's "binging") the greatest new program to come to television "MTV".

A career in the military is known for having a lot of perks, financial well-being is not one of them. This is especially true for junior enlisted Soldiers like I was. We soon discovered why military towns are full of pawn shops and payday loan establishments. I fell into these financial "traps" like so many Soldiers before me. A simple explanation will go a long way here. The payday loan "system" works something like this. These establishments know that no matter what a Soldier may or may not have, they do have a regular income each and every two weeks. So, for the small interest fee of 25% they will give you a "loan" until your next payday rolls around. Virtually no questions asked. So, when I needed money for groceries, gas, diapers, formula, or at least as frequently, money to party with my buddies, down to the payday loan establishment I would go. I could borrow $20 anytime I wanted if each payday I took $25 dollars back to repay the loan. The pawn shops worked in somewhat a similar fashion, with a small amount of collateral (the pawn) to be placed up front as security for the money you needed. Virtually any item of value can be used as a pawn. Guns, stereo equipment, jewelry, watches, anything could work. That was assuming the item being pawned had at least equal to or more than the dollar amount you wanted to borrow. For example, you take your watch which has an aftermarket value of $75 to the pawn shop. The pawnbroker will probably offer to lend you up to around $40. He then keeps your watch as collateral for that $40 until the day comes that you do one of two things. The first is to return withing 30 days and repay the pawn broker his or her $40, along with the 25-50% interest which automatically accrues at day one. So if you return within the 30 days with $50 to repay your $40 loan you get to put your watch back on your wrist and go home. Things start to get a little trickier from there. See, that interest rate doubles from day 31-59, and then finally on day 60, if you have not repaid your debt, you just sold your $75 watch to the pawnbroker for $40. By applying a little simple math here, it doesn't take an individual long to realize that a young Soldier, whose paycheck is a few hundred dollars, very quickly doesn't have enough money left after repaying these types of loans to get them through until the next payday. The vicious financial cycle repeats itself.

Now when you add financial difficulties to a young newlywed couple who never really got along that well in the first place, the increased strain in our relationship was incredible. Now add on top of that, the stress of having a new infant in the house, my problems with alcohol abuse, the relationship became almost impossible. This situation would finally diffuse like the other times in Lisa and my past when the Army, by the nature of the career, would separate us for a while. In hindsight it was like the bell between rounds in a boxing match I suppose. I had been chosen for a little 3-month T.D.Y. (Temporary Duty, I don't know what the "Y" means) near Fort Devens in Massachusetts. The First Sergeant (also affectionately called "Top", an E-8, the head N.C.O. of an Army Company second only to the Company Commander) at A-Btry T.C.B. assembled all of us in the auditorium one morning and said "Which one of you rats can spend all day working in 90 degree heat in M.O.P.P. (heavy chemical protection gear) 4?" Naturally, me being the smart ass I am, raised my hand. First sergeant chuckled, "Oh Specialist Roberts do I have something for you!" A week or so later, I was a test subject (think lab rat) at Natick Army Research Laboratories in Natick Massachusetts. This ended up being a great little assignment. At Natick everything the Army uses, except for things that go "bang" is tested at Natick. This includes clothing, food, equipment, you name it. What I was there for, was to be a part of a group to test a new drug to prevent altitude sickness. It wasn't a new drug actually it was Decadron and had been used for renal treatment for years. Somehow scientists deduced that this drug may alleviate altitude sickness so there was only one way to find out. A typical day there would start by reporting to the lab at 8 am. There was no P.T. or anything even resembling military structure there, you were essentially a civilian while you were a test subject. You would then be wired to every type of physiological machine known to man inside a steel room, the door closed, and the atmosphere artificially decreased to a pressure equating 20,000 ft. Then we would be asked to pedal a stationary bike for 20 minutes or so. You could go faster or slower, but the only requirement was to finish the 20 minutes. Once that "test" was done, you were dismissed for the day. I guess they wanted to make sure fatigue would not skew any results of any other tests so usually it was one test a day. You could volunteer for other small tests as well if you got bored. I particularly liked the food tests. You would be in a sealed booth; a slot would open and a tray of food would appear. You simply eat the food and fill out the questionnaire. "What did it taste like?" "Sour, sweet, bitter.." "How was the smell?", you get the picture. After testing it was all beer and poolside surrounded by all the hot civilian female employees in bikinis. Natick is even more laid back that Ft Sam Houston and that is a hard act to follow. But alas, all good things must come to an end and a couple of months later I was returned to the drudgery of Lawton, Oklahoma. This separation, albeit shorter than others have been, would be the furthest distance we had ever been apart. Even that short separation had Lisa and I back in at least temporary wedded bliss. I continued to work for A-btry and soon enough I received orders for my next duty station. You see, in the early 1980's in the Army every enlistment had two distinct parts. I, like everyone else, would spend half my enlistment in C.O.N.U.S (sick of acronyms yet? This one is CONtinental United States) and half my enlistment somewhere overseas.

Despite the United States Army having a presence in virtually every nation on the globe that wasn't behind the "iron curtain" (term referred to any country who was under the sphere, guidance and rule of the U.S.S.R.) Soldiers with my M.O.S. went to one of two nations, South Korea and West Germany. Normally, I would not have cared where I was going if it was overseas, and I would be able to see more of the world. These locations bore two very different criteria as far as I was concerned. South Korea at the time was "unaccompanied", and Wet Germany could be "accompanied". Even though my marriage was headed for the rocks every time we had to spend more than 6 or 8 months together, it didn't mean I wanted to spend 18 months away from Lisa and my new baby. So, I held my breath and waited for my orders to arrive. As luck would have it I was being assigned to West Germany, officially called the F.R.G. (Federal Republic of Germany) I always thought it was funny that communist East Germany was officially the D.R.G (Democratic Republic of Germany). West Germany was the "The front line" is what history would refer to in the years to come as the 'Cold War".

At this point in my life, except for my Army duty assignments, I had never really been outside of the state of Michigan or Maryland. It was almost like a dream to be heading to Europe. I have no doubt that if I had not joined the military, I would have never had the opportunity to go and visit Europe. Even if I was visiting only to work. Once I received my orders to go to West Germany, I had another decision to make. A married Soldier had two choices once they were assigned to the F.R.G. You could choose to go accompanied or unaccompanied. Going accompanied had advantages. The Army would pay all of you and your family's expenses to get you to Germany. They would also provide post housing at the Kaserne (Germany's word for "post") and ship your household goods and automobile to the Kaserne were going to be assigned to. There, of course, was a caveat. If you chose to travel accompanied, you had to agree to stay in Germany for 3 years, if you chose unaccompanied, you only had to stay 18 months. Even if you went unaccompanied you could still bring your family with youm but it would be at your own expense. Staying three years anywhere when you're a young family seems like an eternity so I chose to be unaccompanied, and would send for Lisa and my daughter once I was settled in. I took another two weeks leave and off to Europe I went. Once you arrive in Europe, at least in the Army, you stay in Frankfort in a "Replacement Battalion" until a unit somewhere in the country decides they need you, and then you go from there. I think it was only a day or two and I received my assignment. I was going to be assigned to the greatest Army division of all, the First Infantry Division. Affectionately, it was called the 'Big Red One" but soon enough though and all of us referred to it as "The big red weenie." This was the "weenie" which was being stuck to you daily. There were three locations that the 1st Infantry Division occupied in the country, Goppingen, Kitzingen and Neu Ulm. I got assigned to Headquarters, headquarters battery of the 4th battalion of the 5th field artillery (H.H.B. 4/5FA 1ID, official annotation) at Wiley Barracks in Neu Ulm. I was told I got lucky getting the best assignment of the 3 as Neu Ulm was smack dab in the middle of the beautiful Black Forest. I still remember the very first taste of German beer I ever took in country. Before being transported to my unit, I was going to have to spend the night at the replacement battalion in Kitzingen. I just remember the location as being on a rocky outcrop in the middle of nowhere. At least, approximately one block down the road, you could easily read a sign saying “Gasthof.” Gasthof, in the German language among other things, translates into “bar” for us G.I.’s. Despite the fact we were told by the C.Q. to remain inside the building for the night until our transportation arrived in the morning, two fellow Soldiers and I knew we had to do a little exploration. I remember walking into the bar and the waitress asking us “Eine” or “Doppel”, and my thinking that meant “small” or “large.” What I did not know was that it was the glorious time of the year when “doppelbock” beer was being brewed and that was what she meant. Did I want “the regular” or the “extra strong” beer. Of course, all three of us held up one finger and replied “Doppel”. I soon got my second lesson in the German language when the waitress brought 6 beers for the three of us. In Germany (this makes complete sense when you think about it) the thumb is counted as a finger when ordering, so when you want “one” of anything, you just give them the thumbs up. Your index finger indicates “two”, middle finger “three”, and so on. Another interesting fact around the world, no matter how language may differ between cultures, the middle finger is almost universally recognized as an obscene gesture. So, when you want to place an order for three of anything in Germany, you raise all three digits instead of just the middle fingers so there is no “miscommunication”, quite likely to lead to confrontation. The next morning, a jeep arrived to take me the hour and a half or so down the road to my new home for the next year and a half at Wiley Barracks.

Neu Ulm was a great little town, the newer community added when the very old town of Ulm expanded beyond the capability of public services to care for the city effectively. Of course “newer”, meaning only

300 or 400 years old, unlike its original neighbor Ulm which was well over 1000 years old. Both communities were full of wonderful, eclectic, old European style with restaurants, museums, bars and nightclubs. The Ulm establishments were more for the "locals" while most of the entertainment hot spots in Neu Ulm were geared more to providing for our American tastes. The one "must see" in Ulm though was the 900 or so year old cathedral, still a functioning church, named the Muenster. Although being built around the year 1200, it still has the distinction of having the tallest single standing cathedral spire in the world. As I recall, it was over 700 or so steps to the top. I struggle with the words to try to describe this. I climbed that bitch, which was no small task considering I have a bad case of claustrophobia. This spire, and it's over 700 stairs, is so steep and winds so tightly upwards that it is difficult for two people to pass each other on the stairwell going up or down. The spire also winds so tightly that all you can see as you climb up it, is about to the knee level of the person above and the head and shoulders of the person below. It was also very dimly lit, as there were no real windows in it, only "arrow" slots every 20 or 30 steps, and a platform to get off and stand every two or three stories of the 10-story total height. Claustrophobic or not, much like a ski slope, once you start the climb up (or get on that lift) you are committed to completing the climb. Inside the chapel was an almost incomprehensible beauty. It was filled with solid walnut pews, arraigned row by row, and at the end of each pew was a hand carved diorama of life in the 12th century. Interred inside of the walls of the sanctuary, as was the custom for generations, were the vertical tombs of the bishops and religious figures who had been the lead vicars in years past. In one back corner of the Muenster was a small museum with pictures and the story

of Muenster during World War Two. Although it is hard to recognize today, every metropolitan center of Germany was utterly flattened as the Third Reich was brought to its knees and Ulm and the Muenster were no exception. The Muenster did manage to remain unscathed well into 1944 as the Allies were still trying to save some of the cultural heritage of Germany as it was able. The Army Air Force finally received intelligence that the Wehrmacht (German Army) was mocking them, as they were able to "flatten everything except the largest most prominent thing in the city, the Muenster". What the Wehrmacht did not realize was that it was not being targeted on purpose due to the fact its location was being used to triangulate every other strategic target in the area. To prove this fact the Army Air Corps performed a "special mission" and bombed the Muenster. They bombed it with flour that is, just to make a point. Unfortunately, the Muenster was ultimately bombed and flattened by the end of the war. There are pictures of all this history in that corner and it was hard for me to grasp how that pile of rubble that remained at the end of the war had been reconstructed back to its original splendor. The only reminder of that destruction is only noticeable today by the different aging colors of the bricks. You can see this difference if you look closely enough. I'm sure in a couple of hundred more years the colors will have blended again, and no one will ever know. Flowing through the center of Ulm is the Danube River. In Germany however, it is referred to as the Danau. This added special beauty and splendor to the parks and walkways there. This "hillbilly" had never seen anything, like any of this in my life. I remember each adventure into town being filled with wonder and amazement. In the summertime every little village and town hosts their own little "festival" the highlight of which is the beer tent complete with the "Oompah" bands playing away the polka music. Many weekends we spent just cruising in the countryside looking for which little village might be hosting their festival that particular day. Interesting thing to note, despite how far away some of these villages may have been from American posts or G.I.'s Every single festival we went to, we were treated as hallowed guests and felt comfortable and welcome.

I could write ten books describing Germany and the wonders therein, but many writers, greater than I have covered this over the years. There were two Kaserne's in New Ulm, Wiley Barracks, home of the 4/5th Field Artillery, and the 1/118th Air Defense Artillery. The second Kaserne was Nelson Barracks home of the 2/4th Infantry Regiment. Much like every little town has its own private establishments which the local gentry like to frequent, each Kaserne had its own bar in Neu Ulm, which we called our own. The 4th of the 5th's little hole in the wall was a small bar called "Christian's". It was named not for the religious preferences of its patrons, but because its proprietor was named Christian. Virtually every evening, and most weekends, after working our duty hours, all of us would naturally just migrate there for an evening of beer and German "munchies". Money wasn't a real problem for me then either because your small paycheck goes a lot further when I was getting almost 4 Deutschmarks for each dollar. The local German girls were nice too, Germany has the same lovely girls as the Scandinavian countries do for the record. I somewhat felt sorry for the German men over there because anywhere that there was a Kaserne full of U.S. G.I.'s that was pretty much where all the girls were congregating. They loved nothing more than fucking G.I.'s and apparently American men have a few things sexually, such as "staying power, that German men lacked. I know a lot of the German girls were willing to give up anything, sex was just one of those things, in order to snag them a nice American husband. This was their "ticket" to the "land of the free" which they automatically thought was a much better place to live than Germany was. I never understood this as Germany was fine by me. What happened most times, unless a local gal was lucky enough to end up pregnant, then her chances of marriage were greater, was that the G.I.'s were just fucking everything they could get their hands on and at the end of the tour the girls got the "Well it's been great sweetheart but...." Then a little debriefing and back to C.O.N.U.S., and their wives and girlfriends they went. The local saying about the United States Servicemember was "over paid, over laid, and over here" and it was well deserved I suppose. It is amazing to me that as much alcohol as I consumed over the course of the 18 or so months I was in the country I can remember any of this at all.

In a month or so, I was able to save the money to have Lisa and my daughter flown over to me in the country. I had secured a small apartment in a little community about 25 kilometers from the post called Untereschligan. Untereschligan, was of course just a little further down the road from Obereschligan. Sadly, a lot of Soldiers, when assigned to different countries, never wanted to leave the barracks and preferred to be surrounded by as much of "America" as they possibly could be. We all referred to these troops as "barracks rats". I was just the opposite. During any of my travels abroad I always enjoyed immersing myself in the local culture, language, food and so on. This was to ensure I could squeeze in as much knowledge as possible from my new location. This was a much easier task when I lived in the local economy. Our little apartment was an upstairs apartment, located on top of the landlord's house. Paying rent was easy and affordable as well. In Europe, as well as generally anywhere else overseas that U.S. Soldiers are, the "black market" thrived. Taxes in European countries were astronomically high even in the early 80's. And on luxury items like alcohol, tobacco, coffee, gasoline and sugar the taxes were even higher yet. My landlord was a businessman above all else and much to my good fortune had a taste for good old Kentucky bourbon (Jim Beam to be exact) and Marlboro cigarettes. As an American Servicemember I was able to purchase these items U.S. tax free on post at the Class Vi store. There is a Class VI store on every post, just think of it as the "store of sin" as this was where you purchased your booze, cigarettes and other goodies. My rent was supposed to be 700 Deutschmarks per month (about $200 U.S. at the time), but my landlord and I had a unspoken agreement that if a gallon of Jim Beam and three cartons of Marlboro cigarettes magically appeared on his doorstep each month, a receipt for 700 marks would appear in my box. My cost for the aforementioned items was around $35 U.S. dollars, $5.25 per fifth of Jim Beam x 4, and $3.25 per carton x3 of Marlboros. My landlords cost for these items on the German economy would have been around 900 D.M. so we both ended up saving some money. This was the way of black market. I am sure there was a lot of this that was occurring, but C.I.D. (Criminal Investigation Division) was much more concerned with finding and apprehending those individuals who were earning two and three times their military pay by purchasing and then openly selling rationed items on the regular market. I knew of at least two or three cases involving very high-ranking individuals who were caught, fined and in some cases jailed for this activity. One particular low-ranking individual involved in this I remember well. His name was Eddie Bugamdi. Eddie was from Guatemala and was a G.I. just like the rest of us. Eddie was also a businessman as well. Eddie ran a little store out of his wall locker and had anything anyone would ever want to buy readily available. If you got drunk on a Saturday night and stumbled starving into the barracks, why for a few bucks Eddie would sell you a sandwich. Need to borrow a little cash till payday? Why Eddie had that too, and for the low, low interest rate of 25% compounded by the minute, you could borrow some cash too. More than a few Soldiers went to complain to "Top" (affectionate term for the First Sergeant) that they owned their whole paychecks to Eddie because of his interest rates. Now while it isn't a nice thing to do, taking advantage of your mates, there was nothing illegal about doing it. Top's reply to all who bitched was always the same, "Then don't fucking borrow money from Eddie." Two things Eddie was doing that was illegal were selling marijuana and hashish (Germany is right next to Turkey which is renowned for its high-quality hash) out of his wall locker. He was also paying other G.I.'s for the extra stamps on their ration cards to buy products he could then sell on the black market to German civilians. Why it seems Eddie had quite a little enterprise running out of his locker. Even as slow as the wheels of military justice may turn, they aren't entirely blind and eventually C.I.D. (Criminal Investigation Department) got wind of Eddie's "side business." Eddie was smart with his money though and used some to purchase friends in the right places so before C.I.D got wind of Eddie; Eddie got wind they were coming from him. I am told he went to the bank the following morning, withdrew his $55,000 in cash (in 1983 dollars) threw his military I.D. in the garbage can, used his Guatemalan passport and bought himself a one-way ticket to Taiwan. Eddie obviously also did his homework as Taiwan had no extradition laws and was, for Eddie anyway, safe haven. I am told the following Christmas season Top received a Christmas card from Eddie in Taiwan reading simply, "Merry Christmas Top! I hear you looking for Eddie, sorry I can't make it but here's my address in Taiwan, if your ever in the area stop and say "Hi." He was untouchable and probably still living the highlife there in Taiwan. Despite Eddies happy ending, most stories of this nature did not end that way. I always wondered if that money was worth the careers the higher echelon troops had just flushed down the toilet.

In Untereschligan there was no English spoken, no English signage, no English anything out there. While I enjoyed this environment and viewed it as a challenge, Lisa had completely the opposite experience. She found it isolated, foreign and frustrating. While I enjoyed kicking around in my little town, hanging out at the Sportplatz (think Sports Bar), or getting sloshed working on my language skills with my landlord, she generally stayed at home and quietly took care of our daughter. We did have some fun hosting parties out there for some of my fellow Soldiers and I know she enjoyed these times as it felt a lot more like "home" to her. There was one exception to this enjoyment though. After one particularly brutal work week I had a hell of a backache. I had received a prescription for robaxasol for some relief. Well, so I am told, after a few dozen German beers and probably a few of those robaxasol (it's amazing how drunks lose track of time and don't count so well, not really) and I was fairly incoherent and having trouble breathing. It is all still a blur to me as I remember none of it. What I do remember though is waking up in the psychiatric ward at the Army hospital in Augsburg for 3 days of observation. I also remember an IV in my arm and feeling like rubber. I guess they like to make sure, compliments of plenty of Valium, that Soldiers do not cause any troubles. A few days later I was deemed fit for duty and sent back to my unit. I did not receive any official administrative punishment for this but a stern warning to "get your head out of your ass". Life moved on. Lisa and I also had this great 1971 BMW 2002 automobile. It was pumpkin orange, had a 4-speed standard transmission and 4-cylinder engine. Those automobiles would be considered pretty spartan by today's standards, but this thing was great!! It would pretty much keep up with most automobiles on the autobahn and was reliable as the day was long. I had my doubts the first time I looked at it though, when you look at the rear tires while standing behind the car, you'll notice the tops of both are slanted ever so slightly into the fender well. I soon learned that this is a unique BMW design to assist in sharp, fast corner handling. It is not a broken axle or bad wheel bearing. "Side Note": If you look at any BMW today you will see they still employ the same engineering design. This little car would serve as Lisa's sole lifeline during the frequent times I had to work "away from home" while stationed with the 4th of the 5th. Working "away from home", is the civilian phrase for the Army's "headed for the field" As I have said earlier, the Army's sole function is to fight and win our Nations wars, and like all good things, this too requires practice. This practice is obtained by doing Army stuff in the hills, woods and countryside. Think of the field as camping without the marshmallows, hot dogs, campfires, alcohol, fishing poles or any other activity that could be regarded as fun. For my unit, going to the field involved emptying out all our equipment out of the motor pool, loading all of our vehicles, tanks, trucks, howitzers, and what have you and head to the train yard. Once we arrived at the train yard, also known as the "rail head", every vehicle was driven onto the train cars and chained down for transport. We would all then climb into the few passenger cars, basically cattle cars on rails, for the 20-hour trip to the Grafenwoehr combined training center. Now Grafenwoehr was only a 3-to-4-hour trip by P.O.V. (Personally Owned Vehicle, your car), but everything in Europe travels by rail and a train loaded with United States Servicemembers and their equipment has a lower priority than the garbage scowls. Therefore, you may spend 6 or 7 hours moving in a forward direction, only to stop and go in a reverse direction for 2 to 3 hours so a different train could pass you. Upon arrival to "Graf" you would unchain everything and head into the woods there to a predesignated location and set up your perimeters. You now were part of a make believe "front line" waiting for an assault or battle which (hopefully) will never come. We would stay in one location a day or so, set up aiming posts, put our camouflage nets over everything and wait for the next order. The cooks would set their mobile kitchen up and at least once a day we would get a hot meal. I developed a new love for that all-American food staple S.P.A.M. In case you didn't know as I didn't for many years, S.P.A.M. stands for Spiced Pork And haM and the Army loves it! For our hot meals breakfast would be scrambled eggs and S.P.A.M, lunch was a bowl of Mrs. Grasses chicken noodle soup with a S.P.A.M sandwich and dinner was a nice slice of baked S.P.A.M with pineapples. I do remember it being cold as hell, but the food was hot and when it was served it was wonderful. If you were a gun bunny of the lowest caste, your sleeping arrangements consisted of sleeping on the ground sharing a shelter half, (Each Soldier is issued one half of a pup tent called a shelter half) with another of your crewmates. Since we were the support mechanics and rated a little higher in the caste system, our accommodations were a little better. We had a deuce and a half truck converted into a sort of a camper complete with electricity, heat, coffee and radio. Although it was cramped for the 6 or 8 of us and our equipment, it was inside a makeshift room, heated, had our own coffee pot and we were thankful for it. I am told Graf does have a Summertime, but I don't believe it. Each and every time I was there it was one of two temperatures. either cold, or colder. Our time in the field would vary from at least a week, to sometimes as long as a month. Around 10 days was the average. It was on return from one of these field maneuvers that Lisa informed me she had had her fill of Germany. Considering the time, I had to spend away in the field, and my behavior when I was in garrison (any time you are not in the field you are considered in garrison) or home, I understood what her reasoning was and promptly made arrangements for her to return to C.O.N.U.S. Just like the separations before, this separation delivered another reprieve to our rocky marriage. It would only be 3 or 4 months and I would be joining her back in the "World". I had no reason to make any attempt to behave or stay reasonable sober once she was gone and after all I was getting "short". Now the term "short" has been used by U.S. Servicemembers for at least a few generations. Being "short" had nothing to do with your physical stature but the time an individual had remaining indebted by contract to Uncle Sam. Once I had less than 60 days left on my enlistment I could start referring to myself as "Short". Being "short" also carries a particular attitude with it. People who were "short" made every attempt to do as little work as possible and have as much fun during that time. One Saturday evening after Lisa had gone back home, I had traded my little BMW with another Soldier for his 1972 Ford Gran Torino, sport model. This car was a monster by European standards, it was every bit as wide as most of the lanes are in Germany, and with the 302 V-8 power train much more power that was ever needed. It was time to add another item to my ever-growing list of "things that don't go together". That would be getting good and drunk, having a huge powerful car, and a carload full of your buddies on a Saturday night. I then added an excellent rock soundtrack to the situation (38 Special, "Hold on Loosely" to be exact) and it was an accident waiting to happen. It didn't have to wait long, I was whizzing down a great, divided paved road at around 60 miles an hour. This doesn't sound like that fast until you find out the road has a speed limit of 45 KILOMETERS an hour. 45 Kilometers per hour translates into about 30 miles an hour for readers not at all familiar with the metric system. I was still doing a good job keeping my car on the road until the 15 km/hr left hand curve I went careening into. The car slid perfectly into the curve, and I thought we were home free. What I did not know was the road instantly became a divided road and the side of my car caught every bit of that guard rail there. With sparks flying and metal screeching I came to a halt. My buddies and I all got out of the vehicle laughing like hell at our good fortune of not totaling the car. The entire driver's side of the car had been split open down the side like a can opener. Gasoline was pouring out of the gash in the rear of the vehicle by the gas tank. I told my friends, you better head back to post before the Polizei (German for police) arrive. Another thing I did not know was that my little fender bender occurred almost directly in front of the police station. It only took about 20 seconds, and my friends were sent home. Meanwhile I was taken into the police station in a set of handcuffs.

Normally, it is a terrible thing to get arrested in a foreign country, but you get some leniency for being a U.S. Servicemember. Germany and the United States have this arrangement called a "Status of Forces" agreement. In a nutshell, if a member of the U.S. Armed Forces did not commit any capital crime, murder, rape, particularly violent assault on a German National, et cetera.. the German authorities would just turn your dumb ass over to your unit for punishment. In hindsight, I'm not sure wither this was good or bad in my case. I was certain that it was bad when Top came into the station. His first words were for the German police officer who was behind the desk were "Where's the fucking receipt for prisoner?" His next words, as he turned his head towards me and I am certain I could see flames coming out of his eyes, "Get in the fucking jeep". A few short minutes later, I was in his office and the ass chewing I was getting at 0600 hrs on a Sunday morning could be heard by every building on the Kaserne. Long story short, I received my first Article 15, and was demoted to E-3 Private First Class, fined $140 and given 45 days restriction to barracks, chow hall and place of worship (grounding for grown-ups), and 45-day extra duty. Extra duty sucks ass. Extra duty means each day, after your regular workday, your ass reports to the C.Q. who then puts you to work doing cleaning, or some other mundane tasks until 2300 hrs at which time you can hit the rack for the night. This was my routine for the next month and a half. A month or so after that, that magical date of 16 September 1985 arrived and I was officially a civilian. While I wasn't' considering it at the time, between my latest fuck up and that little weekend in Augsburg, typed on my DD-214 (a DD-241 is the final document an enlisted Soldier receives in military) in addition to my dates of service, the few medals and awards I had received, was a small code “RE-3” this is a “bar to reenlistment.” But again, at the time, that was the least of my worries as I was happy to be a civilian again. A few short days later I was with Lisa back in the ‘world”.

CHAPTER 4: “Home Again, at least briefly”

One thing any Servicemember will tell you, at least while they are in the service, is that all they want to do is get out of the service. Shortly thereafter, all those memories become the best time and best job you ever had. Being "free" was a new and not necessarily comforting feeling for me. My days of a regular, steady paycheck every two weeks, 30 days paid vacation a year, housing and clothing allowances, all of it was now over. As I never did make a lot of money in the Army, and what money I did have extra I pissed away, I had no savings to live on until I found gainful civilian employment. I did have a few hundred dollars in my pocket from cashing in a few weeks paid leave I had accrued while stationed in Germany. Since there really was nowhere to travel to, no family to visit and so on, you really didn't take any "official leave". The Army, just like civilian employers, does allow you to "bank" paid leave days that if left unused, can be exchanged for good hard cash at the end of your enlistment.

I used this money and Lisa, our daughter and I got a small, ramshackle apartment right inside Reed City. I was an ancient house, in an incredible state of disrepair. In more urban settings, this most certainly would have been slum housing. Beat up as it was, it was home, it was clean, and it was ours. If it were to remain "ours" I was going to have to get my ass out there and find a job quickly. I did just that. Another small factory that had been set up in Reed City was Bentek Corporation. The founder of the company had discovered a small niche market to exploit and a place where he could get factory floor space and labor at the lowest possible cost. The company purchased used, burned up, non-functioning automobile parts from the big three. The focus was on the small, electric motor driven parts such as starters and alternators. They also added an assembly line for automobile fuel pumps and oil pumps as well. These parts were brought in on huge steel bins, filled to the top with these filthy, oily, burned up and stinking items. These items were then separated by type, then sent to the appropriate area of the shop. Once they arrived they had to be cleaned, stripped down to their nuts and bolts and remanufactured. All the old metal, wiring and piping was torn out and thrown into other huge bins to be sold to recycling plants, The empty "shells" were then loaded with new wiring harnesses, bushings, brackets and so on and sent to the paint shop. After painting off they went to the test benches. This was to make sure these now "remanufactured" components were in proper working order. If those parts passed all the testing, they were packed into spiffy new boxes, marked "remanufactured" and sent to the regional distribution centers and then off to the major auto parts suppliers such as Auto Zone, O'Reilly's, Parts Plus and NAPA.

For those resellers, as well as tens of thousands of backyard mechanics all over the country, these parts were a blessing. My experience with these parts was a lot different. I have always tried to look at the good and bad parts of every situation in my life, the "pros" and "cons" you may say. This job, like the dozen others I would have over the next few years, had both as well. The "Pros", it was close to home, I could walk to work, and if I went every day I received a paycheck at the end of each two-week time frame. The "cons", it was filthy, hazardous, degrading, drudging, low-paying, hard, minimum wage work. I could look at the minimum wage rate up in 1985 to accuracy, but as I recall it was around $3.75/hr. Whatever the figure was, that is exactly what all of us made working at Bentek and there were no benefits whatsoever. No Sick Pay, no vacation, no 401K, nothing. You went to work, you punched the clock, you got paid, the end. Like any menial, low paying workplace, the employee turnover rate was way over the National average. This wasn't exactly factory work like I described earlier, but it was nearly as bad. A few short weeks later I would add myself to that turnover rate and walk out that door. It wasn't a just but a few years later even residents of Reed City demanded higher pay and a decent work standard of living. Rather than have his profit margin go down and shower a little bit of his good fortune on the good residents of R.C. (as they have effectively put tens of thousands of dollars in his pocket), without notice, he put a chain on the factory doors, fired everyone and moved the entire operation to Mexico, compliments of N.A.F.T.A (North American Free Trade Agreement, President Bill Clintons giant fuck of the American worker) So much for everybody getting a happy ending eh?

There weren't a lot of happy endings headed my way for a few years to come. Without the escape of another Army assignment, and the money problems just getting larger my marriage was really going down the drain. Regardless, I kept trying to work my way up the economic ladder. I went through more jobs over the next few years than I honestly can remember. I believe my next job was a brief stint as a garbage man. To many folks this sounds like a horrible job, but really it is not such a bad gig. My first day to report work was the Tuesday after a Labor Day weekend. To this very day I have never seen as much garbage as I did that day. I was on a rural route in Mecosta County with another garbage man as a “partner”. Our garbage truck was not the large, standard rig you would normally think of, but a 1-ton Chevrolet 3500 pickup truck pulling a 13-yard dumpster on a trailer. Garbage is measured by the cubic yard for the record, I believe a “yard” is equal to three cubic feet square. What I do know though is 13 yards is a large fucking dumpster probably 12 feet long, 8 feet wide and 6 feet high. I remember on that Monday that we filled that dumpster completely at least 6 times during our ten-hour shift. I have had a lot of strenuous, physically demanding days throughout my life, but that day will always be in at least in my “top five”. Each day on the garbage crew started at 3 am, which was great because for the first half of your shift it was nice and cool (or freezing cold depending on season) and there was no additional traffic to have to contend with. As much as I remember that first day, I remember the second morning even more clearly. I was so physically sore and stiff that I was completely unable to get myself out of bed. I had to have Lisa assist me out of bed by essentially rolling me out and onto the floor. The money wasn’t bad for this job, and you could have fun if you put your heart into it a little bit. It really was a lot like the movie of the era “Men at Work.” A few weeks came and went, and I knew that this was not life for me though.

There was a movie that came out around this time called “The Color Purple.” One specific quote from it comes to mind “Cletis beat Olive, Olive beat Cletis and between the beatings the chillin’ kept coming.” I was reminded of this since somewhere between the arguments and discord in my marriage, there must have been at least a few good minutes. Lisa was pregnant again with our second child. I was only 20 years old and felt like I had lived an entire lifetime by then. Little did I know.

I was about to start a new line of work that would earn me a lot of money in my "pre-college" years, I took a job working on an oil rig. Unbeknownst to many, Michigan is a very prominent, oil producing area in the United States. Unlike the oil that is pumped in Texas or down south, which was black, thick and deep in the ground, Michigan's oil, is thin, florescent green, and relatively shallow. This translates into a lot of work for the Michigan "roughneck." Since Michigan oil is relatively shallow in the ground, the oil rigs there are set up, torn down and moved to new locations on a much more frequent basis. If you were wondering why Michigan oil is florescent green, it is because the water content in it is much, much higher. It still smells like crude oil and dead worms though for the record. My first job on the oil rigs was with a company out of Texas named Penrod Drilling company. They were very successful down South and thought maybe they could expand their fortunes up North. I was hired at their lowest pay grade at the time $12.48 cents an hour. This was the best money I had ever earned at that time since it was 1985 and the minimum wage was still under $5 an hour I believe. I would be starting work about 3 hours north of where I lived in the Gaylord area. I would generally stay up North during the work schedule and then go home when I had a few days in row off. This separation, the excitement of having a new child, and a reprieve from the money troubles worked wonders for our marriage. At least in the short term we were progressing along and in December, the next "love of my life" arrived. This baby had her story as well. She was born with her bilirubin count a little on the high side which was not entirely unusual for newborns. This was easily enough remedied by a few hours for a day or so exposed to ultraviolet light. Now since this light can damage a newborns sensitive eyes they are given a little pair of "punk rock" sunglasses to where while in the sunlamp. Somewhere out there I have a picture of my baby, also "sunny side up" (this time referring to her little butt though) lying on her belly with her punk rock glasses on, looking like she didn't have a care in the world. I wish I could find that photo today, the extortion power I could wield with that against my daughter would be priceless. At least the laughter she and I would both share over it would be worth it more than anything. A quick 48 hours and my baby was perfectly normal.

Then reality came home again. We were now a family of four, and although the money working on the oil rigs was good, it came with a "hitch". "Roughnecking" (Oil rig work is performed by men most often referred to as "roughnecks", I never worked with a female on the rigs) is physically demanding work that requires attention to detail. That was if you wanted to stay alive and keep all your fingers and limbs attached anyway. On an oil platform everything is steel and iron, heavy and in places, moving fast. One slip up could cost you at least a few fingers or a broken bone, at most, your life. I saw each of the above happen during my tenure in the "oil patch." I had my share of close encounters "of the worse kind" while roughnecking. The first incident I was working on the deck, hooking up the collar to pull the next section of pipe out of the hole. When the pressure was applied to the line, the collar broke loose from the pipe and swung back smacking me squarely between the eyes, just beneath the brim of my hardhat. My little brother who witnessed this said

I flew 15 feet through the air and my hardhat was launched 241 feet through the air (my brother also measured that out) as well. My nose was broken, and my skull was fractured in numerous places around my frontal sinuses. The only blessing in disguise from that accident was that I was able to fly through the air with nothing behind me. This is because if my head would have become wedged between the collar and another solid object, it would have certainly cleaved my skull and two and I would not be writing this text now. Another fun filled incident awhile later occurred a year or so later. Our crew was retrieving a section of pipe out of a well while in the process of sealing it with cement. Once an oil well stops producing oil it must be dealt with. Sometimes an oil company can use it for a while as an "injection well". That is a well that instead of pumping oil out of it, wastewater, brine and other byproducts of crude are pumped back down into the ground. Eventually the Department of Natural Resources says enough is enough and forces the oil company to plug the well. To plug a well, you must pump cement into it from the bottom all the way to the top to prevent any contamination from creeping up into the water table and poisoning people. While we were pumping that wet cement down this pipe to the bottom, a "dry plug" of cement had occurred in the drill pipe. We then had to pull out and disconnect each section before the cement above that plug dried inside the pipe. Naturally, each section above which was filled full of wet cement, quickly saturated the jeans I had on. One of wet cement's primary ingredients is lime and it is very caustic. After about 20 or 30 minutes, just about the time it took me to start feeling some discomfort, the layers of skin had been "burned" off both of my legs from my hips to my ankles. These would be called 2nd and 3rd degree chemical burns at the hospital. I spent six weeks on crutches coated with Silvadene cream and wrapped like a mummy from the groin down both legs healing from that. I bear the scars from that to this day. Another less dramatic drawback to "roughnecking" was that it was not a steady job most times. Even in my little universe of Northern Michigan my employment, or lack thereof, was dependent on the global price of oil. Let's say for the sake of conversation that the price of a barrel of oil is $25 per barrel. If the price goes above that, it is too expensive for the United States to buy abroad and us field workers in the U.S. would be busting our asses to meet the burgeoning daily demand for "black gold." When the price goes below $25 per barrel, then it is cheaper to purchase it abroad than it is to produce it domestically. This, for me, meant unemployment, maybe for a few days, maybe for months. That arbitrary value works like a pendulum. Naturally, the United States would like to see that price remain low. This keeps gas cheap at the pumps, American workers hard at their oil rig jobs and politicians get to keep their jobs at election time. At the other end of the pendulum, O.P.E.C. (Oil Producing and Exporting Consortium) wants to keep the price below, but as close to, that $25 per barrel. This ensures Uncle Sam keeps writing checks to King Saud of Saudi Arabia while at the same time getting as much money as it can for its product. You get the picture. While I loved getting these great big paychecks when I could, the uncertainty of when the next one may or may not arrive forced me to seek work elsewhere.

Fortunately, Ron had just gotten out of the Army himself and had landed a pretty good job working for a propane company called Great Plains Gas. Since he was now a valued employee and another of my high school associates was the manager of the plant, once a job opening occurred I was hired on. We had a lot of fun working there together. After the mandatory "death by PowerPoint" safety classes, I went to work in the yard. It wasn't as physically demanding as work on the oil rig was, and although the pay wasn't as high either, it was better than the all the minimum wage factories in the area offered. My job description was to fill and deliver 100# propane cylinders to rural customers. If we were short of a technician, I could also operate the tanker truck ("bulk truck") and make bulk deliveries. It was a great job, and I had no reason not to be completely happy and satisfied. I was struggling mentally in reality. It seems I had a condition not entirely uncommon to Soldiers who have been active duty, travelled abroad, and then returned to civilian life. Life in the military is very structured. You are "free" essentially, but your day-to-day existence is planned out for you. Where you work, where you eat, where you shit, bedtime and wake up time. In the civilian world it is just the opposite. No one gives two shits where you are, what you are doing, and where you are going with little exceptions. This takes a little getting used to. I had that feeling common to so many veterans "Is this all there is to life now? Am I just waiting to grow old and die"? I also then began to deal with it like so many Veterans have, with drugs and alcohol. I always had a little trouble with authority, but in the Army they have ways of dealing with that shit down to science. In the civilian world you just end up in jail. I did try to utilize the local mental health facilities in Osceola County and get myself on a normal track. Their solution was to drug me even more. I started on a regimen of lithium carbonate and Haldol. Haldol is the brand name for the tranquilizer haloperidol. Haloperidol is the next generation of more "gentle" tranquilizers. The previous tranquilizer of choice developed a couple of decades before was Thorazine, but

Thorazine had some undesirable side effects, like keeping the user in a stupor and drooling a lot. Drooling and staring yes, violent? Not a bit! Haldol was gentler, but you were still in a stupor and stared a lot, but hey, no drooling right. About a week or so going to work delivering propane and handling other highly flammable substances and it was apparent to the management that the current haze I was walking around in, and employment with their company was no longer compatible. Very shortly thereafter I was asked to seek employment elsewhere. I wasn't really fired as I recall, since my friend was the manager, but I had put him in a difficult position. So, he took me off the road and gave me a week or so to find another job.

Lisa wasn't very happy as well having a zombie for a husband, and there was no way I was going to find gainful employment in the shape I was in, so I quit those medications and cleaned my head up. Sometimes in life you fall into a great big pile of shit and climb out of it smelling like a rose. This just so happened to be one of those times for me. I landed a job as the regional manager for the Detroit Free Press, a large statewide newspaper. At the time the paper had a circulation of at least a few hundred thousand Michigan residents and everyone who purchased one in a 5-county area of North Central Michigan was going to have to get their news "fix" from me. I would oversee handling the distribution of 4 or 5 thousand copies each day, seven days a week. I purchased every newspaper that came into my region at a discounted rate and then sold them at the retail price. I remember that I paid 8 cents for a paper that sold for 15 cents and 40 cents for the Sunday editions that sold for 75 cents. I was to accomplish this with the help of 4 motor carrier drivers, and I had my personal motor carrier route in addition to my managerial tasks. I did have to share some of those profits listed above with my other motor carriers. The store owners who also retailed my newspapers got a "cut" of that action as well. Regardless, if you do a little simple math you can see that I was making some decent money once the monthly sales figures were completed. I really enjoyed this job. I would get up each morning seven days a week at 2:30 am and meet all my drivers at our "pick up" point. This location was where a tractor-trailer arrived from Detroit each day to drop our few thousand papers off. I would then load my 180 to 220 newspapers for my personal customers into my little pickup truck and off I would drive into the night. My route took me between 2 ½ and 3 hours each morning to complete, but it was usually a wonderful, quiet couple of hours driving in the country. I did not know it at the time, but in a decade or so I was going to discover that not all long rides into the night are quiet and refreshing. That part of my life is for later in my tale though. Things were still rough during the marriage as we were discovering more, year after year, how personally incompatible Lisa and I really were. We still managed to try to work it out every so often and during one of those ever so brief reconciliations she became pregnant with our third child. It was 1988 and I was 24 years old. I really have trouble writing the next section of this book as it is the most shameful and selfish moment of my life. As much as I'd like to have been able to say I was faithful during my marriage to Lisa I was just as much a part of the activities I described earlier in Germany as the rest of the Soldiers were. If there was some way in my shame that I could omit the next few paragraphs of my story, I certainly would but they lead to an essential turning point in my life. One of the "flings" I had in Germany was with an

American dependent girl from California. It was simply one of those incredible physical attractions that everyone experiences at one time and I was unable to resist in 1984. I was obviously no more able to resist her in 1988 than I was in 1984, and despite Lisa being 6 months pregnant, I told her I was leaving and headed to California. I did not know when I was coming back, so it would have been impossible to tell her those facts as well. After a few days in California and this little rendezvous, I had a moment of human compassion and decided I should go back to Michigan and "clean up loose ends." I returned to Michigan, the paper business I left behind, Lisa and pretty much the entire rest of my life was shattered. If there was to be any chance of a reconciliation to my marriage even after that, it ended completely when a letter arrived from this girl in California. Although it was addressed to me, Lisa opened it only to find a "thank you" letter for my visit and describing the "best sex she had ever had" in print. As you can imagine, and rightfully so, this was the coup de etat for my marriage. Lisa and I barely co-existed for the next few months and fought viciously until I finally moved out. She gave birth to my son, and he came into this world already in the possession of an absent father and a broken home. Lisa started dating a guy that was once of my employees from the newspaper. Despite the fact we were getting a divorce, and my actions described above, this still drove me into a rage. It is odd, how despite the fact you may not be interested in a person as far as a relationship, you still cannot bear to see your old high school sweetheart with someone else. In one particularly crazy, angry episode, I went down to her place of work in Reed City and naturally, she shut the door in my face. Then, in a drunken stupor, I put my fist through the window. Again naturally, she then called the police and after a brief struggle, none of which I remember, I was arrested and hauled to jail.

What I do remember was waking up, face down in the "drunk tank" of the Osceola County jail. At the moment I opened my eyes, I did have one moment of clarity. That moment was my realizing, "Well now you've done it, you have truly hit rock bottom" Shortly after that moment, I remember hearing a voice from outside the bars saying simply, "would you like to talk about the Bible Son?" It was like a lightning bolt struck me in the forehead. I instantly thought of the moment that Saul, torturer of the Jews, became Paul, disciple of the Lord following a touch on the forehead by Jesus Christ. A few days later, I was arraigned and stood before the honorable Judge Frederic Scott Circuit County judge for Osceola County. Now normally breaking a window wasn't a capital crime if that window, or any property in Michigan was valued under $100 at the time. The window I smashed was exactly $106.22 to repair and that $6.22 was just enough to elevate my crime from a misdemeanor to a felony. This was in addition to the charge of assaulting the police officers who were sent to arrest me and haul me into the jail. It is funny, they seemed fine to me and was the only one who woke up with an ass whipping and bruised. Such things happen when you decide to have physical encounters with the law. There was going to be no plea bargaining for me before Judge Scott. He was going to prosecute this as a felony for one reason and one reason only. "I am charging you with this felony as full, for two reasons, the first being so I can incarcerate you for 30 days to think about your actions and secondly because if you ever end up in my courtroom again I will be sending you to prison" "Am I clear?" A quick "yes your honor" later and I was off to my new accommodations for the next 30 days. I would see Judge Scott again, but more about that later. If you think for a minute that the military is a structured existence, I can simply state for the record it does not hold a candle to being incarcerated. Being in jail sucks, just plain and simple. I did utilize the time constructively though and got myself enrolled in Ferris State University and that thirty days would be what changed my life for the good and forever. I think of my life as two separate lifetimes the" before" and the "after" Another thing I did manage to accomplish in jail was letting Lisa go. As far as she was concerned, she was free of me, physically and emotionally. I had seen to that with my behavior. For me that transition was more difficult, this was the woman with whom I have had a relationship with since I was 15 years old. This was the woman who I lost my virginity to and had carried three of my children in her womb. Despite how I pretended and acted so many times that I didn't care about her, and maybe I didn't, but somehow in the back of my mind I assumed she would always be there and that was not to be the case. That I think is what I mean mostly by saying "I let her go." It was something I had to do, or I would never be able to get on with my life. I was 27 and it was about time to turn the page.

Ferris State University was wonderful. Despite my behavior and trying to do everything to prove otherwise I was not a stupid person. At an early I.Q. test, I tested well above average of with an I.Q. of 148. It is said that the line between genius and insanity is thin and grey; I guess I just needed to walk on the grey side for a while. I have been asked by my children and other acquaintances over the years "Why did you go to college." My reply is always simple and true, "I went to college because I had nowhere else to go." When I first applied for admission to Ferris, I took the S.A.T (Standard Aptitude Test, the one MOST kids on a normal career path take before they leave high school) and scored exceptionally high on it. I was sitting in front of the school counselor, and he was holding two different sets of paper up with a perplexed look on his face. He finally spoke: "Can I be frank?" to which I replied "Of course." He said, "Well, your high school grades sucked, but you did really good on your S.A.T. so we are happy to give you an opportunity here at Ferris State University." I almost jumped for joy; a chance was all I needed. I had the scores and prior, albeit early, experience in the Nursing field and thought I might like to get into the acclaimed Nursing program at Ferris. There was one minor problem with my career decision. At that time at Ferris State, there was over a two-year waiting period to get into the nursing program. This was not because of my grades or anything else I could change, but simply because it was such a popular program and there were only so many students who could be taught at one time. There were far more students who had applied than slots available. For me, that made nursing as my career of choice not viably possible. Because I was already 27 years old, and approximately 8 years behind the "curve" of my peers, I was ready to get started with the rest of my life. I was determined to get back into the health care field. I had already experienced all the outdoor, dirty, hard, physical work for a career that I wanted or intended to. I asked my career counselor, "So what degree programs have an opening in the upcoming quarter (Ferris was one of the few universities still on the "quarters" year instead of the normal "Semester" year) and there was precisely one. That one opening was in the Nuclear Medicine Technology program. Now how fucking cool does "Nuclear Medicine" sound? I thought it sounded really fucking cool, so I enrolled in it and as luck would have it I was right in time to start with the new cycle of the fall of 1991. All the two-year A.A.S (Associate in Applied Science Degree) programs in Health Care were good, solid choices and fairly simple from an academic perspective. The first "year," or 4 quarters, are spent in classrooms on campus. This was the part when you did all the math, science, English and other prerequisite courses. Every degree program does require at least some of these classes. No center of higher learning is going to grant you a degree if you do not have at least a basic knowledge of these. I shared all those courses with every other "College of Health Science" student. It was good to now be able to associate with students from Radiology, Ultrasound, Laboratory Sciences and so on. The second year all of us would part ways because that year was entirely comprised of each discipline's internships. The goal of the University at the end of the programs was to have each of its students be able to successfully take, and pass, the certification exams for each respective discipline. Unlike most of my peers there, I was older, experienced and already a father three times over. I was surrounded by 18- and 19-year-old "kids" almost exclusively. Much like my search for the fullest experience when I travelled abroad, I wanted the full college experience as well. As a 27-year-old father and Veteran the normal social activities that college students migrate to, such as fraternities, were not really my "cup of tea." Since I couldn't realistically join a standard fraternity (as well as afford, it does cost a significant amount of money to buy friends) I decided to start a "social program" of my own. Although I was different from the average college student, I was not alone in this regard. There was a small, but not insignificant number of students who were categorically in the same position I was in. I decided to get a bunch of us like students together and form the "Non-Traditional Students Association" or the "Non-Trads." To become a member of the "Non-Trads" an individual had to be over 25 years old, a parent, married or any combination of those criteria. Soon enough, we had a respectable sized group of 20 or 30 individuals. All of us were searching for the complete college experience and soon adopted our own Greek letters for our organization. We officially became "Omega Sigma Xi", and I was its first president. I still have those letters on my Ferris State class ring today to remind me of those wonderful times. We held fund raisers, and implemented programs such as study groups, sharing babysitting hours, and other things that would help us succeed in what was a new environment for all of us. We became active members of the student council body and I like to think we made a difference. Even if fraternity or sorority parties were not our "thing" anymore, we all still managed to get together, have some drinks, maybe go inner tubing or do some fun things when our noses were not in the books. Although I did my share of drinking in college, I did manage to keep it under control as I knew that if I failed at this endeavor I would be doomed to a life of drudgery. I was able to borrow enough from student loans to pay for my education, and the rent to my small basement room I rented in town, I did not have enough money left over to pay my child support. I had been court ordered to pay $145 per week in child support at that time. This was a king's ransom to me and there was no way working for just over minimum wage, and part time around my school schedule, that I would be able to afford this. Unlike the times today, if a person did not pay their child support back then, the police arrived at your door and arrested you. Your bail would be whatever the amount of back child support you owed.

Going to jail would have put an abrupt end to my education so I would have to figure something out. I contacted the Osceola County Friend of the Court (F.O.C.) and explained my situation. The supervisor at the F.O.C. was completely understanding and came to a solution. They would reduce my child support to $25 per week, on paper only, during the time I was attending college. As long as I was making satisfactory progress towards graduation the rate would remain $25 per week. Now that reduction was not truly a reduction of the support order, but just a temporary respite from the $145 per week. This meant that I would still owe, and essentially go in debt $125 per week each week while I was in school. That was still OK by me because the arrears could be quickly caught back up once I graduated and landed a job that paid a professional wage. This worked out well, and although I did end up a few thousand dollars in debt to the F.O.C. I managed to catch up that back up quickly once I went back to work.

Things were going my way and my grades were exceptional, despite the lackluster performance I had shown in my high school years. Apparently my success did not go unnoticed by members of the fairer sex either. Although I had a few "flings" along the way in college, I was much more focused on my education than a full-time relationship. A 28-year-old divorced man with 3 kids is not necessarily a huge calling card for college aged young ladies either. I was also living in the basement of a large house in the college town of Big Rapids Michigan. The house was divided, as all the old, original historic buildings in Big Rapids were, into two apartments. The lower floor was one 3-bedroom apartment, and the upper floor was another 3 bedroom apartment. The landlord gave me the basement at a greatly reduced rate ($75 per month I believe) in exchange for being the house "superintendent." That was essentially just making sure no one was destroying the place during their stay. One Saturday night, in fact it was the first weekend of the new school year, the music was playing out of the upstairs apartment at about 215 decibels. I figured it would be a good time to go up and introduce myself as the building "super" and inform them of the noise regulations at the house. I walked up the stairs, was invited into the ongoing party. As I glanced in front of me I saw a student penciling in the final touches on the 3' square "Ferris State Bulldog" mural he was drawing on the nice, fresh, white wall I had just painted 3 days before. I bit my lip and didn't say a word. This was partly due to the fact it was very good and I also just figured they could repaint the wall at the end of the year. The reason I even mention this was because as I glanced around the room I noticed a pretty, tall girl with the most beautiful, long curly brown hair I had ever seen. Her name was Mary, and I had no idea how much this encounter would have on the next decade or so of my life. My life had completely turned around for the better. In addition to having a lot of fun in school, I managed to learn a few things as well. The days in class were going well, my work at night was going well, and for a change I was enjoying a normal social life. It was a lot to juggle but I am at my best when I am multi-tasking. For work, I fell back onto my health care experience, and with my Army knowledge, took and passed the test to become a certified medical assistant. I was working in the geriatric facilities in Big Rapids and earning enough to keep my reduced child support obligation paid and groceries in my fridge. A large expense for college students is the cost of books. It did not take me long to discover that, except for my Nuclear Medicine texts, I did not even have to purchase books. There were very few actual reading assignments in my classes and if I attended class every day and took some notes, I would have all the information I needed in order to maintain a decent grade point average (G.P.A.). Praise the Lord for my parents as well. My parents harbored a private shame that they were never able to financially assist me with my education. The assistance they provided me with was far more valuable than money. As having an automobile was a luxury I did not need and could not afford, my "world" was limited to wherever my shoes or a bicycle would carry me. My children were living with their mother in Reed City which was 12 miles away. My mother would pick me up and take me back to my parents' house in Reed City. There I was able to spend my visitation weekends with my kids. It haunted me constantly that I was not able to spend the time with my children I wanted to. They were growing up quickly, and I was missing most of it. I had reasoned that although I was missing time with them now, I would be able to spend more time with them in the future after graduation. In addition to the extra time, I would also be able to financially provide for them in a respectable manner as well. It was a difficult decision, but it was, in hindsight, the correct decision. In addition to ensuring that I was getting to spend visitation time with my children, my mother also made sure I had access to laundry and a decent meal. After my now regular diet of ramen noodles with egg, instant pancake mix and hot dogs, a nutritious, home cooked meal was heavenly. My mother did tell me about a "scare" she had gotten in the mail the other day though. She had received a letter from Ferris State University addressed to "The parents of John S. Roberts Jr." Naturally with my track record at centers of education, she opened the letter with great reservation. She thought to herself, "What did he do now?" What "he" had done was made the 'Dean's list" at school for having a G.P.A. greater than 3.5. She said she almost fell out of her chair.

That year in class at Ferris did go by as all years do. I remember when my class ring arrived, (I did scrape up $48 for a stainless steel F.S.U. class ring, I wear it to this day) looking at the year on it being 1993. This was in 1991 and I thought to myself, "1993 will never arrive.." but it was coming faster than I imagined it ever would. Mary graduated from Ferris with her bachelor's degree and landed a job in Michigan's capitol, Lansing. I was in my second and final year of my curriculum and this meant internship. Ferris State did have internship locations throughout the state of Michigan and students were assigned these by a combination of interviews at the location, as well as "luck of the draw." For me, luck of the draw wasn't necessary as not too many students in my class wanted to work in Lansing, so I was able to get an internship at Ingham Medical center. Mary and I were officially a couple then, much to the dismay of her parents. We got a small apartment together and were very happy. My internship was not going as well though. I still was required to pay my child support and other bills, so I needed to find a job. Some students have the good fortune of being able to perform "on-call" work, once trained, at the hospital where they were performing their internships. This would have been a great bonus for me, since working as a Nuclear Medicine Technologist earned at least double the wage I would be able to earn as a medical assistant. Unfortunately, Ingham Medical Center did not permit students to perform paid work while still officially a student. I was ok with this decision until a decision was made by the Nuclear Medicine Department there. They were short of a technologist to perform on-call work in the department and since they did not want to hire an additional technologist, it was decided that they would simply cross-train one of the Radiologic Technologists to perform that on-call. This ingratiated me at a couple of levels. To simply cross train another technologist from another discipline implied that my career was nothing more than that of a "button pusher." Also considering I had spent the last couple of years learning this craft, not to mention essentially working for free 40 hours per week as an "intern" that was an insult. The real stickler was, for me, the fact they wanted me to train the individual. Now the way I saw it, they would not hire me as an employee, because I was a student and presumably did not possess the skill and experience to perform the job. If that were the case, how was it that they felt I had the very same characteristics necessary to train another individual. The stress in the clinic was palpable. I did land a pretty good job working a few blocks down from our apartment at our local inner city hospital Lansing General Hospital. I noted that Lansing General was the inner-city hospital because that was the facility that all the people who did not have health care insurance, transients, junkies, and drunk were sent to. Lansing General may have lacked a few niceties other health care facilities had, but one area it did not lack was in its mental health department. Lansing General's entire top floor was a psychiatric ward and it had received nationwide accreditation. It was because of this fact "crazies" could be added to the list of folks automatically sent to Lansing General be the ambulance and police crews. I was on the midnight crew and had the good fortune of being the only male "nurse" in the facility at night. This meant that every aggressive, angry and or psychotic patient that arrived, I was called to help restrain until the doctor on staff could tranquilize appropriately. I had more than a few memorable "wrestling matches" in the Emergency Room there. I also remember that Lansing General had the first A.I.D.S. (Auto Immune Disorder Syndrome) patient I ever had to care for. This is notable because A.I.D.S. was still very mysterious and frightening to health care workers. This poor gentleman would be admitted every other week or so as his disease progressed to his ultimate demise. He would be admitted and be spiking fevers of 103-105 or so, to the point of having seizures. You see, when an individual has A.I.D.S and no means to defend against even the slightest of viral infections, their bodies do like everyone else's body does and that is turn up the temperature. We would pack him in ice, make sure every 3 hours or so he got massive doses of acetaminophen, and get him through that crisis. On his door were page upon page of "Caution", "Warning", "Universal Precautions" posters and everyone went into his room fully garbed in protective clothing. This patient did ultimately secure a victory for A.I.D.S patients because he threatened to sue the hospital if they did not remove the "wallpaper" that was all over his door. His premise was, "I get treated like an alien and differently than everyone else because you know what I have, there should be at least as much caution taken for everyone as a patient because you DON'T know what they have." He was correct, and soon the "plastering's" were all removed except for one simple "Universal Precautions" sign. This is the same policy in practice in every health care facility even today. My status as an intern at Ingham Medical was ever more tenuous. Each time the supervisor would send the X-ray technologist in to observe what I was doing; I would simply stop work. At the end of the day, I became the first Ferris State intern to ever be dismissed from an internship, and Ingham Medical Center, never received another Ferris intern to exploit. The department head for Nuclear Medicine at Ferris State completely agreed with my position therefore I was granted a second internship location in order to finish my degree program. I was sent to the Veterans Administration hospital 40 miles or so down the road in Ann Arbor Michigan. There were more than a few raised eyebrows at the V.A. as to exactly how I had arrived mid-term, but I was accepted and fit right in. Being a veteran myself, this was an environment that I naturally felt very comfortable in, and 6 months later successfully completed the requirements for my degree. I had also completed the requirements in order to take the A.A.R.T. (American Association of Radiologic Technologists), and C.N.M.T (Certification of Nuclear Medicine Technologists) examinations. One of the happiest moments of my life was wearing that black cap and gown,, walking down that aisle and receiving my first college degree.

In addition to fulfilling my needs for employment and education, the city of Lansing brought another gift to me. Between the hours Mary and I were working, and going to school, we found a way to make some magic and Mary was pregnant with my child. By this time, her parents had discovered that, despite my age, divorced marital status, and having 3 children, I treated their daughter well and that she was truly happy. The fact I was now a college graduate certainly helped forge their decision as well I am sure. Mary and I had talked about getting married a time or two before anyway, so all the pregnancy would do is accelerate the planning process a little bit. In addition to my happiness, Mary also treated my (soon be hers as well) children like her own and even though she was a bit younger, she was a great stepmother. I do believe my kids loved her as well. I had just graduated with my A.A.S. in May of 1993 and Mary, and I were married the following month. We had a wonderful outdoor wedding at her parents' home on the lake.

Nuclear Medicine Technology was a great career choice and I had already secured employment at a major medical center even before I graduated from college. Everything in my life had fallen into place. I had secured a job at William Beaumont Hospital in Royal Oak Michigan, a moderately affluent suburb of Detroit. Mary kept her job in Lansing and was moving up the corporate ladder in her career as well. We bought a nice little house in Lansing and our daughter was born. My other children now had a sister and were ecstatic about it. I too couldn't have been happier as well. I was worried at first during my interview for my position at Beaumont because although I had been hired, the day that they wanted me to start work happened to be the exact same day I had planned to be married. Having to ask for your first week of employment as time off is not necessarily a good start to a working relationship. Fortunately for me, my new supervisor just laughed and said, "no problem." I always loved being a father, but when you are a 19-year-old father struggling to make ends meet in a troubled marriage it was not as wonderful as fatherhood could be. But now my new experience as a 27 year old, financially secure father was everything happy I knew being a parent could be. Fatherhood for me at this time had a special bonus as well. Childcare has never been inexpensive and unless an individual has a job that pays enough for the bills and the childcare, many times it is just more financially responsible to just have a parent stay at home with the child or children. Mary and I found a way around this dilemma. She had a job that was second shift from 3 pm to 11 pm, and I was working days 6 am until 2 pm. Even with the 70-minute commute back and forth from Lansing to Royal Oak, I could still be back home in time to take care of my new baby girl. From the moment I got home from work, the baby was all mine until we both went to bed a few hours later. I feel sorry for any father who does not get to experience the bonding that I got with their new child. The greatest moments of my life were on the visitation weekend and holidays when I had all (now 4) of my children down at our little house. I was saddened by the fact that I was not able to attend a lot of the school functions and activities that my children in Reed City were having, but that was a 3-hour one-way commute there. With my work schedule it was impossible for me to be in two places at once. Even if I could not be as much a part of their daily lives as I might have liked, at least I was able to comfortably provide for them. They would not have to suffer the financial difficulties that so many of their friends in the Northern Michigan area had.

The years moved along much quicker now but at least it was all in a good direction. I remember one moment in time, when as a boy, I asked my father how old he was. He replied, "I am 32 years old" and I remember thinking how old that seemed to me at the time. He then stated the following "But you wait son, the older you get, the faster time goes." If I did not realize then how correct he was then, I certainly do now. Even if they were passing quickly, these were some of the best years of my life. I loved working at Beaumont. Instead of working with people who essentially had no future, few dreams and were living financially from paycheck to paycheck, my associates now were all happy, educated and had real hopes and dreams that were obtainable. I was now like them in this regard. For the first time in my life to that point, I looked forward to going to work. I liked everything about it. My associates were not only my co-workers but my friends. Each day I perfected my craft and like to think I helped a patient or two feel better about their situation in life. My friends and I took care of a lot of people who were having the worse times of their lives. The hardest part of my day-to-day tasks were the few occasions I had to care for pediatric patients. I could understand adults getting sick and dying but children, it seemed so unfair. There was one test that I really had an issue performing. It was called a V.C.U.G. (Voiding Urethrocystogram.) This test involved essentially restraining a child down to an imaging table and then artificially filling their bladder to within 80% of its calculated maximum (via a foley catheter) and then measuring how much refluxed back into the child's kidneys. This generally involved a lot of screaming and the test itself took at least 30-50 minutes. It may not have been so bad except that the very same test could be performed with an x-ray technique to obtain the same results. Most pediatricians for reasons unknown to me usually ordered both tests. Fortunately, not more than two or three of these tests per year ever came through our department. Another questionable activity I had to perform was my rotating on-call requirements. We did perform a few exams, lung scans for pulmonary embolism, biliary scans for acute cholecystitis, and G.I. (gastrointestinal) bleed scans which are self-explanatory on an emergency basis as needed in the middle of the night. I don't necessarily enjoy being woken up in the middle of the night any more than anybody else. On-call did have one benefit though, it paid handsomely when you had to go in. Unfortunately for me, I was still commuting almost 80 minutes one-way and by the time I arrived and finished the exam, I would have to just spend the rest of the workday at the hospital. During the Wintertime, when the roads were going to be particularly treacherous, I would just pack an overnight bag and stay in the department on the nights I was on-call. This was not as bad as it seemed. I had everything I needed for a comfortable stay at the hospital. We had a wonderful break room complete with futon, refrigerator, microwave and T.V. The hospital had showers as well, and a well-stocked cafeteria where I could always get something to eat. I often wondered if an individual decided to "move in" to the hospital, not spend too many nights in the same place, and actually move around a little bit, how long it would be until anyone noticed that they had made the hospital their new "home." One thing I particularly enjoyed about working at Beaumont was the camaraderie of my fellow technologists. We had a superior feeling of esprit de corps and always pulled together to make sure all the work was accomplished timely and professionally. There may have been a couple of folks who liked one another either more or less than others, but for the most part I never noticed any real hostility. We had some great social events too. In the department we would have a monthly breakfast which I would usually at least help prepare in our breakroom. Another favorite at work was our annual "Hawaiian Shirt Day." The entire department was done in island décor, each of us wore our favorite beach clothing (NON swimsuit to be sure) and a contest was held to see who the best was dressed for the event. Naturally this event also included a luncheon in our breakroom. I know that the Patients who received services that day in our department enjoyed the lighthearted fun and cheerful environment. William Beaumont Hospital prided itself on being an academic institution and was also a clinical education location for many health care vocations. We had our own “Certificate in Nuclear Medicine Technology” program, we were recognized by the appropriate accrediting agencies. Upon successful completion of our program, an individual was qualified to take the appropriate examinations and become certified Nuclear Medicine Technologists. A few years later, our program, along with others, became affiliated with the local Oakland University. I was made an adjutant professor there as I was one of their instructors in our program. Shortly after this affiliation I received a letter from Oakland University. It read simply “Congratulations on becoming an adjutant professor, while you can put this on your resume, this, unfortunately does not entitle you to any benefits, parking, discounts, or perks (to include tenure in any form) whatsoever.” The end. It did look great on my resume if nothing else and I got a great laugh out of the letter. The highlight of our social calendar year, without a doubt, was the annual “Graduation Party” we would host for our newest crop of technologists who had just successfully completed our 12-month program. While parents and family members were officially invited to the formal graduation ceremony at the hospital, they were not officially invited to the informal party to be held at a bar or reception hall later that evening. The only way to really describe these parties was to simply say they were a fun, festive, drunken bash. More than a few somewhat morally questionable activities occurred during these parties. Discretion was the watch word for all of us the day after, and essentially everything was done in good fun. Another of my favorite festive activities at Beaumont was Christmas time. I do not remember how I was nominated, blessed is a better word, but for a few years, I was the official hospital “Santa Claus.” I had a couple of “Elves” from the Human Resources department to accompany me throughout the hospital as I made my "rounds." The joy I may have brought to some of the children and patients there will always pale by comparison to the absolute joy I received by performing this task. Besides being Santa had special benefits too. A close second place in our social calendar, behind the graduation party, was the annual "Holiday" (We really did not call it a Christmas party as many of our staff physicians were Jewish and they funded a good part of the event) party which was also held at a local banquet hall in the area. I was able to borrow my Santa suit to perform my official "duties" at this party as well but let's just say I was much more the "naughty Santa" there. The greatest highlight of all these parties was the one year when my co-workers pulled a chair into the middle of the dance floor and planted me in it. One of my co-workers, an exceptionally gifted one, LeeAnn Scarpini stepped out in her finest, tightest, red sequin "elf" dress onto the dance floor. She then proceeded to give me the finest lap dance to the tune of "Santa baby" I have ever had. Truth be told here, I have never in my life, even to this day paid for a lap dance, and have no desire to. Even if I ever decided to, I have no doubt that none would ever live up to the performance LeeAnn gave me that evening. After this, I was speechless, my co-workers and peers roared with laughter, and I was thankful that at least my Santa suit was not form fitting.

Mary was still progressing well up the corporate ladder in Lansing, but soon the walls in our little house felt like they were closing in on us now that we were 3. We began our search for a new, larger house. We were hoping ideally for a location somewhere more geographically centered between Lansing and Royal Oak. This would have us searching in the communities of Brighton or Howell Michigan. As urban sprawl was occurring in the Metropolitan Detroit area like all cities, the home values of any location that was within easy commuting distance was higher than what our home budget was. We ultimately found a wonderful, 100-year-old, historic house in the little town of Fowlerville. Although it was 10 or 15 miles closer to Lansing than it was to Royal Oak, it would suit us fine. Mary and I fell in love with this huge old house, and despite our original hesitation the small tight-knit community of Fowlerville. The only drawback was this added an extra 30 minutes to the commute to pick my other children up from Reed City. Although it was now fully a 3-hour trip, when the kids arrived in their new home they each had their own bedrooms and plenty of place to play. I think this made the little extra car ride worth it for all of us. Fowlerville was and is still a wonderful place to live and raise a family. It is large enough to have all the necessities, gas station, grocery stores, auto repair shop and hardware store, that anyone needs, but still small enough that everyone knows everyone else's names. I have such wonderful memories of that time. One of my greatest joys is always the holidays with all my children. In our large, old corner house in the village we had wonderful Christmases and made the most out of the weekends when we could all be together. Mary and my daughter made friends and started school in the Fowlerville school district where she made even more friends and could walk the few blocks up to the school. A had started a little side gig while I was working at Beaumont and that was doing computer assembly and repair. I got pretty good at it and was eventually making as much money doing that as I was at the hospital. With that in mind I leased a small building in downtown Fowlerville, turned in my notice at work, at opened a computer store named "JR's Computer Solutions." That small town had a disadvantage in the sheer number of customers a proprietor of any business could have, It did have the real advantage in that although the numbers of customers as a whole may be lower, a local proprietor held a higher percentage of them, as in a small town, everyone tries to do business locally. It was nice being able to walk to my little store and unlock the door each day rather than have the over 2 hour daily commute in rush hour traffic. Business was really picking up and thinking I had found a successful business model in a small town, I opened a second store in the next little town over, Stockbridge. This was a disaster. I did not know everyone in Stockbridge and found out shortly thereafter than a local kid was doing the same work I was out of his home. Guess where all the computer business in Stockbridge went to? At the time I opened the original store in Fowlerville, small, independent computer manufacturers like me held about 30% of the market share. The two mainstream manufacturers Dell and Gateway at the time took note of this and steeply slashed their prices to regain some of this share. They succeeded and within 6 months although I was a decent computer repair "guy" my sales plummeted. And even though I was an okay computer guy like I said before; I was not a very good businessman. Money was getting tighter, and I was beginning to drink a lot more. As I was self-employed and my store was empty of people a lot of the time, I had no problem "drinking on the job." This caused a great deal of stress between Mary and I, and I have no doubt that greatly accelerated the demise of my business. In the time frame of about 18 months I had folded both the stores up. I went back to my original occupation and went back to Beaumont with my tail between my legs to humbly ask for my job back. I not only got my job back but ended up with approximately a $3 per hour raise out of the deal. All was back to as it should be again. I had three employees when I owned the stores and there were many, many times when I wrote them larger paychecks than what money I would have left over for my paycheck. Although I was commuting again, I remember that first punch "back on the clock" as being a happy day knowing that in a few short weeks I would be getting a regular paycheck again. A paycheck that was not dependent on whether I had a good sales week that is.

It was sure great to be back to work again with my friends as well. As I was essentially a new hire, I had to refill all my employment paperwork out again. A few days back into my "frest start" I was called into my Chief Technologists office. He said in a quiet, serious voice, "I am supposed to fire you" Of course my reply was "WHY?." "A felony showed up on your background check and you stated that you had never been charged with one," "falsifying employment documents is grounds for immediate dismissal" I told him the whole story and how I did not put it on the first application either as I thought that those automatically go off your record after 7 years. My Chief Tech said, "Your lucky I play sailboats with the President of the hospital and was able to call in a favor he owed me and not fire you" "Get it taken care of immediately." A couple of notes for the record here. Felonies NEVER just go off your record. To remove them you must apply to the court that imposed it and hire an attorney and essentially open another case to get your record expunged. Remember how I said earlier that I would see Judge Scott again? Well, here I was in his courtroom 9 years later humbly asking him to officially and permanently remove that felony stain from my record. I was now college educated, gainfully employed, and a family man who has had no other brushes with the law. Judge Scott asked "the state" if they had any objections to this removal. “the state” did not so Judge Scott simply said “You should be proud, you have turned your life around, I wish I could say this for all of my felony offenders,” “which after today a group of individuals to which you will no longer belong.” The gavel slapped down hard on his desk and I was no longer a convicted felon. I took my document of exoneration back down to my Chief Tech and went back to work. I was very happy again and the next ten years went by quickly. I had no idea that the “two parts” description, the “before and after” I have thought of my life in was about to become “three parts.”

I was in the break room with my co-workers at 9:00 am one morning and flashing across C.N.N. was a picture of what appeared to be a jet aircraft slamming into the side of the World Trade Center in New York. We all first thought it was a horrible accident, “How did that thing even get into that airspace?” The news then stated that it was believed that this was a deliberate act. Shortly thereafter a 2nd Jet careened into the second Trade Tower. This action was now confirmed to be the result of an act of hijacking and terrorism. While everyone was struggling to grasp what was happening in New York, the news broadcast that a 3rd jet airplane full of innocent people had just crashed into the Pentagon building. Another jet crashed shortly thereafter into a field in Pennsylvania where it was presumed to be on its way to the White House. 9/11 just permanently became a dark part of the American lexicon. I told my co-workers, “You will remember this day as the Pearl Harbor of our time, mark my words.”

CHAPTER 5: "Adventure, Again..."

It is hard even now 20 years later to describe what happened to America that day. For the first time in recorded history, a few hours later there was not a single civilian aircraft in the skies over America. Police, firefighters and emergency services from all over New York City streamed to the World Trade Towers, joined by their counterparts nationwide in a few days. Play by play and hour by hour we watched those heroic folks trying everything imaginable to try to save the towers and the people in them. They were unsuccessful on both accounts. Individuals trapped on the upper floors leapt to their deaths 100 stories below rather than be burned alive. A few hours later all that remained of the World Trade Towers and the unfortunates trapped inside were a few hundred thousand tons of rubble. Scores of children remained at daycare centers around New York waiting for parents who would never arrive to pick them up. America was confused as well. Gas, groceries, and water prices at least quadrupled over the next few days as unscrupulous business owners tried to capitalize on that fear. People wondered if this was going to be the beginning of World War III and were hoarding necessities as a hedge.

America would not see this kind of behavior again for another 20 years, until the advent of covid-19.

Like everyone else, I was in shock. The images of those "jumpers" and the thoughts of those children haunted my thoughts day and night. I was also angry that this attack was performed by a bunch of cowards who only attack groups of folks who are most vulnerable. Like a few thousand office workers in the middle of N.Y.C. I was having a lot of trouble coping with these visions and feelings and tried to vent my emotions to Mary. She was not very receptive to say the least as were living the American dream and did not want anything to interrupt that. This was unusual to me as Mary was a military veteran herself. She had spent a 6-year term in the Navy Reserve herself a decade prior. How anyone could be blasé about what had happened was a mystery to me. Even my co-workers were angry and wanted to lash out at whatever evil had done this. I have always believed that being angry or vengeful towards someone or something and not acting upon was like "Drinking poison and expecting the other person to get sick." Despite this believe, the fury growing inside my head would not subside.

A few years prior I had humored a notion of rejoining the Army Reserve or National Guard. Like I had written earlier, the times when you are in the active military were usually miserable time and all you do is mark your calendar counting the days until your "release" Once you are again "Free" all you think of is the good times and what a great experience you had. I never honestly considered re-enlisting before 9/11. I just attributed the idea as being part of a larger, mid-life crisis. One thing I did remember about the Army was that during times of crisis it throws a bunch of 18- and 19-year-old kids into uniform and into harm's way. When 9/11 happened, I was 37 years old and had a virtual lifetime of experiences to fall back and rely on. While I was always ready to give my life for my country, I did not to ever want to see a teenage American being sent back in an aluminum box with a flag draped over it. In my way of thinking if, by my service, I could prevent this from happening even once, then I would have done something useful in this world. Much to the dismay of Mary, the following day I went to the local Army National Guard station 7 miles away and signed the paperwork to reenlist. I was again, a member of the United States Army. I did not throw my entire world to the wind and go back to active duty though. I joined the Army National Guard and was assigned to my local armory as the newest member of the 1462nd Transportation Company. By doing this, I was able to continue working at Beaumont, spend every evening at home with Mary and my daughter and keep my little house in Fowlerville. Mary continued to work in Lansing, and I felt as though I was able to contribute my part to America and not disrupt my wife's "universe" too terribly.

As America struggled to find out who was responsible for the unprovoked attack on our Nation, I attended drill weekends and all of us watched the news intently. Since I was a prior servicemember I did not have to attend basic training or any other training immediately. As I was assigned to an M.O.S. (described earlier) that I had not attended formal schooling for, the time would come when I would have to go away for a couple of months to get that accomplished before I was able to become a permanent, traveling member of the 1462nd. A National Guard unit has some very different characteristics than an active-duty Army unit.

Probably the most significant was the fact that a guard unit can be comprised of individuals from any (or none) of the other branches of the Armed Forces. There were prior members of the Marine Corps, the Navy, the Air Force, and of course prior active-duty Army people like me. I really looked forward to my drill weekends. We through some incredible parties and still managed to keep the unit's vehicles in a high state of readiness. We had our old motor pool area with its 3 bays, and a huge, paved parking lot behind the armory where we could park the approximately 60 or so semi-trucks which were the "trusty steeds" of the 1462nd. All my peers there were very surprised when they found out that when I was not rolling around in diesel fuel and grease, I was dressed in a white coat administering radioactive materials to patients. Of course, after duty hours we had a little section of the garage partitioned off and converted into a "bar." Our bar was complete with the long hardwood bar, and all the décor one would think of in any bar. We could all sit around and reminisce our stories from when we were on active duty and the places we all had seen in a prior life. These were a great bunch of folks and I naturally fit right in. Only once did the local Howell police department ever stop in on a Saturday night. That was because we decided to have a small bonfire out back and learned quickly that once you get 30 or 40 oak wooden pallets lit up together it creates quite a high flame. The civilian neighbors were concerned that maybe we had set our armory on fire or something.

I think approximately a year went by and the United States had supposedly, finally pinned down who was ultimately responsible for the 9/11 attacks. It wasn't like the public didn't know exactly who was responsible for the actual attack. The cowards who did these hijackings died along with the thousands of innocents they murdered. Those individuals would unknowingly add another term to the American lexicon, the "Suicide Bomber." It was a given that these individuals would have required a great deal of logistical and financial support to do what they did. Those support people and their home countries was where Uncle Sam turned his focus of vengeance to. Osama bin Ladin, no stranger to American Intelligence, was determined to be the mastermind and one of the financiers of this attack. He was tracked back to the almost inaccessible, mountainous regions of Afghanistan. This area was bombed relentlessly for over a month. On a few of these bombing missions Uncle Sam thought it would be appropriate to drop a few tons of ordinance (things that go "boom") manufactured from reclaimed steel from the destroyed World Trade Towers. Another few hundred tons of this steel would be used in the construction of the U.S.S. America a new Grunwald class guided missile destroyer. The next majorly responsible group was determined to be the regime of Saddam Hussein. He was then the dictator of the nation of Iraq. This determination would be the one that would also, unknowingly to me at the time, be a force of great change in my life. At that time, the C.I.A. (Central Intelligence Agency) had credible evidence that Saddam Hussein did in fact help, finance, and train the perpetrators of 9/11, His Nation was also supposedly in possession of, and developing additional (yep another new lexicon word coming up) "Weapons of Mass Destruction" or W.M.D's. I would find out years later that all of this was complete bullshit. It has been speculated that the real reason for President George W. Bush Jr's attack on Iraq was because of an assassination attempt that was being formed by Saddam to take out his father. His father was, of course, previous President, George H.W. Bush. America, nor I, will ever truly know the truth behind all of this. None of that would matter to me then as it would not have made any difference in what was going to happen in my life. Shortly after what would be called a "shock and awe" campaign, blowing the shit out of military (and unfortunately some civilian) targets in Baghdad and all over Iraq the ground invasion was set to begin. The original intent of this was to be a simple regime change in Iraq, but like everything else, this "goal" would change. Further intelligence showed that Obama bin Laden was the leader of a shadowy, global organization called Al Qaida. This organization was discovered to be planning its global operations from loosely knit groups or "cells" located in Iraq as well as Afghanistan. Now the goal of the upcoming war in Iraq and Afghanistan would be multi-faceted. It would now be to apprehend Osama bin Ladin, depose Saddam Hussein and his despot sons from Iraq, and ultimately dismantle Al Qaida once and for all.

The United States military, like virtually every military through history, requires logistics. More specifically transportation of troops, munitions, fuel and everything else an Army needs to win a war. General Nathan Bedford Forrest, Confederate States of America (and first Grand Wizard of the Klu Klux Klan, but that's another story) was quoted as saying "He who arrives first, with the most, wins." That statement about war is as accurate today as it was in1863. The 1462nd Transportation Company from Howell Michigan was soon activated and deployed to the Middle East as part of that plan. Since I still had not received my formal schooling for the M.O.S. I was working in the 1462nd, I would not be able to deploy with my friends. This caused me a great deal of grief as I loved each and every one of these folks and if they were going to be in harm's way, I intended to be there with them. The Army had different plans for me, and I would never be a member of the 1462nd again. Unlike my first enlistment in the United States Army, I was now in possession of a college education. This made me eligible to become a commissioned officer. The Army was in desperate need of what was referred to as "Company Grade Officers." These were officers in the ranks of 2nd Lieutenant, 1st Lieutenant, and Captain. These are the leaders of the most basic operational group of the United States Army. This is usually 80-125 Soldiers and is referred to as a "Company." In a Company the Lieutenants are the platoon leaders, and executive officers and Captains are the Company Commanders. Without a qualified group of these people the Army is unable to function. It was going to be up to me as to which military career path I wanted to choose. I could have remained an N.C.O. and headed to another mechanics school at Ft Knox. My other alternative was to attend Officer Candidate School and receive a commission as a 2nd Lieutenant. If I chose the Commissioned Officer path, I would have to get enrolled into the course as quickly as possible. To become an Office there is a requirement by the Army that an individual must receive their commission before the age of 40. Supposedly this was so the individual could serve a full 20 year career as an officer before reaching retirement age. As I wrote earlier, my goal with reenlistment was twofold. My first goal was simply exact a little "payback" against the individuals who were responsible for the death of over 2700 of my countrymen. My next goal was to try to keep some young people from coming home in an aluminum, flag draped box. I knew that I would be in a better position to succeed at both of these goals while serving as a commissioned officer. There are two avenues that an individual in the

Army National Guard can choose from to receive their commission. The standard method is to perform the coursework in a reserve time frame. That meant reporting to an O.C.S. (Officer Candidate School) every drill weekend and pretty much getting your ass kicked piece by piece over the next 18 months. Enrollment in the 18-month course would have placed me over the age of 40 upon completion, this was not an option for me. I would have to attend the "accelerated O.C.S." which condenses all the course work into a 12-week block of instruction. The Alabama Military Academy was an entity created from the remains of what was Ft McClellen in Anniston Alabama for just such a purpose. It was 2002 and the 1462nd Transportation Company headed to Iraq for what would be named "Operation Iraqi Freedom." Maybe the name was derived from the mission to free the Iraqis, and the rest of the world, from Saddam Hussein? At the same time I was headed to Accelerated O.C.S. at the Alabama Military Academy (A.M.A).

248 Soldiers from National Guard units from every state arrived one sunny day and were soon standing in front of the Commandants building. My life was about to become very uncomfortable for the next 3 months. The Commandant stepped out onto the podium in front of everyone with a small stack of papers in her hand. She simply read 18 names from the papers she held and said, "I kept the busses here for just reason, if yours was one of those names I read, climb right back on that bus to go back to your state" "You came here with a physical profile and you cannot successfully complete this course with any physical limitations whatever." That set the ominous tone for the course and our 248 Soldiers were now 230. "Time" was the cadre's, (referred to by us as sir or ma'am,

and we were simply referred to as candidate) most valued possession. Time would become the candidates worse enemy. Every single minute of the next 12 weeks was to be accounted for and was on the training calendar with a purpose. This was important because the next thing the Commandant said to us, after the eighteen "broke dicks" were on their way back home" was, "You can miss exactly 120 minutes of training, should any of you, for any reason whatsoever reach minute 121, you will be joining those 18 individuals back to your state." In the military if you are sick, you report to "sick call." This involves that telling your supervisor you don't feel well, and then they write you a "sick call slip." The soldier then walks their ass down to the local aid station. Once there you sit in the waiting room with any number of individuals, like you, who were also not feeling well. After usually an hour or two later, you get to see the P.A. (Physicians Assistants, REAL doctors NEVER saw Soldiers at sick call) who would then determine what medicine you may need, any physical restrictions to prevent further injury or illness you required and for how long those restrictions would be in place for. The P.A then writes their impressions and instructions on the sick call slip and sends the soldier back on their way to their unit. By this time three or four hours had passed by the time they return to their respective unit. The time requirement imposed by the A.M.A pretty much assured that if you had to go to sick call, you could kiss your opportunity to become an Army Officer goodbye. For the few that attempted it, when the cadre handed them their sick call slip, they also clicked the button on their stopwatch. That time was also written on the sick call slip. The stopwatch clicked back off when the Soldier returned to training. You will usually hear Soldiers talk about basic training as the toughest course of instruction they ever had.

That was the regular Soldier anyway. Now naturally some of the special forces (Green Berets, Airborne, Air Assault, Pathfinder, etc....) courses are far more demanding, but only a select few will ever be accepted to those types of instruction. I briefly entertained the notion that "This course could not be that difficult, its intended for a group of college educated "Cadets." I could not have been more wrong. It's hard for the average person to grasp how much physical duress can be caused in any environment where there is no physical hitting, or beating and even obscene language is forbidden. The group at the A.M.A. had developed new and successful methods of torture down to an exact science. The Army does have guidelines for training and exactly how much of what is required to be provided. Sleep for example, I believe it is written that Soldiers must be allowed at least 5 hours of sleep each night, but that number can be reduced to 4 hours for limited periods of time. One of those limited times would be the first three weeks of this course, and 4 hours of sleep were the maximum that I would get. Lack of sleep for me is like Samson's hair in the Good Book, without it, I rapidly become ineffective. My training day started at 4 am each day. Unlike basic training, there was no brutal wake up, it was just expected that by 4 am, I would be part of the formed unit, dressed, shaved, bed made (to standard of course) my personal items all put away (again to standard) and ready to train. To accomplish this, I had to make sure that I was awake by roughly 3:15 am or there was no way I could have everything done. This was no easy task since it was after 11 pm at the earliest that I was able to sleep. After each demanding training day, the cadre would have us all lined up, in front of our bunks standing in our underwear, holding our rifles at arm's length on the tops of our hands. Now just about the time that this position was becoming painful and impossible to continue, we would be instructed to lift the rifles over our heads. Blessed relief it was, for exactly the two or three minutes until that position too became painful, then weapons back in front of us and so that "rotation" went while we were given stories of the glorious and heroic Army Officers who had proceeded us in history. I could write 20 pages alone about my block of instruction in Anniston Alabama, but this was simply a means to an end in my life. We were marched, drilled, instructed, trained and moderately tortured day in and day out in all kinds of weather and terrain. We were taught water evacuations by being kicked off a diving board into a pool, completely dressed. In addition, we were also blindfolded and had our M-16 (Individual weapon of choice of the US Army, a rifle) with us. To succeed you simply had to make it back out of the pool, minus all your gear except your M-16. I had no trouble with this, but surprisingly even in 2002, have a few individuals who could not swim. I will never forget one candidate, a tiny black gal named Jessica, who struggled through the whole course. She damn near drowned during the pool portion and had to repeat that particular exercise no less than 5 times before she was succeeded. She also contracted pneumonia at one point and was very sick. Despite this she still never went to sick call, never faltered and never quit. She was my inspiration! I imagine she is probably a Colonel now and any Soldier would be very lucky to have her at the top of their chain of command. But all this training was done for one purpose and one purpose only. That is to ensure that when it was completed and we were commissioned as a 2nd Lieutenants, each and every one of us would be capable leaders of Soldiers. Being a leader means different things to different people, but in the Army there were a few expectations that had to be met. A "leader" leads from the front, every time. A "leader" does not expect Soldiers under their command to perform any task that they cannot or would not perform themselves. Most importantly, a "leader" always places his Soldiers needs before their own. These are absolutely inviolate statutes. Every servicemember who has ever been in a uniform can easily recollect leaders in their service who did not meet or make any attempt to meet these standards. I made a personal vow that I would never be one of those types of officers. As I write these pages, I do know that I did what was expected as a leader of Soldiers. This was not simply because I was a nice guy. It doesn't take a rocket scientist to figure out, that by placing your Soldiers needs and care above your own, you Soldiers will also not only perform the missions that are required of them but will look out for your welfare as well. Another word that officers leading Soldiers in combat will always think of is that dirty little work called "Fratricide." Fratricide essentially is a way a Soldier, or group of Soldiers can rid themselves of leaders who are not looking out for their best interests. There are more than a few instances where an Officer has been killed in combat by their own troops. I had no intention of becoming one of those statistics as well. Time moved quickly on, praise the Lord, and despite the hardships I was one of the 159 or so individuals who successfully completed the course. Our official "commissioning" (the act of having your new rank pinned on you and getting your official covenant with Uncle Sam) was performed back at our home units. This was so you could have this done in front of family, friends and peers. The Army is steeped in tradition and the act of commissioning is no different. My favorite tradition was the one involving two silver dollars. You go to choose an individual who would pin your first "butter bar" (the affectionate term for the 2nd Lieutenant gold bar rank) on your uniform, and the second was for the first enlisted Soldier who presented you with your first official "salute" outside the auditorium. I chose my father to pin my rank on, and when he came up to the podium and pinned it on, I saw a tear go down his cheek. It was exactly the second time I had ever seen my father shed a tear, the first being many years ago when his mother died at age 54 of cancer. It was his, and one of my, most proud moments. I presented him with his 1921 Peace dollar that I brought for the occasion. Naturally there is swarm of enlisted troops outside the auditorium waiting to whip that salute out and get their silver dollar from the new "Officers" and honestly I can't even remember who got my second one. I will always remember the first one with my father though.

It wasn't but a few weeks later and I had to leave again for my first assignment as a United States Army Officer. Unlike enlisted Soldiers with an M.O.S. Officers job descriptions are referred to as "Branches." Branches are a lot less specific than M.O.S are. Some of the branches an Officer can choose are Infantry, Artillery, Armor, Medicine and my choice Transportation. I was no more officially job trained as an Officer than I was as an enlisted Soldier so my first task would be to get my education as a "81-D" the official designation for a Transportation Officer. I said goodbye to Mary and my little girl again and was ready to ship off for the next 4 months. Things in my marriage were, unbeknownst to me at the time, going downhill as Mary was not doing well having her husband gone so much. As she so eloquently stated "I did not sign up for this." The proverbial writing was on the wall, and I was too blinded with visions of heroism and grandeur to see them. I was headed for the home of Army

Transportation, Ft Eustis Virginia. Ft Eustis is in the middle of a beautiful part of the country. It is the very first stop on the peninsula that starts with historic Jamestown and ends at the very tip with the beautiful community of Virginia Beach. Between Jamestown and Virginia Beach were Ft Eustis, Ft Lee (Home of Army Administration) the giant Norfolk Naval Station and finally Virginia Beach. On the west side of the peninsula was the James River and on the East was Chesapeake Bay. Unlike the rigorous training course I had taken at the A.M.A., the Transportation course at Fort Eustis was a "gentlemen's course." In addition, I was now officially a United States Army Officer. I had a blast there. The days were filled with lectures, calculations, and learning via planes, trains and automobiles how to move everything a modern Army needs from point A to point B. I learned not only how to load a train at a rail head but got to drive the little diesel electric locomotive around the post for a couple of laps. I learned how to load a giant freighter with equipment and how many chains of each size were required on every corner of a truck to keep it secure while sailing the seven seas. I was taught what an M647 pallet was and how to load it correctly so it could be strapped down and take to the sky in a C-5 Galaxy Air Force Jet. Between all this training were the evenings and weekends of fishing, sightseeing and drinking with all my new officer buddies. I am certain more than a few officers watched us and shook their heads. Again, time passed quickly and a few months later I was a trained 81-D Officer ready for my first assignment.

The 1462nd was still in Iraq, in the heat of combat and naturally I wanted to join them. That is not how the Army works though and I was given another assignment. Although I was only a 2nd Lieutenant, I was probably the Army's oldest living 2nd Lieutenant. I was assigned as the Company Commander for the 113th Maintenance Company based in Detroit. It was my first experience as a Company Commander, and I enjoyed it. It was also a good place to start polishing my techniques. The 113th had some personnel challenges being an inner-city unit and I think I was placed there to see how I would handle such situations. I had the benefit of having been an N.C.O. before I became an officer, and that experience served me well. Absenteeism and tardiness were rampant in the 113th Maintenance Company. I developed remedies for each one of those. Now absenteeism was easy enough. The usual "song and dance" was "Oh my car won't start, and I can't make it to drill weekend." Once I started having my First Sergeant and Operations N.C.O. driving to Soldiers homes to pick them up for work, the absenteeism rate dropped down to single digits. For tardiness, I utilized a time "repayment" system that I had been exposed to at the A.M.A. In the attic of the armory, I found a large 2' high bronze statue of an eagle perched on a globe. For every minute a Soldier was late to one of my formations, they would "repay" me that minute during their lunch breaks or after regular duty hours by shining and polishing "The Old Man's Eagle." My office was at the end of a long hallway, and I had soon found a can of forest green paint on the premises. I had my Soldiers paint a 1' wide green path on the concrete floor leading right to my office door. Just like the movie with Tom Hanks "The Green Mile" if a Soldier had to report to my office, the other Soldiers would laugh that they were "Walking the Green Mile." Both these techniques, while effective in remedying my problems, were still lighthearted solutions. The leadership of Michigan Guard had noticed I had brought the 113th up to Army Standards. I was still in the National Guard though and only had to perform these duties during drill weekends and Annual training and the rest of the time I was free to return to my civilian employment. I went back to Beaumont and returned to applause and accolades for my dedication and accomplishments helping to make America safe again. The war raged on in Iraq and as soon as the 1462nd Trans returned from O.I.F 2, I was "activated" to regular Army service and headed to Iraq with a different company as a platoon leader. The Army was struggling to fill the ranks with company grade officers in order to maintain enough strength to fill the ranks and many officers were assigned to different units as "fill ins." It was one of these "fill in's" that I was assigned to. I became the Platoon Leader for a platoon of Soldiers from the 1461st Transportation Company based out of Jackson Michigan. Another platoon from the 1460th Transportation Company out of Midland Michigan joined us. Now that we were two complete platoons, we were "Patched up" with one platoon of Soldiers, the company command leadership and the Company Commander from the 137th Transportation Company of the Kansas National Guard. Now why, since there were two platoons from Michigan and only one from Kansas, did we not have that Kansas platoon join us in the Michigan Guard with command and logistics from the same was a mystery. One thing I did learn long ago was that if you expected everything the Army did to make sense you would just be confused and disappointed. The term "Military Intelligence" is an oxymoron of the highest level. This kind of arrangement was as new to the Army as it was to us. It seems the Governors of the States have "volunteered" our services to the active Army in any way that Uncle Sam saw fit to use us. Despite the challenges of different unit crests, command and control centers, and equipment utilization and all, we made the best of it and came together as a solid fighting unit. There were a few moments of "Those Kansas folks" or "those Michigan people" that occurred but only rarely at first and not at all shortly thereafter.

The 137th Transportation Companies mission would be to replace the 430th Transportation Company from Puerto Rico, already in place in a place called Taji, Iraq. A disadvantage to a National Guard unit is that they essentially only "play Army" one weekend a month and two weeks a year. It didn't mean that we were any less dedicated to the mission at hand, maybe just not as proficient at being full-time Soldiers as the active-duty Soldiers were. One glimmer of "intelligence" the Army used was the recognition of this. Fully over 60% of the Soldiers in our company had no active-duty service besides their basic training and their M.O.S. school. Over 90% of the Soldiers in our company, many with decades in the National Guard, had never been deployed. Deployed is a term used when a National Guard unit is activated, or placed on active-duty status, in order to perform a specific mission. Units in the past have been deployed to assist with law enforcement during times of crisis, assisted local emergency services during periods of disaster. Some of the units in the Southern United States had even been deployed to assist the border patrol along the Mexican border when Customs Officers were particularly inundated. Obviously a remedy had to be implemented before guard units were sent into combat. This was accomplished by creating MOB (mobilization) Stations to send units to in order to receive specific training for the new environment we would soon find ourselves in. Our MOB station would be located on Ft Riley Kansas. This was a bit of a treat for me, because Fort Riley was the home of the First Infantry Division. Home of the “Big Red One” and its signs were all over post. As I had said earlier I was a proud member of the “Big Red One” in Germany, but alas had never spent so much as a minute in its actual home of Fort Riley. In 1985 the Army changed its method of Soldier replacement from individual Soldiers to a system called “Battalion Rotations” for U.S.A.E.U.R. Instead of cutting orders for each Soldier, every 18 months an entire Battalion of troops (all 700 or so of them) would be exchanged. They would just take over the equipment from the battalion they were replacing. For me, instead of the upcoming battalion rotation between the 4th/5th F.A, and the 2nd/F.A. stationed at Fort Riley, I ended my time in service and never got to see Fort Riley then. Fast forward to 2003, an area just outside of post at Fort Riley was specifically designed and constructed for our training. This area had miles and miles of open roads in the middle of nowhere that could be utilized for convoy training. There was even a small Iraqi village constructed (think Hollywood prop) for receiving training on urban warfare and interaction with the “locals.” Buildings inside this village were of different types, floors and construction materials in order to practice “clearing” houses, apprehending “bad guys” and collecting intelligence. Active-duty Soldiers from post were specially trained and dressed like “local nationals” (Iraqi citizens in our case) in order that the training and interactions would be as realistic as possible to the real thing. With one main exception, if you fuck it up there, you won’t bleed as much or probably die like you will if you fuck it up in Iraq. Our focus at the MOB station was the convoy operations. My Soldiers were mainly professional truckers back in the “world” but trucking on the highways and byways of the good old U.S. of A. is nothing like trucking in an area of this area of the world. This was where a majority of the folk’s main purpose is to prevent you from getting from Point A to Point B. Their preferred method of preventing us was by blowing us to shit and turning our convoys into grease spots. The focus of convoy operations training was twofold. First, we learn ways of reducing our chances of getting blown to shit in the first place. Second was, in the most likely event we were attacked, what to do afterward. Preventing, or at least reducing the risk of being attacked, is accomplished in several ways. Your convoys arrangement, what vehicles go where in the line, where the locations of your fire power is and how and when to use it, specific things to watch for on the roads and so forth. Naturally what to do after being attacked will vary, sometimes widely, depending on the success of the attackers. I loved this lesson at the A.M.A. and remember it well; "If you manage to drive into a well-planned ambush, your chances of survival are low and you should just attempt to drive straight through it", pretty straightforward. As the commander, my focus was on three things, my Soldiers, my equipment, and getting the mission accomplished. If I managed to succeed at the first two, the mission was automatically successful. Nature helps a little bit in the regard with our "flight or fight" reflex. Fortunately, the flight will win every time if that opportunity is presented. If bad guys took a shot at us, or something went boom and we were not damaged first rule of thumb was to get the fuck out of "Dodge" easy! If we were damaged things got a little trickier. I would have to quickly assess the extent of damage to people or equipment and decide what could be done. My priority was always first and foremost "my kids." If possible evacuate injured personnel into other vehicles and then have all other convoy assets stop at a pre-determined safe "rally point" Once the threat is passed then, if can be safely accomplished, attempt to either recover the damaged vehicle or cargo, or destroy in all in place. You never leave anything whatsoever to the enemy. The most accepted way to become proficient at anything in life is repetition. Stephen King wrote in one of his novels "Hell is repetition." Fort Riley's MOB training for all of us was no exception. While we did get some free time during MOB training, this was by no means a "gentleman's course" There were written standards and grades given by the instructors for each task to be trained on and until our entire unit met these standards. There really was no other focus there except training. I can't say that I was scared, I always had a lot on my mind, but fear wasn't part of it.. My greatest fear, above all, was something happening to one of my Soldiers. Some Officers may not take the lives of their Soldiers as their personal responsibility, but I most certainly did. Shy of the fear of hell, I had to greater fear that a mistake on my part would result in the death of one of my troops. In a few short weeks our 137th Transportation company was considered "trained" and cleared to departure to "theater." Another mystery to me is how anyone could call an area of combat a "theater." None of them I've ever seen were anything anyone would intentionally buy a ticket to that's for damn sure. One morning that call finally came and the following morning, the 137th, all our equipment, people, weapons systems, everything, was assembled on the tarmac at Volk Field in Kansas to board the huge "Ryanair" jet that would take us 6000 or so miles across the "pond". The last thing I did on the American soil I stood on that day was to stand in line at the scales. This was making sure that I, or anyone else getting on that aircraft, was under the 400 pounds we each were allocated. When I think of the tons and tons of men and machines that were packed on that plane, I am still amazed it ever left the ground.

It was 2003, I was just shy of 40 years old and was in the air with the lives of 47 or Soldiers in my hands. My mind was reeling. 6 or 7 or so hours later, we completed the first "leg" of our trip and landed in Leipzig, Germany. I remember two things about that. The first was that the place looked like a slum. The second was that I was now standing in what would have been a forbidden place 19 years earlier as Leipzig would have been smack dab in the middle of the D.D.R. (East Germany). I didn't have long to reflect on that because a few short hours and a hundred thousand pounds of aircraft fuel later I was back in the air. Our next stop was in the Middle East. Commercial air traffic into Baghdad was still not permitted yet as there was still active fighting throughout the country. All arriving U.S. flights would land at the Kuwait International Airport, and we were no exception. Naturally I would never see the inside of the airport building proper as all military arrivals are always kept in the middle of that special section of every airport across the globe. This is always to keep away from the prying eyes and possible discomfort of the civilian comings and goings. I also remember a couple of things about this arrival. One is that it was hot, an oppressively, incredibly, humid, very uncomfortable type of hot. You quickly learn why the men and women over there both wear flowing white dresses instead of the combat uniforms we were all dressed in. The next thing I remember was the smell. The smell was a mixture of jet exhaust, perspiration and human feces. Once we left the airport area, the exhaust and perspiration smells went down a little bit. The smell of human shit did not. It was a smell that I just got used to. This is because the entire Middle East has that smell, no matter where you go or where you are. I guess when you're in the area of the globe where people have been walking around for the last 6 or 8 thousand years it will leave a mark. Kuwait is comprised of two things, Kuwait City and the desert. I bet you can guess which one we would be staying in until our departure to Iraq. If you guessed Kuwait City, you are either too stupid to be able to read, or you guessed correctly and we were bussed into the middle of the desert. An hour or so later, just about the time I began to wonder if we were somehow on the surface of Mars we arrived at a big gate and sign. The sign read simply "Camp Virginia." There were around three large Quonset hut type buildings and row upon row, acre upon acre, probably mile upon mile of large tents. One of these tents would be our temporary home. Except for us, rattlesnakes, scorpions and camel spiders, there was no other life in this area of the desert whatsoever. It makes me feel a little ill to know, despite liberating these people a few short years before from becoming and remaining Saddam Husseins 19th state of Iraq, that they were charging Uncle Sam a lease fee for this huge chunk of nothing. Life at Camp Virginia was about as mundane and ordinary as is humanly possible. You wake, shower, dress, eat, an occasional meeting for us officers, and repeat, day after day. All I could think of was that my mates in the 1462nd were up north in Iraq fighting and I am sitting here in the desert doing essentially nothing. I don't recall it being more than a couple of weeks and the 137th received it marching orders to begin the convoy into theater. We put together our first combat, pre-convoy briefing and rolled down the road. The desert was everywhere. I don't even remember there being a specific line or gate at the border, but hearing across the radio that it was time to pay more attention as we were now officially in Iraq.

Once we had travelled 20 miles or so inside the country one of my vehicles broke down and was in need of repair. Two things would happen here. Unfortunately, we were still around 180 miles from our destination in Iraq and my platoon was not going to make a single mile of it until my vehicle was repaired. Fortunately, we did make it into a coalition area where we could, in relative safety, await the service technicians to get us back on the road, even if it would take until the next day to get it accomplished. My platoon and I were about to find out what caliber of Company Commander we had been given from the Kansas National Guard as well. A couple of things about our Commander, Captain "Randy" Tong. First was that he had no active-duty Army experience whatsoever and had joined the National Guard in order to fund his education as a lawyer in the "world." Second was that Captain Tong primary concern was Captain Tong. He called me off to the side while we were waiting for our truck to be repaired and informed that the rest of the company would be leaving immediately to continue their journey to our new home in Taji. 20 minutes later, the other two platoons along with 75% of the firepower we had to defend ourselves headed down the road. My Soldiers were terrified. I was a little apprehensive myself, but it was not the time to show any of that apprehension at all. I watched a lot of war movies in my day, and cheesy as the idea may sound, I did pull some "pearls of wisdom" from some of them. The "pearl" that popped into my mind at that moment was "The Commander ALWAYS knows what to do, even if he doesn't, doubt can sink a ship" or destroy a platoon I suppose. Once my vehicle was ready to travel again, without a minute's hesitation, I called my N.C.O.'s together, updated them and gave them our new pre-combat briefing. A briefing which more clearly reflected our current status, and soon enough we were on the road again. The Lord was looking out for us I suppose because despite, because of our reduced size, and looking like an easy target we did not encounter any problems on the way. We all safely arrived in Taji without incident.

Taji was a large outpost situated around 15 miles North of Baghdad. Before the war, this had been the home of “Chemical Ali” one of Saddam Husseins generals. It was also the location where Ali had his laboratories and the things he needed do develop W.M.D’s. New biological and chemical ones to be specific. How much of his “experiments” were just poured out on the ground upon his hasty departure I could only guess. None of us wanted to be breathing or rolling around in the dust very much though. Taji now belonged to the coalition and was named Camp Cooke. It was divided into two sections. The first section was the part that was in the best state of repair and was occupied by us and other coalition forces. The other section of the camp was little more that rubble and was occupied by the ‘New Iraqi Army.’ Now that Saddam Hussein was gone, a temporary government was installed, and plans were made for regular elections and to rebuild an Iraq that its citizens could live safely in and prosper. In order to keep this now fledgling nation, it would also have to have its own armed forces again. This fact would become very important to me in the near future.

We had pretty good accommodations as far as the Army goes. My troops occupied one large bay, narrow and lined with bunkbeds along each side. At either end of the building were “common” areas where there was a big screen TV, a couple of very well-worn couches and lounge chairs, and a small dormitory style refrigerator. One end of the bay was the entrance, and at the other end of the bay was a private room. This was where my Platoon Sergeant, E-7 (Sergeant First Class) Wylde stayed. The only inconvenience in this living area was the fact that there was no bathroom in the building. Like almost everyone else on Camp Cooke, the regular Soldier had to make the small walk to the nearest row of porta-johns which were set up almost everywhere. I got really lucky when it came to my "luxury" accommodation. About 20 yards or so out, along the outer wall of our compound area was a small brick building. This building was comprised of two private rooms, each with a bunk bed and desk, and it had its own bathroom and shower in between them. Being an officer does have its advantages and I absconded one of these for my "residence." This could be considered almost like college dorm living. With the exception I was 6000 miles away from home, in the desert, and surrounded by people who were trying to kill me. It doesn't take long to notice how different everything is in the Middle East. Everything is the opposite of what it is here in the States. The hot and cold faucets are on the "wrong" side of the sinks, the doors open in the "wrong" direction, even the Arabic language is written right to left and from bottom to top. It all takes a little getting used to. There were no functional public utilities available anywhere on Camp Cooke. I think it was because we blew the shit out of the place during the opening salvos of the war. Everything, and I mean everything, was portable and had to be hauled in and out. All the water on camp for each building was kept in a large rubber bladder somewhere near the building. All the electricity was provided by the large Caterpillar diesel generators which ran day and night. Very soon, you never even heard them running anymore. You would certainly perk your ears up when they were not running though. On those rare occasions (fortunately) those diesel generators would fail, all life stops for us. As I had said earlier, I lived in a small brick room with a single pane window. The sole purpose of this window was to hold the little portable air conditioner which was the difference between life and death when its 114 degrees outside. When the generator stopped, I could sit and watch the little thermometer I had mounted on the wall rise. The food was also completely trucked in and out of each camp in theater. There was one main mess facility on Camp Cooke, and it was a few blocks away from where we were staying. Although it was always hot outside it was always worth the walk. The food was great, plentiful and always had a variety of selections for pretty much every palate. All the Soldiers needs in theater ware met by an independent contracting company K.B.R. (Kellogg, Brown, and Root) based out of Texas I believe. A lot of people were questioning the governments choice of K.B.R. to be the Militaries sole provider for all things necessary in Iraq. K.B.R., being from Texas, did have some loose affiliation with the Bush family at one time in the past. Questions were raised because the entire operation was not put out for bidding like every other government contract. The Bush administration simply replied that only K.B.R. had the means and financial ability to provide everything that would be required in theater. America may have had its doubts, but I can tell you having seen everything that K.B.R. did for us there, that Uncle Sam was correct in his choice of them for this contracting mission. We also heard through the grapevine that people back home were bitching because K.B.R was charging the United States Army $135 per soldier, per day for every meal served. I felt pretty pissed off over these rumors as I know every other Soldier who learned this did as well. While we were performing our duties for God and country we were forbidden to consume alcohol, certainly weren't getting any regular sex (most Soldiers anyway), or sitting "back on the block" watching Sunday football. I would have gladly traded this one small luxury we were provided with, which was the good food, for any of those. And this food was still only available when we were back in garrison. Once we left the "wire" (common combat nickname for the borders of our compound) the only shit we were eating was out of a brown, plastic bag with M.R.E. (Meal, Ready to Eat) writing in bold black print across it. And just like combat across the ages, we were "on mission" a lot more than we were in garrison.

"Missions" were what we were in Iraq to do, and we did a lot of them the first six months I was in country. My platoon consisted of 42 Soldiers, 15 P.L.S. (Palletized Loading System) trucks and 2 HUMMV ("Hummers", to this day I don't really know what the acronym stands for) as the command and communication vehicles. My "chariot" was the HUMMV which would lead the convoy. This isn't the greatest place to be in combat because it was known that over 70% of all attacks on convoy attacks occur at either the front, or the back of the convoy. Very rarely were we attacked in the middle. This was due simply to the fact that once we were rolling, nothing or no one was allowed to fall into the middle of our convoy for any reason. Another statistic was that daylight attacks happened around 6 or 7X more than night attacks. I think one reason for the day versus night statistics was because of money. A lot of the attacks on coalition forces were simply for money, not ideology, not hatred, but simply, cold, hard cash. The same way the 9/11 attacks were financed by a third party, a lot of the ongoing war in Iraq was as well. Rather than do the dirty work themselves, the wealthy, "ideological" folks (and of course

Iran) would just find other poor locals to do it for them. These true cowards would always find the poorest citizens, and there were plenty of them as the economy was in shambles, and then provide them with the materials and money to get the job done. They only required one item before they would pay out these "bounties." They required an actual video recording of the attack in progress. Since poor people generally do not possess night vision cameras or infrared film the only way they could record their deeds was during daylight hours. Simple economics kept the war going.

My war would be fought at night. Our missions would begin when CPT Tong received an order from the Battalion. It might be simple as "Take 4 tons of dog food from Baghdad to B.I.A.P (Baghdad International Airport). Then the good Captain would decide which of us three "Convoy Platoons" to assign the mission to. A standard Army "Company" is usually 4 platoons, 3 of which are mission specific, for example we were one of the "delivery" platoons. The 4th Platoon in the company is always the command and support platoon. The Companies Commander, First Sergeant, Unit Clerks, Armorer, Mail Clerk, Administration folks and medics are member of the 4th Platoon, most commonly referred to as "Headquarters Platoon." Captain Tong was very okay with this arraignment. This ensured he could look all important and commanding, while never having to leave the relative safety of the compound. Once the mission was assigned, assuming my platoon received it, my work would then begin. My first task was to assign a "WARNO" or "warning operation" to my Platoon Sergeant, this was a simple "hey we just got called to do this tonight so get ready to make it happen." The Platoon

Sergeant would then decide what vehicles would be needed, personnel would drive and operate them, support assets and so on. While they are getting to work on that, I usually would go to Battalion to the S-2 briefing and find out what kind of shit I could expect to come across on the highways and byways on the mission. A brief explanation of S-2 moniker is required here I suppose. Once a functional unit of the Army is at a Battalion level or higher, their functions become less mission specific (Like transportation, or infantry, so on) and more about support functions for mission specific companies. Battalion sized units and larger were divided into sections rather than platoons and each section had a specific function there. In a battalion each section has a function detailed by which letter it was a part of. For instance, S-1 was Operations, think of them as the headquarters platoon of the battalion, S-2 was Intelligence, everything to do with intelligence operations was handled at S-2, S-3 was logistics, what had to be obtained, from where and so on for the battalion, and S-4 was supply. S-4 handed out all the goodies throughout the battalion that S-3 procured. Division sized elements also are divided by sections but they are detailed by the letter "D" (Army has to keep shit simple you know) and has a couple more sections like a "D-5" and "D-6" but they were well out of the scope of anything I was responsible for and since I didn't have anything to do with them or know about them; I don't have to explain them. Ok, now that you have the grasp of that, back to my work at the Company. Each evening Battalion S-2 would gather all the information from its other companies and operations throughout the theater. They kept their thumb and eyes on the news ticker you might say. They would combine this information with other information they obtained from other Companies in their command who had been on road missions and put together a daily “intelligence briefing.” Despite the hundreds of “Death by PowerPoint” briefings I had received in the Army to that point, believe me when I tell you, my ass paid attention to the daily S-2 briefing before I went on the roads in Iraq. It’s amazing how closely related to your well-being certain news may be, the closer your eyes and ears are glued on it. From this briefing I would learn where attacks had come from in the past, which roads and areas had been or were most likely to be attacked, and most importantly the current S.O. P’s (Standard Operating Procedures, yep assholes use them too in combat) the bad guys were having success turning coalition forces into grease spots with. All the time I was gathering my intel for the night my Platoon Sergeant was getting everything ready back at the company area.

Because of the reasons I have stated earlier, virtually all of my missions were at night. With our possession of night vision equipment and other technological wizardry, just like in Vietnam, “We ruled the night.” Besides the obvious advantage of less chance of getting attacked, driving at night had a lot of other benefits. One of these was reduction of the oppressive heat. No matter the temperature outside, if we were outside the “wire’ it was in full battle dress (also referred to by many as “battle rattle”), which was long sleeve shirt, long pants, flak jackets with ballistic plates front and rear, helmets, gloves, eye wear, boots and all the essentials pinned to the outside of that. The flak jacket of the 21st century was a little different than the one my uncles and friends had known in Vietnam. It was thicker, heavier and two “ceramic” plates were placed in slots in the front and back of the vest. Although I wondered how a ½” piece of ceramic that came in a box that said “fragile, do not drop” and had boldly written “this side out” on one side would stop a 7.62 bullet or artillery fragment, we were shown numerous training videos of these in “action” and that left little doubt these things could save your life. Even knowing this, it is hard to convince your Soldiers that it was in their best interest to keep all this shit on while riding in an armored vehicle with a outside temperature of 93 degrees (it was nighttime so it was cooler from 107 or so) Our vehicles were required to have air conditioning in them, but even the most powerful A/C unit could only reduce the temperature inside a vehicle to just below 90 degrees or so. Another great thing about running missions in the nighttime hours was the obvious lack of traffic. Traffic is bad in every respect in Iraq. The roads were fucked because in the opening salvos of the war we, coalition forces, had blown the shit out of the good ones along with the water, sewer, and electric utilities. The roads that were almost remotely serviceable were so packed with cars during the daylight hours that people regularly invented their own” lanes” in the center areas between any divided roads. Any and all drivable areas on the sides, in between, pretty much anywhere else you could maneuver an automobile from point A to point B were filled with cars. Despite how impressive my 17-ton, 8-wheel drive, diesel powered behemoth P.L.S. vehicles were, they could not fly and would be packed in traffic sardines like everyone else in this situation. Unlike everyone else, when a convoy cannot move, that is when bad things happen. The bad guys in Iraq, not only had no concern with any innocent locals they may kill while trying to get us, but they also actually thought by killing innocents in their fervor they were doing them a favor. In their view, anyone who died in the pursuit of killing an infidel was guaranteed a ticket to heaven. Long story short, getting stuck in a traffic jam was not good for your well-being by any measure.

An ideal mission was plan, assemble, load, roll out the wire locked, cocked, and ready to rock around 23:00 hours. You always remember your first encounter with the enemy. That evening started at midnight just like so many others to follow would. We were hauling 10 P.L.S filled with I don't even remember what to an outpost downtown called F.O.B. Warhorse. To get to this F.O.B. you had to take arguably the most dangerous stretch of road in downtown Baghdad. This road wall called route "Pluto." All the roads had special names like "Miami," "Pluto" "Purple" and so on. Route Pluto took you right through the east side of Baghdad which was called Sadr City. Now Sadr City alone was probably the size of a big city in the United States and the most significant feature of it was that it was one giant slum. It was named after an individual called Muqtada Al Sadr who was a Muslim cleric, rabblerouser and troublemaker. He harbored a hatred of all things western and "non-Muslim" and all of Americans most specifically. Like most slum areas, people tend to be easily swayed by anyone who stands on a podium and tells them they have the cure to your lot in life. Long story short, Sadr City was full of probably a million or so folks who all hated us being there. It was around 2:30 am and we were rolling neatly along until we came to a main corner in the area we had to take. Once my lead HUMMV (with me inside) made that corner the fireworks began. A green streak tore through the night and skipped off the road about 10 yards in front of my vehicle. It was easier to tell the good guys munitions from the bad, because the Soviet manufactured shit the bad guys used, had green tracer rounds instead of our red. Of course, my driver instinctively slammed on the brakes. That is the WORSE thing you do when you are being fired at in a convoy. The bastard who had just missed us with the R.P.G (Rocket Propelled Grenade) that skipped off the road may not be as unfortunate with the second one he was sure to have. We would only be helping his aim if we were standing still, so I slapped my driver on the back of the head and yelled "Step on it." And as we continued to proceed through the ambush area, green tracer rounds were flying everywhere. I opened my side window to get my .45 out and return fire in the direction we were being shot at from. While emptying my clip out the window (I know, so much for fire control) I felt a burning in my right forearm. I yelled at my platoon sergeant sitting next to me "I think I got clipped." Once we all out of the ambush area and safely formed in a circle with all vehicles a couple of hundred yards away, it was time to assess any damage our convoy may have sustained. I rolled my sleeve up, only to discover a piece of hot brass from my .45 had blown down my sleeve and burnt my arm. My platoon sergeant cracked up, "Yeah you got clipped alright" and we all had a huge laugh about it, once we knew no one had been hurt during that exchange. Eventually though with this mission and all the others, you arrive inside the wire of your new compound where you had to deliver the goods you brought. You then unload, make your way to the new F.O.B's "staging area" where you could get lined up for the way home, and find some quest quarters for the night. Once you were at a new location, you were under their rules as to when and where you could leave again. Most of the time we would have to just stay for the remainder of the daylight hours where we were and then depart that night. This has great perks. First, unlike many Soldiers in theater, we got to see all different parts of the country while we were there. Each compound, depending on size, had its own little PX, shops, amenities and things just different from where we were. Each compound had its own M.W.R. (Morale Welfare and Relief) stations which could be used to contact loved ones back home via internet, or V.O.I.P. (Voice Over Internet Protocol) phones. We would all then try to get a few hours back to sleep, roll out the wire that night and, hopefully sooner than later, make it back "home" to Taji and Camp Cooke. A transportation platoon can usually be expected to perform missions every or every other day. At the very least we would run a few missions a week. Driving on the road was where most of the Soldier individual stress occurred. Since Taji was so close to Baghdad, and half of it was under the "New Iraqi Army" control, you could be counted on to be occasionally shelled or mortared while kicking back in your hooch in garrison, but this didn't happen too often, and we did have some air defense and rapid response units to help keep things under control. On the highways was a different matter. The bad guys, (insurgents, assholes, ragheads whatever you chose to call them) always had an array of different methods to try and wipe us out. Their favorite method of all though was the infamous I.E.D. (Improvised Explosive Device). The entire country of Iraq was littered with ordinance left behind by the fleeing Iraqi regular forces and stockpiles of artillery and mortar rounds of all shapes and sizes were found everywhere. The bad guys would take one (or three, or five) of these artillery rounds, take the fuses off them, wrap them together somehow and then wire a dynamite cap or other little chunk of explosive to make it go "boom." This was then set this by the side of the road, buried in a newly dug shallow hole in the ground, or strapped to the inside of a guard rail where it couldn't be seen. A cell phone was then attached to this I.E.D. with the “hot” wires of the explosive wired to the speaker wires on the phone. So, when the bad guy sees an American convoy come into close proximity, he dials the number to the cell phone below, a small amount of voltage goes to the “ringer” on that phone and “boom.” If we had kept regular time, and routes of travel it was also an easy enough method to wire the “hot” wires again to a simple appliance timer and when it was “time” was reached on the dial, yep “boom” again. One use of a garage door opener you won’t find described in the owner’s manual is how they make great I.E.D. detonators. Simply put each infrared sensor on either side of the road, and when anything (hopefully U.S. convoy, sometimes stray donkey or grandpa taking a walk sadly) interrupted the beam, instead of lowering the garage door, that current was fed back through the “hot” wires and yep, you guessed it. Now we had countermeasures for most of this stuff, and this was the kind of good stuff you learned at the S-2 briefing. For starters NEVER run convoys on the same routes or same times. This made using alarm clocks or appliance dials for detonators impractical. For the garage door beam, we would put a 10’ bar on the front of the lead vehicle of a convoy, affectionately called a “Rhino”, with a piece of chain dangling down. That little piece of chain would break the beam, detonate the I.E.D prematurely greatly reducing the damage to the convoy 10’ behind. The cell phone operated ones were the easiest (and could be the most fun!) to counter if you had the right equipment. We were equipped with this device called a “duke.” A “duke” was attached like a fat antenna to one of the HUMMV’s in your convoy and essentially blocked every cell phone signal for a few hundred yards in every direction. I’m sure there was more than one pissed off Iraqi who had their call dropped suddenly. The “fun” part about the “duke” was at the same time it was blocking cell phone signals from other sources it was broadcasting multiple signals in every direction. We would be rolling down the highway, hear a loud bang, see a puff of smoke and sometimes arrive to a crater surrounded by a few limbs, tatters of clothing and other small bits of human flesh left by the individuals planting the I.E.D. They must have been attaching that last "hot" wire when a "duke" dialed up the number the cell phone they were using. So instead of finding a comfortable place to anxiously await our arrival and get their video recording, they got to go meet "Allah." I bet they never realized they would see their creator long before they would get to see us. Those of you old enough to remember the old "Spy vs Spy" (one dressed in black, one dressed in white) cartoons and all the creative ways they would try to destroy each other for laughs. Well, Iraq on the highways was like this, except for maybe the laughs. Our battalion S-2 section had even incorporated the logo of those two characters into their official motto.

While this was my day-to-day life on missions, I did attend some of the sponsored extracurricular activities at Camp Cooke. I had stayed in pretty good shape and started running when I quit smoking for the last time at Ferris State. One of my goals was to successfully run a marathon. I never imagined that I would do this while stationed in a combat zone, but this was where the opportunity presented itself. The Chicago marathon was being run (in Chicago of course) and M.W.R. had coordinated to simulcast the marathon to us overseas. They even sent actual race numbers and T-shirts to any of us who wanted to run the marathon at its now "satellite" location. For us, 26.2 miles was 6 laps completely inside the wire of Camp Cooke. Thank goodness with the time difference, our start time was 11 pm when the temperature was cooler. A very long and grueling 4 hrs. and 54 minutes later I had completed my first full marathon. I wish I had kept and framed the t-shirt I received, as it was only given to individuals who completed the marathon, but I was proud of it and wore it out years ago. I did manage to do a small triathlon (10-mile run, 2-mile swim, 20-mile bicycling) event while I was there too which was fun. I always trained hard because, as I always told my Soldiers, that if I ever had to roll around with one of these assholes to fight for my life, the poor bastard who tangled with me better be at the top of his game, because I most certainly was going to be. In the meantime, I was trying to keep in contact with Mary and my daughter and my other children. You can only imagine the apprehension and fear they felt daily imagining the danger I may be in. Of course, seeing the images of American convoys in flames and seeing the names of my fellow transporters who were not so lucky certainly didn't help. In addition to this, my marriage was ending, even if only emotionally now. As Mary had said before "she didn't sign up for this" and now in addition to worrying about my physical wellbeing, she was sick of being a single parent. Statistically marriages aren't exactly compatible with military life. During deployments, divorce numbers go even higher. For National Guard and Army Reserve Soldiers the statistics are higher yet. I guess Mary isn't the only woman who didn't "sign up for that shit." Both of us knew that it was over all except the paperwork. For the remainder of my tour, she would sell the house in Fowlerville and buy another house further South in the state nearer her parents. One little known fact of marriage law in Michigan and its antiquated "dowry laws", regardless of whose names are on the mortgage paperwork, a husband cannot sell property without his wife's signature. A wife can sell property without her husbands' signature though and Mary did just that. I really didn't care anyway. I had plenty enough to focus on in Iraq to spend too much time grieving over my 13-year marriage. When you are wondering whether the next day may be your last, or even more importantly for me, the lives of my 40 or so Soldiers, how things are going to transpire upon return to the "world" matter little. Between missions and seeing the Iraqi countryside, what could be seen at night most of the time, there was some entertainment and relaxation on Camp Cooke as well. Like I said before the food was great, and if you got sick of eating mess hall food, a few entrepreneurial businesses set up little shops in the center of the camp. Burger King, Cinnabon and Green Beans Coffer were the main ones I remember. I guess Starbucks was not brave enough to set up shop in a combat zone, but Green Beans was just as good and had no problem risking their asses a little bit to sell suckers a cup of coffee for $5 cup. Camp Cooke had one unique entertainment venue that was the envy of every other camp in theater. Each Wednesday evening at Taji was "Night at the Fights." In the middle of camp, a full-sized boxing ring was set up next to the dining and post exchange facilities. This "arena" was complete with a television camera, professional sound, everything. And it was all amateur boxing. Anyone who wanted could sign up, fill out the medical waiver, and try their luck in the ring. Every attempt was made to match everyone up with an appropriate opponent in size and skill level. Easily, a few hundred Soldiers would be there every Wednesday for the entertainment. It was also co-ed and one of my females stepped in the ring to try her luck. It was a great match. I thought it was going to come to a quick end at the end of the second round when she stepped straight into a glove square in the face at the bell. With tears in her eyes, she shook her head, got a drink and was back in at the sound of the third-round bell. She did end up and finally won that match by decision. Tempted as I was to try my luck, my neck had already been damaged during one close encounter with an I.E.D. and getting it completely broken in the name of entertainment just didn't sound too appealing. Not to mention, all the evening's events, good and bad, were broadcast via closed circuit television in the mess hall and all over post for the rest of the week. If the thought of getting my neck broke deterred me, taking an ass kicking never did, apart from having to relive the moment all week long in the mess hall.

Being overseas has a strange uniqueness about it. Despite having access to news, newspapers and television, you never quite feel "attuned" to everything that is happening in the "world" Although you are only in a different country, you may as well be on another planet. You just end up so wrapped up on keeping yourself alive, your Soldiers alive and missions accomplished that you don't pay a lot of attention on anything that is happening back in America. This point, for me, was particularly evident after watching the news one weekend in my hooch. It seems that there was a hell of a storm in America. There were pictures streaming of bodies floating in the water, levees breached and entire neighborhoods underwater. I just remember thinking "Boy, that must have been one hell of a thunderstorm". History would come to call that "thunderstorm" Hurricane Katrina, and I would not have any idea of the real destruction it wrought until I returned to the states in a year or so.

My life in Iraq was about to take a strange turn as well. Our platoon was chosen for a special and unique mission. This mission would reassign our command-and-control leadership from the 137th Trans Co to the M.N.F (Multinational Forces) Iraq, centered in Baghdad. More specifically we were now part of the M.I.T.T (Military Instruction Tasks and Training) team. We would live with the 137th, but each day our "work" would take us to the Iraqi side of Camp Cooke. Someone higher up the Army food chain must have noticed how effective we were running our missions and we were assigned to train the new '1st Iraqi Transportation Regiment." The 40 of us would work to turn the 500 or so new Iraqi Soldiers into "transporters." This would be our task for the remainder of our time in Iraq. As much as I may have enjoyed immersing myself in local places when travelling abroad, this is not what I had in mind. We were given a large auditorium building and free reign to develop all training doctrine necessary to accomplish our task. In addition to our Soldiers, we were given a set of equipment to train these troops with as well. This equipment was comprised of 30 or 40 1940 era, U.S. 2 ½ ton trucks (Deuce and a half's) and a few Russian vehicles in lieu of HMMMV's for lead vehicles. Our weaponry would be the standard AK-47's, and the Russian version of the M-60 machine gun, the PK. This was going to be a challenge. A couple things to note about the Iraqi Soldier. Virtually none of these Soldiers had any military experience whatsoever. Any of the old Army troops under Saddam Hussein were either granted immunity and returned to civilian life (many into the bad guys who were trying to kill us) or were killed. We did have maybe a handful of old N.C.O.'s from the old Army who convinced the new army that they wanted to be a part of changing the country. Their loyalty was questionable at best. The rest of the Soldiers were simply handed a uniform, promised a paycheck and an occasional meal and told where they had to be to get them. Just imagine a group of kindergarteners, who do not speak English, in a uniform and handed a gun. For me, this arraignment presented a whole new arena of risk that I had to worry about for my Soldiers safety. Most of these Soldiers could not even drive a car. The first matter of business was to establish how to communicate with them. We did get assigned a couple of interpreters from the M.I.T.T team in order to translate all our lectures and training materials into Arabic. All training materials we would create would become new Iraqi Army doctrine to be taught to all Iraqi Transportation regiments. I always thought that was pretty cool to leave something positive in Iraq besides wreckage and corpses. The first couple of months were a lot of lectures, marching and assembly of functional transportation groups. Then came vehicle maintenance and drivers training. These troops would have to learn the most basic driving skills before they could be taught defensive driving techniques in combat. My platoon was co-ed which was an alien phenomenon to the Iraqi troops. Having women among them, not fully garbed in burqas and being escorted by a male relative was shocking enough to them, but to regard a female as an instructor was almost impossible. My females were regarded in the minds of these new troops as sluts, or at least woman with loose morale standards. On more than a few occasions I would see a couple of the "Jundi's" ("Jundi's, Arabic for Soldier) in a small group giggling pointing towards one of my females. I would ask the interpreter what was going on and he would inform me how they were making lewd references about them. This had to end. My females were tough, I have no doubt they could hold their own toe-to-toe with any American Soldier, let alone these smaller, underfed little Jundi's. I finally, in front of the whole Iraqi regiment in our auditorium, I had all my females step forward. I had the interpreter inform all of them that the next lewd comment from any of them and I will have my Soldier, who they just insulted, beat the absolute dog shit out of them. In front of all of their peers and friends. To an Iraqi "man?"; This would be an almost insurmountable insult and embarrassment. He would never be able to be in the presence of his peers again. That was the last time any derelict comments were ever made about my female Soldiers. At least in our presence anyway. All this training was taking place in the Iraqi side of Camp Cooke. This area was a lot closer to Baghdad, and therefore a lot easier to lob mortars and shit into. We were teaching away one fine day in our auditorium when the building shook, a loud boom and dust was everywhere. Once we went outside we saw what had happened. Some insurgents had gotten lucky and managed to launch a Katyusha rocket into our area. It hit the ground next to our building, slid across the parking lot and slammed into one of the deuce-an-half's that was parked out there. It then detonated and blew both the rear axles off that truck. Only by the grace of God it didn't hit the building we were in or at least a few dozen of all of us would have been killed or wounded. Guess it just wasn't in the stars for me that day.

Now that the Jundi's were getting a little proficient in the operation and maintenance of their vehicles it was time to start teaching some combat operations. One well known fact of combat is that it involves violence and guns. Like everything else, an overwhelming majority of the Jundi's had never fired a weapon. An extended trip to the rifle range was going to be necessary. I was not looking forward to my 40 Soldiers being surrounded by a few hundred potentially enemy Soldiers with guns. More than a few times in theater a "new" Iraqi Soldier, police officer, or civilian worker on camp, had turned their weapons on their coalition associates killing some before being gunned down themselves. As I was determined this was not going to happen to one of my Soldiers, I quickly implemented a safety rule. I made sure all my Soldiers had plenty of bullets and gave them a quick but precise briefing. Should any of them see a Jundi raise his weapon about the 45-degree mark from the ground, in any direction whatsoever near any of us, the Jundi will be shot dead. I had the interpreters explain this very clearly before we went to the range. While I really did not want to kill anyone, or certainly have anything happen to one of my Soldiers, I lived by one simple fact. I would kill a hundred Jundi's before I will even risk the safety of one of my Soldiers. I thank God that from the look of my face at the Jundi's lecture, and the tone of the interpreter, the Iraqi troops got the idea and knew none of us were joking. It was time for the range day. All of us convoyed, without issue during the day no less, to the nearest rifle range which was under the auspices of a United States Special Forces group. Everybody managed to have some fun, burn some cordite, and even get a little proficiency. All was fun and games until it was time to get ready to go. The rangemaster was performing the mandatory inspection of the range to approve our departure. I was called into his office and with as much disgust as a human being can muster he explained the situation to me. Behind every bunker, tree and bush on his range was a nice fresh pile of human shit and pile of plastic water bottles. Another little-known fact about the Iraqi Soldier is they have different toilet practices than most other cultural groups. You see, despite having multiple porta johns throughout the range, Iraqi's won't sit on a toilet seat. They regard it as unclean I guess, so at first, the troops who use those will stand on the seat, thereby blowing shit all over the inside of the walls of the porta john. After that, naturally no one else is going to use that facility so the other couple of hundred who had to shit would have to go elsewhere. Did I also mention that despite the great food we were receiving in garrison, the poor Jundi was fed shit I would not give my dog. We were warned NEVER to eat in their "mess" facility. Bloody diarrhea and hepatitis A were endemic and back at the range shit, figuratively, was everywhere. I was informed in no uncertain terms there was "No fucking way you're leaving my range until all that shit is cleaned up." The Iraqi Trans Regiment Commander, Colonel Iyad was with us, and I proceeded to explain the situation to him. I did not report to him, but by the status of forces agreement, he did outrank me, and I had to at least attempt to offer him the respect his rank commanded. Guy was a fucking scumbag but that's another book all its own. At first Colonel Iyad was indigent and attempted to state how this was "our fault" for not providing the "proper" facilities for the Iraqi Soldier. I politely but firmly made it clear that this was not a "request" but "demand" and mentioned that I could bring the American Colonel who oversaw the M.I.T.T team, a female for the record, into the conversation. Naturally this would cause Colonel Iyad a great deal of embarrassment, so rather than try to debate this situation with a female (her rank was inconsequential) he informed his troops of what they had to do. There were howls of protest and complaints as to "how are we supposed to pick this up?." They had around three small shovels (no fucking way they were using OUR shovels from our pioneering equipment) and about 75 piles of human feces. So, their 3 shovels went to work, and twenty or so other poor bastards found sticks and plastic baggies and in an hour or so, the task was finished. Then with a simple "Don't ever bring those nasty animals back to my rifle range" the rangemaster cleared us to depart and we headed back to Taji. Now as horrible as the Jundi's might sound, you couldn't help but feel sorry for them. As disgusting as my previous tale was, one should always remember it was a cultural difference, nothing more. I already spoke about the food, and although it was provided for them, I would safely say if it would even be determined in America as "for human consumption" I would be shocked. These guys were given one uniform and one only. Imagine training all day in 110-degree heat and only having one set of clothes? Each day the Jundi's would wash their one uniform and hang it to dry for the next day. They were getting a little paycheck but that was for the first couple of months I was there, and Uncle Sam was writing those checks. It was felt that since we effectively blew the shit out of all the infrastructure of the country, and any means it had to generate revenue, it was only fair that we "helped" them until we could rebuild them. The "give a man a fish……" story you know. Suddenly, the Jundi's were starting to walk up and slide small, handwritten notes to my Soldiers. Once interpreted most said things like "We haven't gotten any money in over a month" or "Please give us some money, my kids need milk." I made some calls up the hierarchy of the M.N.F. to find out why these Jundi's had not been paid. It seems that now that Uncle Sam had repaired at least the oil exporting infrastructure and Iraq had generated a few billion dollars in revenue they could start paying some of their own bills. When the Ministry of Defense (M.O.D.) was called, M.N.F was informed "We don't have any money." Now where in the hell did a few billion dollars disappear to? No one could answer that then, but it didn't take long for anyone to figure out what the deal was. Even though

Saddam, and his raping of the national treasury, was gone, other "rapists" just stepped in and took his place. One gleaming example of this was our little Iraqi Colonel Iyad. Soldiers were paid in cash because lists of names were not very popular in the Iraqi government at the time. That was because if the bad guys got their names on any such lists, it gave them a great way to find out who, and subsequently execute, anyone who was considered to be collaborating with us. That being known, payday worked like this, an Iraqi commander (Col Iyad) would call the ministry of defense, tell them how many Jundis he had to pay, a van full of cash would line up and he would hand that cash out. Each couple of weeks Col Iyad would be asked how many Jundis he had, he would tell them "145", and the M.O.D. would bring down pay for 145 troops. Progress continued to move on in the country, as well as accountability for the government. One payday M.O.D told Col Iyad and said "Were bringing the money down for 145 troops but we want to see them, and they have to put an "X" on the payroll form." Sure enough, the van pulls up and Col Iyad hands the money out and returns with 122 "X's". He is then asked where's the other 23 troops? He replies, "this is all of them", ok then "Where is the rest of the money for those 23 troops at?" He also then replies, without a moment's hesitation or reservation, "Why that's my money, that's my "supplemental" income" He was inconsolable when told that method of "supplement" was no longer allowed, and your "paycheck" was ALL that you are paid. It only bothered him a little bit as another means for him to "supplement" his income was via a little store he had built on his battalion complex. He was the sole owner and proprietor of it, would purchase everything in it and then sell it at a minimum of a 100% markup to his troops. He was told by M.N.F that he had to close the store, (making money of the backs of your soldiers is pathetic) but he refused, and really could not be forced to do so. You pick your battles I guess. In addition to the original payroll services, we provided to the Nation of Iraq, the American taxpayer would vomit if they had seen the new sidewalks, electric companies, train cars full of brand-new Chevrolet Tahoe's painted blue and black with "Police" painted on the sides in Arabic, that I saw. All of this was being paid for from the healthy chunk of change Uncle Sam was taking out of every hard-working American's paycheck weekly. At the end of the whole conflict, we (Americans) would also leave billions of dollars in military equipment, free of charge, for use by the government there. Even the average Jundi there would laugh as to how stupid America was to give so much away, but they were glad to stand with their hands out and will pretend to be our allies as long as we were. This was the political environment at the time, but it made no difference to me as I had no influence over any of it. Time marched ever onward and soon our Iraqi troops were ready for convoy ops. I like to use the training method referred to as "crawl, walk, run". The "crawl" portion was essentially watching us perform the tasks and maybe assist a little. The "walk" was when the task was performed by the Iraqi troops but with assistance and guidance from us, and the "Run" was when they could perform the task to standard without or intervention. The "crawl" and "walk" portions were performed at camp, the "run" now had to be tested on the highways of Iraq. The convoy arraignment was determined, and our cargo was loaded. We had converted two of the deuce and a halves into their "gun trucks" and manned each with 8 armed Iraqi's. We would follow their convoy from in front and behind in our HMMMV's. Naturally once we made our first turn of the route, a couple of bad guys popped off a few rounds at our convoy. Instead of returning fire, all 16 of gun trucks "warriors" simply dropped their AK-47's and hit the deck. Happily, it was not a sustained attack and the convoy moved steadily through the danger area. We arrived safely back to camp and had to regress back to the "walk" stage of training where we reinforced the notion "If they shoot at you, SHOOT BACK." In the meantime, another method of method of stopping convoys was being taught to the bad guys. Thank the Lord for the S-2 briefings so I at least had an idea what to look for before I encountered it with my convoy. Just like in "Hollywood" when it is hot enough in the Summertime you really do see mirages on the roads. Once it's over 100 degrees for a few hours all the asphalt looks like shimmering water. The bad guys could use this optical illusion to their advantage. They would dump 5 or 10 gallons of oil across the pavement on particularly sharp exits, curves or overpasses. When the unsuspecting driver, usually with a large, heavy, fully loaded vehicle drove into that curve, not seeing the oil at 20-50 miles per hour, they would lose control of the vehicle. This usually resulted in the vehicle flipping over repeatedly causing death and mayhem to all occupants of the vehicle. Not to mention complete destruction to any cargo on the vehicle. A "bonus" for the bad guys was that while the rest of the convoy was stopped to assist, they would know right where the convoy would stop at and have an ambush set up for it. At least for the rest of the vehicles which were fortunate enough not to follow the first couple into the oil. A little more training was now needed for the 1st Iraqi training regiment. Soon enough though we were ready for mission number two. On that mission, about the same location, a few shots were again fired in our direction. The Iraqi troops did indeed return fire, in every direction with every bullet they had. They burned through probably

3000 rounds of ammunition in about 14 seconds. A new Army concept obviously needed to be taught. That concept was "fire control." Fire control can be described in one word "proportion" If someone fires at your convoy from the left side, then only the Soldiers on the left side shoot back. It only took a few more missions on the road with the Iraqi's and they were able to perform at least simple combat convoys and at least have a fighting chance if they were attacked. Our time with the 1st Iraqi transportation Regiment was coming to an end. My platoon and I arrived on our last day of "work" and were surprised to find the entire 1st Iraqi Transportation regiment in formation, "Standing tall and looking good." Colonel Iyad was present and then called our group to the front and center in front of his regiment. He placed the Iraqis at ease and had a large, new, wooden crate brought out in front of him. He opened the crate and presented each of my Soldiers and I a brand-new AK 47 bayonet and the new shoulder insignia (patch type) of the 1st Iraqi Transportation Regiment. That is my favorite patch on my motorcycle vest to this day. It was the Colonel and the regiments way of saying "Thank You" for all we had done for them and what was their country. We were returned to the 137th Trans Co for the last two months of our rotation abroad. It was time for me to receive my first O.E.R. (Officer Examination Report), the Army's version of your employment evaluation. I had a good repoire with Lieutenant Colonel Eileen Thorne. She was an active duty, career officer and she was straightforward, no nonsense and to the point. I had only brief interactions with her as we crossed paths at BN HQ, but she usually had a good word for me. I admired her. While I was sitting in her waiting room, awaiting my turn to go in, one of my fellow lieutenants came out of her office after just receiving his O.E.R. He said it went great and mentioned what was a nice picture of Col. Thorne and obviously her wife in the civilian world. Homosexuals were in the service long before politicians decided to try to make an issue out of us. Us regular troops really didn't care who was fucking who as long as they weren't trying to fuck us, or anyone we wanted to fuck. My fellow lieutenant then says to me on his way out the door 'You know what the hardest part of the process was?" I replied "no", to which he replied, "Dealing with the smell of Skoal and pussy on a woman's breath." At that very minute as I was trying my utmost to not break out in peals of laughter, I heard LTC Thorne call me in. As you can imagine trying to look that woman in the eye and keep a straight face was no easy trick. I did manage to do so, received a stellar O.E.R. and headed back to the 137th. Two months and a few hair-raising missions later, our replacement unit arrived, and our primary focus was to "show them the ropes." Two weeks later, we had left our mark in Iraq and were on our way back to the "world."

Chapter 6: Home again (briefly)

I would hope that after what amounted to 22 months overseas the Army would send us back home, but it was not to be. Not for a short while anyway. After mobilizing, then getting sent into a combat theater only one thing can come after that, "Demobilization." Mobilization was to tell you everything you needed to remember when you went into harm's way. Demobilization was to tell you what you would be better off forgetting. It all was a drunken party blur. Except for the other 13 damn vaccinations I had to receive. I guess 19 of the fucking things, everything from Hep A to Yellow fever, I received on the way out weren't enough. Had to get the current flu, hepatitis vaccines, and I don't know, or care, what else. I just wanted to go home. Although we were not officially authorized to drink alcohol until return to our home states, my whole platoon was like wild animals that would not be caged. Every bar, strip joint and shopping center in Wiley Kansas was fair game. I just wanted to keep track of everyone and make sure after the experience we all had been thorough, everyone got back to their families finally and safely. We only wanted to get back to Michigan only slightly faster than the Army wanted to get us the hell out of Fort Riley and on Thanksgiving night in 2004 we arrived in Lansing. Now we arrived on two different bus loads and the second bus had mechanical problems and was going to be a couple of hours behind. Those of us who arrived early just wanted to continue to Jackson and maybe even get a last shot at a Thanksgiving dinner with our families. Michigan Headquarters would have no part of it. We left together and we would be arriving in victory all together. Of course, we thought this was bullshit until we all finally arrived in Jackson. It was almost 11 pm at night, a driving blizzard and horrible weather. Despite that, the city of Jackson coordinated a parade for us to arrive in, and our buses arrived in the middle of the night, in a blizzard to streets lined with flag waiving family members and citizens applauding our arrival. We all assembled for a joyous hour or so of some happy Army ass-slapping. Around 1 am or so we were finally released to our families. We were, finally, completely, home.

I went with Mary back to what was essentially her house in Oxford. I had never seen it before that time. It was time to face the reality of divorce court. I would like to say we tried to put it back together, but things happened that I could not bring myself to get over. Mary also would never get over the fact that I left her and our daughter alone no matter the reason. I could go into detail over all this, but it serves no purpose. We were simply one of the over 60% of marriages that do not survive a combat deployment. We parted ways and managed to make it as amicable as possible for our daughter. I took no pride whatsoever in now being responsible for 4 children growing up in divorced homes. All I could do is try to be the best father I could be. I did make every attempt in my ability to be as present in their lives and activities as they grew up. With my supplemental Army income, I was able to at least financially provide for their needs. A vow I took before the Lord and myself in the mirror that my children would not grow up looking, feeling or being looked at like 3rd rate citizens because of what happened between their mothers and me. At least my youngest was a lot geographically closer to me than my kids in Reed City. I was also determined that she and her sisters and brother would be a family together and always regard each other as such. My children were growing older and at least my two oldest girls were of the age that they could be proud of what their father was doing for the country. I only hoped it would give me at least some forgiveness for the time I was not spending with them. It was a bittersweet return to Beaumont. While I was happy to be back with my friends and coworkers at the hospital, it was also the last time I would be in command of the 40 Soldiers from the 1461st Trans Co in Jackson who I had been through so much with. Although I was never in any official capacity with any of them again, most of us still stay in touch to this day. We share our memories, experiences, joys and sadness, and I feel great pride in each and every one of them. Like Soldiers everywhere, they are the true American heroes. I watch each of them via social media and with pride as they all now have growing families and are making their marks in life.

I also cannot say enough good things about Beaumont as an employer. Except for paying my salary while I was deployed, they provided every other benefit while I was away. They paid for my insurance, held my position, allowed me to continue accruing employment time as well as my P.T.O (paid time off) just as though I had been working. My co-workers were great as well. Many stayed in touch with me while I was deployed and sent gifts and cards. They will never know the joy those things brought me. It was a reminder that the deployment was not the proverbial "end of the line" and my "world" was waiting for my return exactly how I left it. Another of my dearest friends, "Jim" who I had met years before through a mutual acquaintance was also a savior to me in the desert. He worked at the Detroit Diesel company who incidentally manufactured all the Oshkosh motors which were in my P.L.S. vehicles. The technical expertise and parts I had the "inside scoop' to were invaluable through him. More importantly in addition, knowing my love for scotch, he would pack me up a plastic bottle of Dewars scotch and ship it to me overseas. I can't count how many of my "last nerves" after a close call on the road, he saved. He is one of my best friends to this day. He did send me one "special" gift though, it was the weekend before Easter Sunday and since we were back in the F.O.B. I got the platoon together for mail call. Now all of us usually open any packages in front of each other simply to "Spread the love." Naturally, if there was contraband like liquor or anything, you just didn't yank that out of the box in front of everyone else. I had a nice package from my buddy Jim and opened it cautiously in front of my troops. Enclosed was a large 16-ounce bottle of baby oil and a 3-foot inflatable Easter Bunny. Of course, the entire platoon burst out into laughter and the lewd comments ensued. "Gonna smell burning plastic coming from the old man's hooch tonight" and "nothing worse than the sound of squeaking rubber and the smell of baby oil." Of course, I laughed like everyone else, but next time I talked to Jim I asked "Dude, what were you thinking?" He grew quiet for a moment and did not understand. "I knew it was Easter, so I sent the inflatable bunny to cheer you, and I know its dry over there so I sent the baby oil for your skin." It was hilarious, he never once thought of the sexual connotation the two items together could be associated with. We both laugh about that to this day.

I digress though, it does take a while to readjust to civilian life after such an experience as I had just come from. On occasion at my civilian job, I would slip up with a word or deed that, although totally acceptable in the military environment, was not so much acceptable in the civilian environment. My spouting off with something like "That's as fucked up as a football bat" in a hospital staff meeting was just one such example. Fortunately, the hospital administration was understanding, having known the environment that I had just spent the better part of two years in. One thing that I had not counted on was my relationship with the woman who would become the light of my life. She was a gorgeous, young redhead gal with the best smile ever. She had been a Beaumont employee for over ten years and over the past few years she had been assigned to the patient registration department. I was performing P.E.T. (Positron Emission Tomography) imaging during the 2nd shift hours and she would be the one who would register my Patients when they arrived. When we first met, both her and I were married folks with young children and despite a lot of innocent kidding about what would happen "if we were single" it remained just that, kidding. At this particular point in time, it seemed that both of us were in the process of divorce. My daughter was 7 and her girls were almost 3 years and 14 months old. We decided to just spend some time together while she was going through the throes of her divorce. We just casually got together for a drink, maybe took a ride in the country or took the kids to the park. While I was most definitely smitten, she was at the very least "reserved." We talked a lot more than anything. It seemed that we were going to be tested as a couple, even before we were a couple. The war in the Middle East not only continued on but had expanded into Afghanistan. If I could not stay with my troops from Jackson who I had been through so much with, I wanted to return to my original "Battle Buddies" in the 1462nd Trans Co in Howell who had just returned from their deployment. They had gotten the shit beat out of them over there during their first deployment in O.I.F. 2. Although none of them were killed, there were more than a few serious injuries and equipment lost. Neither of these scenarios were meant to be for me. As the conflict expanded in the Middle East the Army was no closer to having enough Company Grade Officer's to complete the missions. That made my chance of avoiding a second deployment virtually nil. I figured if I was going to be redeployed I would rather do it on my terms. I then volunteered to fill a Company Commander slot for the Forward Support Company (F.S.C.) in the 107th Engineer Battalion in the Upper Peninsula of Michigan. The F.S.C. would be leaving for mobilization at Fort McCoy Wisconsin in a few weeks and I would be going with them. It was time to say "so long" to my kids (again) my employer Beaumont (again) and Michelle, the redhead who I had most certainly fallen in love with by that time.

It was clear early on that this was going to be a different kind of deployment than my first one had been. There is a world of difference in job descriptions between a platoon leader and a company commander. I had just gone from the supervisor on the line to the guy in the office at the end of the hall. Although I was still a long way from the guy who had the office with the window on a different floor, I was now still essentially an office worker. And I was an office worker in a different kind of office. I was now part of a headquarters platoon of the type that I had discussed earlier. I was the Platoon leader of that headquarter platoon as well the whole rest of the company. Some things hadn't changed and one of those was the joy of M.O.B training. Our M.O.B. training for this deployment was at held at Fort McCoy Wisconsin. Ft. McCoy was a beautiful installation in North Central Wisconsin, so it felt like my Michigan home for starters. It was also solely a National Guard facility unlike the Active-Duty Army posts like Ft. Sill, or Ft. Riley. Because of this it was operated by the National Guard bureau and the State of Wisconsin instead of the U.S. Army. Michigan had its very own version of one of these training facilities as well at Camp Grayling. In the peacetime these were quiet, sleepy places, almost empty except for the times when all the States National Guard and Army Reserve units sent their troops there for annual training requirements. Since the conflict in the Middle East had continued year after year, not only were many of these reserve troops activated, but these facilities were also activated as well in order to handle the overflow from the Active-Duty M.O.B stations. These camps did have most of the amenities of their larger counterparts; they were just older and not as updated. Unlike many of the Soldiers from the Upper Peninsula, I personally had been to Ft. McCoy before. A couple of years prior I spent the better part of three weeks there for B.N.C.O.C (Basic N.C.O. Course). Like the A.M.A in Alabama, the regular function of these camps, in addition to providing annual training facilities, was to host all the additional extended education courses such as B.N.C.O.C, A.N.C.O.C (advanced N.C.O. course), as well as the First Sergeants and Sergeant Major academies. The biggest thing I remember about Ft. McCoy from before was how damn cold it was. I attended B.N.C.O.C in January and I don't believe the temperature ever went about 30 degrees in the whole three weeks I was there. One of the parts of the B.N.C.O.C course was "land navigation." When it was my turn to perform the land navigation course, of course a good N.C.O must be proficient with a map, it was in the middle of a blizzard. After 3 hours or so of stomping around in 2 feet of snow in the woods, I finished the course and was herded into the back of a deuce and a half. There I sat with 8 or 10 other aspiring N.C.O.'s waiting for the rest of the Soldiers to finish the course. Of course, by then

I was wet from sweat on the inside and the outside temperature dropped. We all had to sit in the back of that truck for at least an additional hour and it was the coldest I have ever been in my life. Fortunately, the 107th Engineers M.O.B. would be starting their training at the end of August, and the weather is beautiful that time of the year. M.O.B. training is specifically designed for whatever type of mission a unit will be performing while in the country your headed for. With the 137th, all our M.O.B. training was about how quickly and safely you and all your equipment can go from point A to point B. The 107th Engineers mission was to go as slowly as possible and clear I.E.D.'s, when found, off the roads before units like my 137th Transportation Company before, ran into them. There are two basic categories of Engineers in the Army. Those were referred to as "vertical" and "Horizontal." The "vertical engineers" were the M.O.S's that performed all things construction. Buildings, Bridges, pretty much everything that rose "vertically" from the ground would be considered vertical. The "horizontal" Engineers were the M.O.S. who worked on things just like the term "horizontal." Earth moving, road building, airstrip creation and those types of things were constructed by "horizontal" engineers. The 107th Engineer Battalion was classified as a "horizontal" engineer battalion. It would also be one of the Army's new "patchwork" battalions just like the 137th Transportation Company was, just on a battalion level. Our battalion would be comprised of 5 individual companies. There would be the H.S.C. (Headquarters and Support Company), this company would contain the Battalion Commander, Sergeant Major, and all the administrative staff needed to support a battalion of 500 or 600 Soldiers. The second company was called the F.S.C. (Forward Support Company), this is the company that held the maintenance, medical, and recovery assets that would leave the wire and provide any support the "Road" companies may require in the performance of their tasks. This is the company that I would be in command of. There were then the 3 actual "Road Companies" that would be performing the route clearance tasks in our assigned region of Iraq. The 107th Engineer Battalion was a "patch up" job just like the 137th Transportation Company was that I had been Platoon Leader in. The "patches" were at almost every level of the organization here though. The 3 "road companies" were the 272nd Engineers from North Carolina, the 177th Engineers from Virginia and 234th Engineers from the state of Kentucky. I guess in hindsight the only complete complement of the 107th Battalion were each of these companies. They were attached to the 107th as entirely complete companies. I would be the commander of the company assets that would be driving outside the wire to help them as needed while in the performance of their missions. This could be with mechanics, or wreckers or anything else they may need in a tight spot. Despite this arrangement, I never had much repoire' with any of the Soldiers in these companies or their Commanders. For the most part they were all a bunch of good ol' Southern Boys. They were tight-knit groups, professional and well-trained while they were at home states and they were eager to get to work. After a month or two going through the motions at Ft McCoy we were on our way back to the "sandbox." "Sandbox" was simply another term of affection that had been developed for the country of Iraq by us Soldiers who had been there. The 107th Engineer Battalion was also a tight knit group as I would soon find out. Although all the Soldiers under my command were "yoopers" I was a "troll" as was my First Sergeant. First Sergeant Meriweather was also a "troll", but he had the benefit of being from the far Northern region of the Lower Peninsula. Unless you are from Michigan, you are wondering what in the hell a "Yooper" and a "Troll" are. A small geography lesson is in order here. Michigan is a two-part state. The lower peninsula, referred to as the "mitten" (wonder why? Just look at a map) The upper peninsula was a large chunk of land connected only to the lower peninsula by a large bridge. That is the Mackinaw Bridge to be exact. This bridge also has the distinction, at 5 miles long, of being the longest suspension bridge on the planet. Those who lived up in the U.P. were the "yoopers" (U.P.ers specifically) and referred to everyone who lived below the bridge as "Trolls." The differences between these two groups of people went far beyond geography. There were many cultural differences between the "yoopers" and the "trolls" to be specific. Every "Michigander" in the lower peninsula had at one point migrated there from the south and worked their way up into the state. The ancestors of the" yoopers" were almost exclusively of Scandinavian descent and migrated either from the north of Canada, Northern Wisconsin, or straight across one of the Great Lakes from their New York embarkation point generations earlier. The upper peninsula has no land attachment to the lower peninsula but is attached at the west border to Wisconsin. The professional teams from Wisconsin, the "Green Bay Packers" "Wisconsin Badgers" and so on were the team posters that were posted on the walls most everywhere in the U.P.

You are asking yourself "Why is he going into so much detail over this dull shit?" I am for one reason, to state one clear fact, and that was that I was an "outsider." With every interaction with my superiors at battalion I was reminded of that fact. I would have assumed that my volunteer status was known and would be met with gratitude. My presence enabled the battalion to make their troop strength requirements to deploy to Iraq. Even if the Army felt I needed to be there, the leadership at battalion regarded me as a minor, but necessary inconvenience. I was not overwhelmingly bothered by this, as my O.E.R. spoke for itself and I had also assumed that once my commanders noticed I was an experienced commander and fully capable I would be "taken into the fold." But at that moment though, I had to focus on leading a 120 or so Soldiers safely and successfully through another deployment in the "sandbox." Our unit had a good location in Iraq, if one was to be had by anyone, at a place called Camp Victory. I was also familiar with this area from my first tour in O.I.F. 3. I had executed more than a few missions there and it was one of my favorite places to go. I believe Camp Victory was the largest coalition outpost in the country. There was a large area in the center of Baghdad, right next to the Euphrates river, referred to as the "Green Zone" which may have been larger, but I don't think so. Surprisingly with the size of the "Green Zone" I only ran maybe one or two missions there before. The" Green Zone" was a virtual prison compound, complete with wire, fences, walls, communication and security. This was because it was the location where the all the headquarters units for all coalition forces were located as well as the embassies for all the countries of the world. The "Green Zone" was also the favorite place for the bad guys to try to drop artillery and mortars on. It was well defended by every means available and only rarely did I hear of anyone getting injured or killed there.

Camp Victory was part of what was the sprawling B.I.A.P complex. In probably a 10-20 square mile area there was the airport, Camp Victory, Camp Liberty, and a couple of other F.O.B.'s (Forward Operating Base) as well as all of which were surrounding the airport. That was by design because the airport needed to be as secure as possible in order to bring everything the "new" country of Iraq would need to begin life again. This was in addition to all the military personnel, equipment and V.I.P's that came and went on a daily basis. It was an ideal location for the 107th as well, since all the sprawling roads and highways in and out of Baghdad were preferred targets for bad guys. It was essential to keep these roads safe for commerce and travel. The B.I.A.P complex was on the outskirts of Baghdad. This was good because it made it a short trip back and forth for everything that had to come into the country. It was bad because it was well withing reach of all mortars, artillery and rockets that the bad guys could launch from the shadier areas of town. As much as all this was important to me on my first mission in the country it doesn't mean a lot to me now. This was because I had now become a desk jockey and would not be leaving Camp Victory very much. I guess if I had to be stuck in a place in Iraq, this was the best I could hope for. Camp Victory had almost all the comforts of home. Being the largest single Camp in the country, it had the largest PX, the most café's, movie theaters and gymnasiums. I would be spending a lot of time in the gym since there wasn't a whole lot else for me to do. Without the adventure of leaving the wire on missions, time moved extremely slowly. This allowed me ample time to think and reflect on life. Thinking is not necessarily a great thing when you're 6000 miles away from home and everything there that you cared about. On my first tour I was a leader, this tour I was a babysitter. Naturally my company was again co-ed and that always presents a special set of challenges for any commander. Thank goodness on both deployments I had been blessed with exceptional, professional N.C.O.'s and my First Sergeant Meriweather was no exception. "TOP" (Army nickname for 1st Sergeants as they are the proverbial "TOP" of the N.C.O. food chain) handled most of the trivial goings on from day to day and only on a few occasions did I have to deal with discipline problems at my level. Major personnel issues in theater were the use of alcohol, some drugs, and fraternization. My company issues were no different. Imagine that you are 6000 miles away from home, have 84 young adult boys and 36 young adult girls, all of which with too much time on their hands. In addition, they are not allowed to do the kinds of things that all young people like to do which is drink, watch pornography and if lucky, screw. Every single one of these activities is prohibited by the status of forces agreement currently in place between the Nation of Iraq and Uncle Sam. In addition to the geographical, temporary prohibition imposed by the U.S. Army, there were activities that, while legal in the civilian world are illegal in the military one. Adultery was one of those activities. That was illegal under the U.C.M.J if you were a member of the military. Boredom was beginning to become as lethal as cancer. You can only "make up" so much work for a large group of people to do. Normally, Army life in the "world" would involve formations, training, and maybe some healthy, organized, group fun. None of this was possible in Iraq, because you needed to try to avoid any kind of activities where Soldiers would be in large groups. That does make sense if you think of it, imagine having the whole company of 120 Soldiers all outside doing P.T. (physical training) one lovely desert morning and some lucky shitbag manages to drop a rocket or mortar round right in the middle of all of you. Not a good scenario. All P.T. was to be done at the individual level, and anything involving groups of Soldiers larger than 5 was discouraged. One early Sunday morning, "TOP" wakes me up and informs me I have a couple of my Soldiers waiting by my office in a set of handcuffs escorted by the Military Police (M.P.'s). I headed down to the office and sign the release for prisoner forms. The M.P.'s then un-cuff my Soldiers and are on their way. So, the 4 of us, myself, TOP, and two female Soldiers, step into my office to get things sorted out. Both Soldiers were drunk as skunks and had been arrested stumbling around the company area. Only one of them was really caught stumbling around, but when the M.P.'s asked the extremely drunk Soldier where she had gotten the alcohol, she replied "Why my friend Specialist Tucker gave it to me." The M.P.s then headed to Specialist Tuckers quarters and promptly arrested her as well. In my platoon from the 1461st, you would have been required to pull out the fingernails of one of those Soldiers to make them "spill the beans" on one of their fellow Soldiers, but this group of Soldiers was a lot different. The females in this unit were, for lack of a better word "catty." Towards one another that is. The U.C.M.J clearly indicates what a commander is supposed to do in a situation like this. It also gives a commander a few alternatives as to what an appropriate punishment might be. I personally would have cut these two Soldiers a little slack since they did not hurt themselves, any other Soldier, or do any damage to any taxpayer funded U.S. Army property. Alas, I would not have any choice in the matter. Even though drunkenness is clearly defined as under the jurisdiction of the Company Commander, Alcohol had become such a problem in Iraq that the Army added some caveats to the U.C.M.J. One of those caveats was that any alcohol related offenses were now to be placed only in the hands of Commanders O-5 (Lieutenant Colonel) rank and higher. This meant my only alternative was to turn these Soldiers over to the Battalion Commander for what is referred to as a Field Grade Article 15. Company Commanders can punish Soldiers up to a certain point, depending on seriousness of offense, with a company grade article 15. More serious criminal offenses had to be taken "up the ladder" to the Battalion Commander for a "Field Grade" Our battalion commander was L.T.C. (Lieutenant Colonel) Legrass and he came down hard on them. Their field grade article 15 reduced them by two ranks from E-4 to E-2 and charged them both almost $300. In addition, they had to work a double shift at the Battalion for the next 45 days. Normally "Restriction" (Restriction, remember grounding for grown-ups) was not necessary since we were in Iraq, as the only places ANYONE could go was your duty station, mess facility and place of worship. I knew there was a lot of alcohol going around with the Soldiers, hell I had mine too, but if it was kept to themselves I wasn't going to crawl up their asses trying to find shit. My policy from my first tour with Soldiers was "As long as I don't have to know about it, I am not going looking for it." Many times, I have hoped the Lord kept a special place in his heart for the individual who developed the plastic fifth bottle for Dewars scotch and Jim Beam. You couldn't get your booze at the PX, so everyone had their own methods for getting a nip or two in theater. I remember scoring my first bottle in Iraq still. I was in Taji and made the walk to the other side of the camp where the civilian workers quarters were at. On every post there are different categories of workers. Even though the military pretty much called the shots, maybe only two-thirds of everyone on camp wore a uniform. There were those of us in uniform, from every branch of the service. In fact, I remember walking to the mess facility one fine morning to see two individuals performing guard duty at the door. They both had "U.S. Navy" embroidered on their uniforms. I asked them "I bet your Navy recruiter never brought this up in the sales pitch did they?" They replied somewhat sadly "Uh... No sir"; those poor bastards. In addition, there were military civilians. They were employees of the individual branches of service, Army, Navy, and so on, but they were basically hired to perform a specific job for a specific period or "contract." A lot of the higher-level maintenance support was performed by these folks. When I had a mission during O.I.F. 3 to take a bunch of my vehicles to have their bulletproof armor added on, it was to a facility right around the corner from us at Camp Victory. It was affectionately referred to as "Big Bob's Armor." This whole shop was prefabricated, packed up, personnel and all from the Army Tank Armory in Warren MI and sent to Iraq. This Army facility was right down the road just a few miles from my new house in Farmington. It's a small world I guess. Then there were the international workers there. Think of these folks as the "cruise ship" workers in a combat zone. There were folks from India, Bangladesh, Thailand and Vietnam and probably every other country in the world. These folks usually were employees of K.B.R. and performed all kinds of ancillary services around post. They did all the manual labor at the water production facilities. In the Baghdad area, remembering we blew the shit out of the infrastructure again, all our drinking and potable water was pumped out of a lake just outside of town and processed through a big facility the Army had built for that purpose. Much of it was then bottled and loaded onto pallets to be shipped all over Iraq. That water was also hauled to the large storage bladders everywhere by tanker truck. These international workers also did of the sanitation work around camp. The crowning jewel of this work was to run the "honey truck" all over, emptying, refilling, and sanitizing the hundreds, if not thousands of porta johns all over camp. This task takes on a whole new meaning when the temperature never goes below 90 degrees. I am not kidding when I say that if the wind was right you could smell the "honey truck" coming, long before you could hear its engine. One of my fathers' favorite sayings was "Smelled bad enough to knock a buzzard off a shit wagon." Even the buzzards would not go near this thing, but the little Bangladeshi's happily whistled while they worked and took good care of these facilities. I stated many a good day by sitting on a nice new, dripping wet with blue water, cool, sanitized porta john for my first morning shit! I can imagine a thousand or so folks reading this thinking "T.M.I" (T.M.I was a term I would learn a few years down the road from my then pre-teen daughters for "Too Much Information"). The final category of workers is the "local Nationals" Local Nationals are, as the title implies, everyday folks that live in the surrounding area outside the wire, in other words Iraqi citizens. They come to work on the F.O.B every day and perform all kinds of tasks for a paycheck. Local Nationals have been used for labor in pretty much every conflict throughout history. Unlike the Israelites, Aztecs and Nazi's though, our Local Nationals were employed by choice and not hauled to work wrapped in chains. There are some good and some bad things about this practice. I have never entirely decided which side I agree with. I can start with the good list because as far as I'm concerned it's shorter. The number one reason they are hired in the first place is to pump hard currency back into the local economy and get it back on its feet following a conflict. I suppose the number two reason would be relationship building. In theory, you give someone a job, pay them some money, treat them well and they like you. That's how it's supposed to work anyway. Another good aspect of having local nationals is that you have a ready source of language and cultural "ambassadors" for whatever part of the world you are operating in. Almost all our interpreters were local nationals. There are bad aspects of allowing what could be "the enemy" right on to your compound. Supposedly each of these local nationals hired has gone through a complete background investigation and screening before they are allowed to work for Uncle Sam. It bears mentioning that a background check is only as good as the organization performing it. The Iraqi police where the ones performing these checks, and many of the local police had very questionable loyalty. Even though a couple of years had passed, no local was still very keen to the idea of having their name or address on any written kind of note whatsoever. I found out during this tour that the Iraqi Sergeant Major of the transportation regiment we trained arrived home to find the heads of both his teenage sons sitting neatly in his driveway. Those were the kinds of things that happened when lists of names were discovered. The local nationals who worked for coalition forces really were putting the lives of themselves and their families at risk. Another favored technique of the bad guys was the use of our local national employees to launch attacks against us right inside the wire. While the locals themselves may have been loyal, any loyalty would go right out the window when you know the bad guys are at your house holding your wife and children hostage. Should the poor individual not do what they were instructed to do, they could count on arriving home from "work" to a box filled with the pieces of what was their family members that very morning. More than a few times a local national worker would find a weapon on post and open fire killing a few coalition forces before being shot dead themselves. I guess to them, they were giving their lives to save their families. There were much more deadly attacks than just simple shootings. In Mosul that year, it seems a group of the local nationals had been infiltrated and each was instructed to carry one small piece of a bigger item to a pre-determined location. One individual then assembled what was then a complete 128 mm mortar round (approximately 2' tall, 6" around with 20-30 pounds of high explosive and shrapnel). That round was then carried into the mess facility there and detonated during the lunch time "rush" killing 128 servicemembers. More than a few times while minding my own business around camp, I would see a local national just standing around looking like they were fiddling around with a cell phone. A car would then zoom up, couple of people would get out in black jumpsuits and hoods on their heads and whisk "Mr. Local" into the backseat of the car and away they would go. I do not know, or want to know, where they all went, but I do know that I never saw the same individual a second time. I did not know that local nationals were not allowed to have cell phones or cameras of any type on post while they were at "work." This was because in today's day and age of G.P.S. (Global Positioning System) and accurate artillery aiming a set of coordinates was all that was needed. Needed to make a precision strike on people or specialized equipment on post anyway. So, as you can see it was a good mix of people from all areas of the globe and walks of life that contribute to the operations on any F.O.B. in theater. Hopefully, you have also noticed how Soldiers always needed to kind of keep their eyes open too.

One of the cool things they allowed on the F.O.B., in addition to the local national workers, were some small, local vendors. It is a known fact that anywhere Uncle Sam is, there is money to be made in virtually every way. Like the "gut trucks" would line up in area where Soldiers congregated back in the "world", these local vendors would set up their little shops as well. Most everything was available then, legal and illegal. I never tried to solicit anything illegal from any of them, but the word had come down that drugs were being offered at some of these. A lot of pills apparently, valium, pain killers, et cetera. Apparently one Soldier had overdosed on some of this medication so all of us commanders received the "scoop" to be aware of this. I simple assembled my Soldiers, brought the topic up and stated, "Would you really trust a pill from a guy who doesn't wipe his ass, has a 3rd grade education and probably makes those pills in his garage?" A little grumbling from the troops and nothing more was said. I never had any problems with local drugs among my troops so I must have made an impression. It wasn't all bad experiences and danger there. Like I had said earlier if you were inside the F.O.B. you were relatively safe. Camp Victory was especially safe since it was part of such a large installation, there were a lot more valuable "targets" like the airport to throw mortars at. I think the closest I ever got to being blown to bits on the F.O.B. was an evening at Taji. I was sleeping peacefully in my "hooch" when I was awakened to the pounding on my door by the E—7 who occupied the hooch next to me. "Did you hear that?", "No" I said." He replied, "that fucker whistled like hell and came right over our roof!", I again replied "Did it hit us?" "No" he said, then I replied, "Then why the hell did you wake me up?" In the morning I discovered that some bad guys had managed to cobble and wire a couple of Katyusha 40 mm rockets just up good enough to launch then and just blindly lobbed them on the F.O.B. The bad guys could barely ever even cobble all that 30 or so year old shit enough to launch without blowing themselves up in the process. Thankfully for us, they either had no guidance systems whatsoever, or a clue how to use them. Those two rockets that night had struck a storage building which was filled with first aid supplies for the F.O.B. My 1st Sergeant and I rode over to see what the damage was, and the sight took our breath away. At first anyway, because inside that storage building was a lot of fake blood and "Resusci Annie's and Andy's" who had been blown to bits. There were arms and limbs and "blood" all over the place. It was truly a scene from a horror film. It was more like a comedy film, and with that second glance came peals of laughter and we all got some great photographs. There wasn't a lot of comedy among the members of our "road" companies though. While Battalion HQ and our two support companies (H.S.C. and F.S.C.) remained in relative comfort and safety inside the wire, our Road Engineers were taking an absolute ass kicking out on the highways. They were getting the job done, finding plenty of I.E.D.'s and getting them off the roads. The bad guys (back to the Spy vs Spy) were also getting better at their "game" of developing techniques of killing coalition forces. A new, favorite technique was to leave an I.E.D. partially visible and easily found by our Engineers. Then, while their convoy was stopped, they unleashed the completely hidden and undetected I.E.D which was a short distance away and aimed perfectly at the convoy. The equipment we were using now was fairly impervious to a tremendous amount of conventional explosives. These held up a lot better than the P.L.S's I had to work with last time. The armor my P.L.S. had at first was just what we affectionately referred to as “hillbilly armor.” This was nothing more than lots of plates of 3/8” steel plate welded over the door sides, fronts and ballistic glass in the windows. I got lucky enough during the tens of thousands of miles that none of my vehicles took a direct hit. We took a lot of indirect hits which inflicted some injuries and equipment damage, but we always walked away. The detonations these newer route clearance vehicles, primarily “Buffalo” and “Fox” type, were exposed to were incredible. None of it ever could penetrate the passenger compartments and everybody was doing well until about a 1/3rd of the way through this second tour. Like every other hurdle we had thrown at the “bad guys” eventually they had come up with an effective countermeasure. This time these came in the form of an explosive called an “E.F.P.” (Explosively Formed Projectile). You really couldn’t refer to these as I.E.D.’s because there was nothing improvised about them. An E.F.P. must be made to very precise specification and using very specific materials. The basic requirements were a chunk of 4-6” diameter pipe, a ½” thick pure copper disk the same diameter as the pipe chosen and a couple of pounds of high-grade military explosive. C-4, P.E.T.N, SEMTEX, or the like was essential for it to work. The copper disk was carefully pressed into a concave shape of a precise 40-something degree convex. The convex side was then placed inside the end of the pipe and attached to it. The high explosive is then gently packed behind the copper disk in the pipe and detonation cap added to it. A steel end cap, with two holes drilled into it for the detonator wires, was then attached to the back of the E.F.P. The concave, copper end was the “business” end of the device. When detonated the entire energy of the high explosive packed inside was transferred into to the copper disk turning it into a molten plasma. This plasma, when seen under high-speed photography, resembled a "nipple" from a baby's bottle. It wasn't anything as innocent though, it travelled at near the speed of a bullet, and could cut through at least 12" of military grade armor steel. I have seen the remains of the one of our road companies' vehicles, a "buffalo", which was struck by one of these set ups. It was struck by 3 E.F.P.s simultaneously, the first one fortunately just cut through the front grill and tires. The second one hit the vehicle precisely in the engine leaving holes that you could look completely through one side of the engine block to the other. The 3rd E.F.P entered the passenger compartment of the vehicle killing two of our Engineers inside. If you were wondering how the vehicle was hit three times with one detonation, I can explain. Like I said earlier while the convoy was halted "interrogating" the I.E.D. in front of them, 60 yards or so behind them was an array of 5 E.F.P.s cleverly held together using heavy construction foam. Once that foam had hardened encasing the E.F.P's, it was then spray painted grey to resemble a large rock. Completely unnoticeable, until it went off, it then became unforgettable. The only deterrence to these horrible weapons was avoidance, plain and simple. The only good part about an E.F.P was that they required expertise not readily available in Iraq so very few were encountered. The ones that were encountered were more likely than not manufactured in Iran by their special forces groups and then exported to their proxies in Iraq. Of course, politically, nothing could be firmly proven to trace them back to Iran, so direct, military retaliation was never really an option. The mujahadeen and ayatollah just got some laughs at Uncle Sam's expense. It was because of these casualties that I had to perform the most emotionally taxing job that I would ever do in Iraq the entire time I was in that country. This was both the first and second tours combined. When a Soldier dies in combat, at least was my experience, a chain of events occurs. During my first tour in Iraq, we all knew when a Soldier had been killed from any unit at Camp Cooke virtually as soon as it happened. This was because the first thing that occurred was all of the internet, cell phones and radio communication is stopped. All the M.W.R facilities are shut down until further notice by the post Commandant. This is to ensure, with the speed of modern communications, that the military has enough time to notify a Soldiers "next of kin" of their loved ones passing before one of his buddies, calls "his buddy" back in the world, whose wife just so happens to know the other Soldiers wife, tells (as they feel it is their "duty") to tell them their husband, wife, son or daughter has been killed in theater. It would be like seeing your loved one was killed in a car accident on the 6pm news before the State Police come to your door. Although that is not a good situation, it happens no matter what precautions are taken. At least the Army could say they were at least trying to be first offering the outstretched hand and shoulder to cry on. Usually within 5 or 6 hours the lines would be turned back on, and you knew someone back home had gotten some bad news. I had received a small block of instruction at Ft Eustis regarding types of duties Officers had to perform for mortuary services, but never had use of them (thankfully) my entire first tour in theater. That was about to change. Of the three casualties the 234th sustained that day I was called into the Battalion Commanders office and assigned to be the "court-martials Officer" for one of them. Once a Soldier is killed they are taken to the main mortuary in theater which was located at B.I.A.P, I guess a short time later the body is prepared (or whatever is left of it) and shipped to the main military mortuary located at Ft Dix New Jersey. Apparently that is the main mortuary for anyone that is killed abroad anywhere in the world in the military. Now is the part where I, as court-martials Officer, step in. It would be my task to go to the poor bastard's hooch and assemble all their personal belongings together, inventory it and pack it in a box and then forward to it Ft. Dix. This may sound easy enough in theory, it is a lot more difficult in practice. Each and every item, no matter how trivial it may seem, must be accounted for and sent to his family. Only the Soldier themselves (now deceased) and their families will know what is emotionally and financially important. My job would be to get it all there. Of course, this Soldier was a younger man, married with two very young children at home. Nothing rips your heart out like going through all the Soldiers papers and finding the homemade birthday card, tenderly written in the hand of their 6-year-old son. "Happy Birthday Daddy" "Love you so much, please come home to me soon." Daddy was coming home alright, just not to the homecoming this poor child would have expected to have. There was also a rubber chicken, the comedy type, there and I could only wonder what story was behind that. It wasn't too emotionally healthy to think too deeply about these items. You also must get to the deceased Soldiers hooch fairly expeditiously as well. This is because there is one thing all Soldiers have in common, that is their bond with each other. Part of that bond usually involves "Hey bro, if something happens to me, take this..." or "I want you to have this." Lovely as that may sound, it poses a problem for the court-martials Officer. As I had written earlier, EVERY item that belonged to that Soldier now belongs to their family. In some cases, it will be all they have left from their loved one besides a folded flag and box of medals received from a "grateful Nation." It wouldn't be fair to call his buddies "vultures" as many of them probably did truly have spoken agreements regarding certain items. No matter what those agreements may have been, I cannot and am not supposed to honor them. I suppose there may have been certain circumstances where a Soldier had a written "contract" regarding an item or two should their buddy meet their demise, but none of them turned up, thankfully, in the case I was working on. My duty involved a little detective work as well. While going through the papers, I found a receipt from the PX for a nice new digital camera this Soldier had purchased just a few days prior. I did have his closest friend with me to supervise the post-mortem inventory, so I asked him where this camera was. "It was with him in the vehicle when it was hit sir." "I need a little bit more than that Soldier, where is it now?." "It was blown to bits sir, but I have this" He then presented me with a tattered, bloody case and a memory card from the camera. That was good enough for me, I listed both the items on the inventory sheet and packed them in a box. There was also quite a stack of personal letters from two or three different women among his belongings. I was very concerned that if this Soldier was involved in some kind of infidelity, I did not want to be responsible for destroying any lasting, loving memory his wife may have. I figured the guy paid enough; he did not need to have his legacy with his family marred by some stupid shit he may have done. Thankfully I was given a "hot line" to the mortuary at Ft. Dix for any questions or concerns I may have had. I was informed that it was there in Ft. Dix where a second and final inventory would be performed before these items were sent home to their families. It was there as well, where they would have more detailed information, such as the deceased Servicemember's family names and such to not ship anything that may not be appropriate to the grieving family. The Officer at Ft Dix did tell me that even they have their problems from time to time with this. It seems one of the deceased Soldiers sent to them was followed by a box containing 20 to 30 fuck films (all on DVD of course!). Naturally those were pulled from the belongings before they were sent to the family. A few short days later he received a call from a kindly grandmother inquiring where HER movies were at. It seems granny was watching out for her favorite grandson and lovingly sent him those discs for his entertainment while abroad. It takes all kinds of families to make the world go around I suppose. I would have to perform this court-martial officers' task one more time before I would depart Camp Victory for the last time.

Finally, my F.S.C company received a mission outside the wire. We were tasked with doing the groundwork, grating, leveling, trenching and so on, for what would be new Iraqi police station in Rustamayah about 15 miles the other side of Baghdad. Thank God I was going to get off this fucking F.O.B. for a couple of weeks. Now normally a Company Commander would not go outside the wire very often, if at all, to perform relatively simple missions like this. The grumbling of my Soldiers attempted to remind me of this. At the end of the discussion, I am the Company Commander, you all have never been outside the wire, and I AM going. So, I would at least get a couple of weeks of a change of scenery. I think once we arrived at the location, and it soaked into the other Soldiers that they were really in "hostile territory" they were glad I was along. None of them really had any idea of any of the things to keep your eye on while walking or working outside of the F.O.B. The "drunken sailor" walk was a must. The "drunken sailor" is an action just like it is described. When you're outside of your vehicle there are two things you always want to remember. First, you never just sit still in one place for too long. That makes it way too easy to become a target of opportunity for any shitbag with a gun. Every coalition Soldier did have a bounty on their head by the bad guys, all someone had to do was shoot one of us, get a picture or video of it, and go get your dinars. As an Officer, naturally my bounty was higher, so I always tried to remember that. Now that you know that you don't want to sit still in one place and that you must start moving around, then you perform the "drunken sailor." Even the most unskilled marksman can pop a cap in someone's ass who is walking in a straight line. The "drunken sailor" walk involves turns frequently, varies their walking speed, makes themselves unpredictable as to what they will do next. That may not completely keep you from getting sniped, but at least makes you a lot less of a "target of opportunity." While my Soldiers worked merrily away, running the road graters, bulldozers, and other earth moving equipment I just moved around keeping my head on a swivel. We were, after all, in the middle of Baghdad, working in an area surrounded by high buildings and everyone in the city knew we were working on a new police station for the area. There is nothing on earth bad guys hate more than law and order, so naturally they would attempt anything to prevent the construction of a police department.

The weather was nice every day that we worked there and each day about noon time a small "treat" would arrive at the construction site. It seems it's not only the United States where proprietors of "gut trucks" and "roach coaches" seize an opportunity to make a buck (or dinar) from any group of people who may congregate every day at the same place.

Each day this Habib would drive up, be allowed through the wire and then pull his or her truck over to the end of the construction site. They would then set up their tables off to the side of the truck, and a couple of kids (I can only assume they were his) would start unloading mounds of food and crates filled with "Pepsi." That heavenly odor would waft across the area and the lines of local nationals, who were assisting us in this project, would form to get some food. At the one end of one particular table was a stack of fresh baked, still warm, slathered in butter, perfectly browned Syrian bread. There was no fucking way I was not digging into that! It was a choice between real home cooked food, or the M.R.E.'s that we brought with us for lunch. No real contest in my book. Of course, my Soldiers, not being quite as "worldly" in Iraq as I was at that point were hesitant to purchase or eat anything that didn't come out of a bag, or one of Uncle Sam's official mess facilities. Since I felt bad for them standing around foaming at the mouth, I explained the facts of the situation so they could make an informed decision whether to get some REAL food. I explained that everyone working in that location would be eating from the same piles and containers of food. If any of it had been tampered with in anyway, everyone would have been poisoned. As long as no vendor pulled a "special" stack or pile out for us, we were good to go. You also did not have to speak Arabic for food. You could always consider the good old "greenback" the "universal translator" anywhere in the civilized world. So, I finally came to the front of the line, pointed at what I wanted, spread a few bills out in my hand and let the proprietor take the 2 dollars I owed him for the food. Then I went off to an isolated corned to imbibe in some yummy local cuisine. My other Soldiers watched me that first day and once they noticed I did not get hepatitis, or had been poisoned, the following day all of them fell into place in the impromptu chow line just like me. It was around a 2–3-week mission and it was a nice reprieve from being stuck on Camp Victory day in and day out.

Unbeknownst to me my scenery was about to change in a tremendous way on Camp Victory though. I had no way of knowing the entire time I had been assigned to the 107th, all the higher up's there, primarily the Battalion Commander and Executive Officer, had already decided that my tenure in their "Yooper" group was going to be temporary. Once their one and only "home grown" Second Lieutenant was promoted to First Lieutenant, the bare minimum rank he could hold to replace me, the process of eliminating me was begun. All they would need was the slightest bit of reason to get rid of me and I'd be gone, and their "exclusive group" would remain just that. Unfortunately, even if I didn't give them a reason, it would not matter. Politically, once an individual reaches a certain rank in the Army, the number of things they can influence regarding their human resources assets grows exponentially. As far as a Battalion sized element is concerned, anyone ranked Major or above is "God." It seems I would be assisting them to get me replaced as well. I had one of my female Soldiers who stated from the very moment we left that "I do not belong here" "I do not want to be here" and "I should not have had to come here" (despite signing the contract and taking Uncle Sam's college money). Long story short, despite being married she started fucking one of our engineer boys, got herself knocked up which was her instant, one-way ticket back to the world. On her out processing briefing which I was required to give her upon signing her release, I wanted to make sure that she would remember to look in the mirror and be proud that she had shirked her duty to her country, screwed around on her husband, and buddy fucked everyone else in the company who would not have to pick up her slack. I believe I ended the briefing with "Get the fuck out of my office." It seems that the calendar worked somewhat in her favor, and she was able to stretch the days just to the point that she could say she was impregnated by her husband on her two-week mid-tour leave. She arrived at home to file a complaint to the State Command that I made "her feel bad." State Command then informed the Battalion Commander of this, and I got an official letter of reprimand. That alone is almost a death sentence to an Army Officers career. A few short months later, I found out (through another of my Soldiers, not the command structure) upon her giving birth, her husband was capable of simple math, and the fact the child looked nothing like him, that she had in fact, not been impregnated by him, or during her leave. He then divorced her ass. That would also mean as far as the Army was concerned she should have been charged with Adultery and dereliction of duty. One would also have thought that the Battalion Commander would have called me to his office and retracted my letter of reprimand. Not only did this not happen, but this incident, along with a bogus "Moral survey" that they conducted showed my Company had "low moral" and just like that I was relieved of command. Naturally their "home boy" was placed in my spot and would be right where they wanted him upon return to the Upper Peninsula. If the letter of reprimand was almost a death sentence to any hope I had of a career, the relief of command was unquestionably the coup de etat. Now that both the 107th and I had pretty much exercised a "vote of no confidence" for each other,

I needed to go somewhere else for the remainder of what time I had to spend in country.

I was assigned to 4th Division headquarters, in the logistics department. Since the division was 3/4th the way into its rotation in country, and they arrived fully staffed, I did not really have an "assignment" to speak of. Pretty much remain accounted for each day and stay out of the way until all of us head back to the "world." I moved my hooch into their personnel area and had a bunch of helicopter pilots for roommates. It made for some interesting conversation, and we had a good time swapping stories about what it was like covering the countryside by land and by air. They were "night rangers" too, as most of their operations came at night in support of the Infantry. The infantry would prowl around the streets and buildings, acting on any intelligence they may have gotten during the day to bring some of the bad guys into custody. The helicopters working at night in the skies over Baghdad were quite a sight. Technically, "not a sight" you might say as they ran completely in "black out" mode. Leave it to the military to use this term ass backwards too. Actually "black out" was "black on" or "all lights off." Although you could hear them prowling all over the city skies, you couldn't see them at all. The exception to that came only when the proverbial "shit hit the fan" on the streets below. At that point all the helicopters would light the streets up with their spotlights like the 4th of July. It seems the pilots were having their own version of "Spy vs Spy" in the air as well. While on the ground the bad guys acquired E.F.P.s to counter our armored vehicles, there must have been some empty room in those shipping crates arriving from Tehran. They filled those spaces with

S.A.M 32's. Now S.A.M.'s (Surface to Air Missiles) have been the scourge of aircraft ever since they were invented. The first S.A.M's were large, slow and hard to move from point A to point B. The S.A.M. 32 was a shoulder fired missile that two Soldiers could carry and only one Soldier was required to fire it. It had a short range, only a mile or so, but it could travel at Mach 2 and had heat seeking capability. Long story short, it wasn't much good for the fighter aircraft of today which could travel faster and further than these missiles, but for a helicopter a few hundred feet off the ground, hovering, leaving a nice blazing hot exhaust from its jet turbine engine, it was a perfect weapon. From a helicopter standpoint, they were virtually impossible to defend against. Like the E.F.P.s though, fortunately, they only arrived in very short supply, and if the Infantry boys on the ground kept their eyes open (It did take a minute or so to set the S.A.M 32 up during which the two Habib's had to be standing still in the open) the helicopters were fairly safe. The bad guys did score a few hits with these though as I recall and killed a few of our pilots. I tried to keep myself in a military manner, learn what I could about Division operations and make the best out of what was a shitty situation. I spent a lot of time at the gym and running in the F.O.B. Running was a great way to take my mind of the absolute screwing I had just received at the hands of the 107th. I will always remember the surreal feeling of running along the inside of the wire on hot evenings as the sun was just lowering down to the horizon. It was usually over 100 degrees and the dusty haze just hung in the air. There was a 15' wall of mud brick and razor wire between me and the "outside world" there, but I could readily see the high rises and minarets that were all around us. To be running in this environment and then to hear one of the "call to prayer" recordings (not sure whether you'd call this a song, a melody?, I it was most definitely original and unlike anything I had ever heard in America) being broadcast. It mostly always reminded me how very far away from home I was. For what it was worth, there was a Physician's Assistant assigned to the 107th (another Army requirement to deploy the battalion) from another State. Unlike me, she did not give them any suitable reason to remove her from their roster so with her they had to completely fabricate a story. Another, albeit brief, Army process explanation is required for this though. When you receive anything in the Army that must be returned to them (Army supply chain), you "sign" for it. Pretty much everything excluding your clothes or personal things go on what is referred to as a "hand receipt." That is, they hand you an item, you sign a receipt for it and then hand that receipt back to them. Off you go with the item now in your possession. Once that item is later returned, you get your hand receipt back and can destroy it if you wish, you're off the hook for the responsibility of the item. Once you sign the receipt for an item, YOU become solely responsible for it until which time it is returned. The item in question here was a drug, Duramorph (Morphine to you un-medical folks) to be exact. The Physician's Assistant signs for a larger amount from the main post pharmacy. They then divide the individual doses out to each of the medics assigned to their unit and receive the hand receipt for them in return. Every so often, being a controlled substance, the P.A. (Physician's Assistant) would ask the medics to come to her office, bring the controlled substances in their possession, as well as any documentation. and all paperwork included with the item. The P.A. would then conduct an inventory on everything. No less than three times did the medic from the 107th end up with less Duramorph than they had "signed" for and had no explanation for where it went. Now normally this would have and should have resulted in an investigation. The result of that investigation would be most likely charges filed against the medic for the loss of the Duramorph. At the very least a drug screen would have been ordered to see if the Soldier in question was using or abusing the stuff personally or selling it on the black market. There was no drug screen ordered but there was an investigation begun. Of course the investigation was conducted by the 107th Battalion and it was against the Physician's Assistant, not the medic. Now despite following Army protocols to the letter and having every signed hand receipt; the 107th was determined that it had to be the P.A.'s fault for the missing items. She must have counted wrong, must have not given the Soldier the items that THEY signed for, or so on. The real truth was that the medic was one of the 107th's "home grown" troops and the P.A. (like me) was an "outsider" and there was simply no way the P.A. was going back to the U.P with the 107th. The P.A. also received a letter of reprimand, promptly told the Battalion Commander to fuck off, and asked to start her own investigation with Division headquarters. That investigation was regarding the absolutely ludicrous process she had just gone through. If you remember a few chapters back about the human resources power wielded by any Soldier ranked Major or higher you'll remember they are literally "God." One thing they (all field grade Officers 0-4 and above) do to make sure this "pecking order" remains in place is to cover each other's asses. There was simply no way an O-6 (Colonel) was going to investigate an O-5 Lieutenant Colonel over the accusations of an O-3 (Captain) no matter how egregious the situation. Long Story Short, the P.A. went back to her state with a stain on her record, just like me, and the 107th had rid themselves of having to bring another "outsider" with them back to the U.P. "Mission Accomplished."

A few more months then passed by and just like before, my time in the sandbox was over. We returned to Ft McCoy for a brief demobilization and then headed back towards our home stations. I did get the other 107th Soldiers' attention when, during one briefing, we were asked as a group what our experiences with the 107th Battalion were. When my turn came to speak it was pretty easy, while looking directly at the Battalion Commander and Executive Officer I simply said "You know, it was horrible, I went out of my way, left my family and job to volunteer to help the 107th Engineers so they could deploy, and these ASSHOLES treated me like shit and worked to get rid of me, despite my performance from the minute I arrived, thanks a fucking lot" and I sat down. You could have heard a pin drop in the room. At least I had my chance to get my say. I had been the Michigan National Guards "golden boy" after my first deployment, my O.E.R. reflected a flawless performance and I had been awarded a Bronze Star, I have even accompanied, by invitation only, our States delegation to the National Guard's National Convention in New Mexico a few years before. I brought the treatment I had received and wrongful letter of reprimand up to the Brigadier General (O-7) who I knew personally from her invitation to New Mexico. She gave me a stern look and said precisely, "I don't want to fucking hear it LIEUTENANT" and walked away. That pretty much summed up what I could expect for justice from the Michigan National Guard. I headed back to the Transportation Battalion located back down in Detroit. I turned my "resignation of my commission" letter in on the first drill weekend, went home and never put a uniform on again. It was a strange reflection for me to put this chapter behind me. I never really thought that after 15 years that I would ever be in a uniform again. I most certainly never thought that I would be an officer. Never dreamed in a thousand years that I would go overseas again, or lead troops in combat. It would end up being the "circumstances' and "side show" that would cause me so much grief and P.T.S.D. (Post Traumatic Stress Disorder) in the future than any contact with the enemy ever would. I have always been a person who detests "loose ends." I like completed tasks, finished things, and chapters closed. I had closed the "Army chapter" before in 1985 and now here I was "closing" that chapter yet again in 2007. I needed to mentally keep these chapters in my life separate, and it was easier than I thought it would be. This was because, despite being in a uniform with a "US Army" tab on the breast, the entire experience was different. There would be no reopening of an "Army chapter" again though because I was now over 40 years old and too old for military service. It was like that realization that every man has at one point in their lives when you conclude that you will never be President of the United States, a professional football player, or a billionaire. It had to be just about this time in my life when I was to receive a serious life lesson. That lesson would be that despite my experiences, the hardest knocks in my life would not be served to me in the military.

It was shortly after I returned home that I received the news about my sister. She died unexpectedly at the age of 54. There were a ton of questions. My sister had always struggled with some health issues but had always persevered. It was one of her great strengths, nothing ever held her back from achieving her goals no matter what they may be. She was even, despite being over age 45 and decades in nursing experience, applying to get into Physician's Assistant (P.A.) school to advance her career even more. One thing my sister always struggled with was her weight. I learned a lot about obesity with her growing up. Most things that people associate with obesity, sloth, gluttony, laziness, lack of concern, NONE of these applied to my sister. I saw her lose the better part of 100 pounds or more two or three times during her life, only to have it return a few short years later. She also struggled with rheumatoid arthritis her entire life. This caused her tremendous pain for many extended periods, but I never saw it stop her from doing what she wanted to accomplish. It was because of these physical ailments my sister always took a lot of medications, pain relievers mostly. Her cause of death was an accidental overdose of narcotic pain relievers. She had a bad habit of leaving her bottles of medication on her bed stand and we all figured that she woke up one night in pain, had forgotten while half asleep, and taken just one too many pain killers. My mother took this knowledge to the grave with her. That was because my sisters "official" cause of death was "narcotic overdose" and it was intentionally taken. In shorter terms, suicide. My sister had taken her own life. It was my niece who pulled me to the side at my sister's funeral services to explain the truth to me. If my mother had discovered that her daughter was a suicide it would have destroyed her. Mom was of the "old school" train of thought and that was believing that suicide was the one "unforgivable sin" or a one-way ticket to hell to put not too fine a point on it. It would serve no good purpose to let mom in on the true details of her daughters death. My niece explained that my sister had contracted a form of Hepatitis C with a particular “delta” variant. Her suicide note, was a simple “I’m sorry, but here are the lab results, I’m not dying that way.” That strain of hepatitis, compounded with that variant, was a death sentence and a particularly miserable death by liver failure at that. Sis just decided that she was not going through, or putting her family through that, and just took an overdose. Like all the conversations I had had with my sister over the years, it was hard to argue with her logic. I love and miss her and just wish there had been a better solution. I’m sure she wished for a better solution as well; even on that last night. I wish I could say that this experience would be my last personal, intimate, interaction with suicide.

Chapter 8: "It's all over"

It wasn't long and I received a call from the Battalion Commander from my transportation battalion. He had been a personal friend of mine for years by this time. This was because I had, in one regard or another, been under his command for over 5 years. I did give him the courtesy of an office visit to hear what he had to say. There was nothing he could do about anything that had happened to me at the 107th, but he did assure me, I could make up for it, time would pass, and that the Army would be losing a great, experienced Officer if I still chose to leave the service. He then asked me to reconsider. It was nice to be hearing something positive, but my mind had already been made up. I was disillusioned and had been used, and I honestly had nothing more to give physically or emotionally. A lot of the speech from my transportation commander was because they were about to deploy as a Battalion to Afghanistan (Fuckmenistan as I like to call it) and knew I could be a great asset to the Battalion if I were to go with them with my experience. There honestly was no way I could ask my kids or Michelle to go through the experience of worrying if I was alive or dead anymore. I was as sure then as I am now it was the right time to hang up the uniform for good. I cannot believe now it has been over 20 years ago. The memories, emotions and feelings I still hold are very vivid. I did make some friends in the 107th as despite the leadership, and a few bad apples, I did have a lot of good Soldiers under my command there as well.

I was a civilian again. Naturally I went back to Beaumont who was again waiting for me with open arms. I have always felt so blessed to never have to worry about what I was going to do for a living upon return to the "world". In fact, one of my very well "endowed" female co-workers had jokingly written on my going away card "Come back alive and I'll show you my boobs" I had a brief moment upon my return where I thought of calling her out on that, but I was deeply in love with my Michelle and didn't think she'd necessarily appreciate that. Not to mention my co-worker's husband was about twice my size and having my lungs pulled out through my nose for looking at his wife's boobs did not sound all that appealing either. A lot of Soldiers were not as fortunate upon their return to civilian life. I did share one thing in common with a lot of them though. My marriage to Mary was destroyed by the deployments overseas. I had read somewhere that statistically over 60% of marriages of Soldiers who deploy end up in divorce. That's more than half and almost hard to imagine. Michelles marriage had also dissolved roughly at the same time mine did. During my second deployment Michelle and I did stay in contact with each other through letters, phone calls and video conferencing. Now that I was officially free from the Army, and single, we did not have to pretend we were going to have a relationship anymore. One might think that with my previous experience with marriage I would want no part of the institution. Nothing could be farther from the truth. I loved this woman and her two little girls and wanted desperately to marry her. She held me off for a little while but within 6 months she finally realized that I wasn't going away and married me. I couldn't have been happier then, or now 17 years later for that matter. I was now 41 years old and essentially starting the rest of my life. Now that I did not have to worry about being dragged away again I threw myself into opportunities with my current employment and education. I had sustained some serious injuries while deployed so I did go to the VA to get my evaluation done. My goal, at the time, was to just be in their books in case something got physically worse in the future. I always thought that the Veterans Administration and the Military were interlinked, and it would be operated a lot like the military. I was wrong. They are most certainly NOT linked, and except for a few items, any information about you, you had to take to them. I did have at least a dozen examinations though of everything from blood, urine, vision and hearing. In addition, there was imaging work of all kinds. It had been discovered my neck was pretty much shattered and would require surgery to fix. The nerve in my right mid-forearm had also been severed resulting in an area on the top of my right hand that did not have any sensory function and never would again. It was also assumed by the results of the M.R.I (magnetic resonance imaging) that I had sustained some mild brain injury which was by this point in time, was being referred to as "T.B.I. (Traumatic Brain Injury). They didn't really know a lot about it then nor do they today for that matter. Besides the constant pain in my neck and numbness in my hands I was determined not to let it come between me and my goals. Prior to my first deployment. I enrolled in Eastern Michigan Universities master's degree program in Education. I scored very well on the G.M.A.T. (just like the S.A.T. for graduate students) and was accepted into their graduate program. I was working on that program the same way I had gained my bachelor's degree from Spring Arbor University. I went to class one evening a week and every Saturday to do the required coursework. I did receive a lot of credit from my "prior life" experience and had completed almost 1/3rd of the classes when I received my first marching orders to Iraq. I was only around 10 days shy of completing the semester when I had to report for duty. The class I was taking at the time was a group project and our class was split up into groups of 6-8 Students. The professor told me that if I turned what I had completed so far over to my fellow classmates before I left she would consider it "complete" and give me the same grade as the rest of the group. Imagine my surprise when I started researching what I had to do in order to get my program restarted only to find out the professor for that class had marked both my classes as "incomplete." I contacted the student dean at the University and their new "Veterans representative". Since now almost 4 years had passed, there was no way I could turn in any partial work to eliminate the "I" (incomplete) There was also no way they would change the professor's grade, regardless of the circumstances, due to what they referred to as "academic freedom." It seems that tenured professors are a lot like the O-4 and above in the Army. They are essentially "God." Here I was again, I was at the receiving end of a good screwing from the 'higher-ups" and there wasn't shit I could do about it. This was even though, at the rate of $740 per credit hour, I had just flushed around $2500 down the toilet towards this degree. I finally took a little while to ponder what exactly I expected to gain from having a master's degree in the first place. The truth was that it really would not do anything to advance my career at Beamont. I would have had to leave Beaumont hospital for a different job, and I wouldn't leave Beaumont anytime soon again. E.M.U did have the audacity to send me a bill for $1650 some 7 years later and they received the same thing from the invoice that I received from them "Incomplete". At 41 years of age, I figured I had achieved as much as I would ever need to regarding higher education.

I threw myself into my job at Beaumont and tried to remain on the cutting edge of all things Nuclear Medicine. One of the things I always enjoyed about the career was the fact that it was always changing and evolving. Unlike X-ray, which hasn't essentially changed since ol' William Roentgen developed the X-ray tube in the 1800's, the more the scientists learned about biologic functions, the more radioisotopes were developed to "follow them along" in the body. It was completely fascinating. I started delving into the research side of the career, and it was easy enough to do since Beaumont prided itself into always being "pioneers" in the medical field. Beaumont also had the financial power to achieve this as well; so, if there was ever any new imaging equipment or technology available, Beaumont was always among the first hospitals to buy it. There were winners and losers in this endeavor as well. Early imaging in nuclear medicine was a lot like X-ray imaging. Photons of energy (the simplest way to describe gamma and beta radiation) would come out of the patient (instead of being emitted by an x-ray tube), then scintillate a chunk of sodium iodide crystal. A simple device called a photomultiplier tube was glued to the back of that crystal. The photomultiplier would then multiply those photons and feed that information into a dot matrix printer which would translate the input onto paper. This would show where the location of all that energy coming out of the body was. This was a slow, inefficient, and only moderately accurate method. Digital imaging would change all of that. Rather than go into a physics lesson, I'll just suffice to say the first few "digital machines" did not quite work like described in their sales literature. Beaumont was not going to miss the opportunity to try this new technology and purchased one of the first digital cameras called the 'digimap 1000" from a company called "Lark" in Canada. Every time Beaumont buys a new piece of equipment they would assign two of their staff technologists to be "resource people" for it. These two would receive all the training, guidance and usually perks from the company until the machine was installed, operating correctly and ready for patients. The selling company would then go their own way and those two technologists would then train the rest of the imaging staff on that piece of equipment. I volunteered to be one of the resource people on this machine. Sometimes even a little travel, and at least a business meeting or two over dinner, was involved in being a resource person. Rather than drivel on and on about the "digimap" I'll just say it was a flop. Like many things the theories behind this equipment were sound, in practice not so much. For starters, rather than use tried and true hardware systems, "Lark" literally invented their own from scratch. The electronics of the day were just not capable of handling the amount of information being thrown at them from these new, all digital, tubes. After about 3 months of failure after failure, hospital administration was not happy and "Lark" was asked to remove themselves and their "Digimap 1000" from the premises in Royal Oak. Digital imaging was very soon afterwards a tried-and-true technology. This was important to me because a whole new science was emerging in the field of nuclear medicine. This was called P.E.T. (yep just like your dog or cat, but the acronym stands for Positron Emission Tomography) This science would open a whole new discipline in the field of radiologic imaging and I was determined to be a part of it. This imaging was straight from the mind of Einstein and his discoveries some 75 years before. I would have never thought that I would ever give two shits about $E=MC^2$ but sure enough it was going to change my life. Again, to avoid delving into a physics lesson in my little story I'll keep it simple. There are types of radioactive material that decay (break down, lose their energy, so on...) by positron decay. This means breaking down by a proton splitting off and out of the nucleus of an atom. Now when two different atoms spit out a proton at exactly the same time (to the millisecond) something remarkable happens. Just like Einstein said, once those two protons leave their nuclei they smack into one another and are completely converted from mass into energy (annihilated in scientific terms). That's what the whole $E=MC^2$ means in case you were really wondering. That energy from the annihilation just so happens to be two, now photons of energy, equal in strength which then travel away from each other in exactly 180° paths. That's where my new P.E.T. scanner comes in, if it detects an interaction from a photon, the computer then checks to see if another photon interacted with the ring of digital detectors at the exact same time and strength. If so, it is counted as an "event", add enough "events' together, you get an image. You get the point. Rather than trying to delve into this adventure with a new and upcoming company, Beaumont decided that it was going to purchase its first P.E.T. equipment from one of the masters of nuclear medicine imaging equipment, Siemens. This would be the beginning of a beautiful "side fling" between me and Siemens.

Beaumont would not only purchase a new P.E.T. scanner but would also construct, in the nuclear medicine department, an entire P.E.T.

“Suite.” In addition they would purchase a linear accelerator (cyclotron, also called an atom smasher) to be set up in the basement of the hospital so we (the new Beaumont P.E.T. center) would never be wanting for the isotopes necessary to do P.E.T. scanning. I would also be getting trained to operate the cyclotron at one point as well. A cyclotron was almost a necessity as, unlike the staple of nuclear medicine Technetium 99m with a 6.2-hour half-life, many of the P.E.T. isotopes had half-lives that were measured in seconds or minutes. I was happier than a fat kid in a candy store. I now had a bunch of new “toys” to learn about and play with. In addition to piquing my interest, once I learned these new skills I would become a member of a very small group of individuals in the country who would know how to do this. I never intended to leave Beaumont, but it was a good feeling to know that I had a very valuable skill set that would keep me in demand should our (mine and Beaumont’s) relationship ever sour. In addition to learning, I did some work on the lecture circuit for Siemens regarding P.E.T. imaging and equipment. These were some lucrative gigs and they helped pay for a couple of impromptu vacations for Michelle and I. One such example was a lecture I was to give at a Siemens symposium in San Antonio Texas. I don’t even remember the topic I spoke about now. I do remember that I was “put up” in my own suite in the “Four Seasons” resort in San Antonio. I purchased the airfare for Michelle separately, and she came along with me for the weekend. My only responsibility to Siemens was giving my 70-minute lecture on Saturday afternoon and then the entire rest of the weekend we were free to do as we wished. During these symposium weekends, Siemens would usually host an “entertainment” event as a corporate gesture, so everyone would get a chance to interact socially as well as professionally.

The event in San Antonio was a huge BBQ meal at a down home "Texas dude ranch." Naturally as a speaker my entry was paid for, I simply had to pay a small fee for Michelle to be able to join me. The best engagement I ever worked for with Siemens was giving a lecture during their "Global Outreach Weekend." Naturally, Siemens "global outreach" would be in their home country of Germany. I jumped through a few hoops to get my passport updated for international travel and I was off for the weekend to Munich. The suite they put me up in there was not a spacious as the one in the San Antonio Four Seasons, but it was ever so luxurious. I did see the room rate was 780 Euros (almost 1000 U.S. dollars at the time) per night. Glad I wasn't paying that bill. Siemens was on their home turf, had international dignitaries and people attending from everywhere. As such, for their "entertainment event" they were going to "do it up right." Siemens rented the entire Paulaner Brauhaus (brewery) for the evening, Paulaner is the oldest continually operating brewery in the world in case you didn't know, established in 1656. It was to be an evening filled with all things Germany. All the brats, brochen, and of course 1-liter mugs of Paulaner's finest beer that you could drink were "on the house." All of this happened to the sounds of the German beer hall polka (Oompah) band playing on the stage. It was a great evening. In addition to my accommodation and travel, I was even financially compensated for my services. Yes, I was STILL PAID monetarily in addition to the perks. I have heard it said "Something too good to be true usually is" but my arraignment with Siemens truly was too good to be true.

For a change everything in my life was in order and moving in a positive direction. Although my marriages to Lisa and Mary were through, we were on speaking terms and I was spending whatever time I could with my kids. Although I did not have a great deal of quantity time, I did focus on making sure what time I had was quality time. I had come a long was from having to have my mother pick them up and haul them, or me, to Reed City so we could all spend a few hours together in the little house on 5th Avenue my parents owned. The one drawback about things going well, is that they also seem to pass twice as quickly. My young "kids" were not so much "kids" anymore but young adults. They were beginning to have their own lives and my part in them was getting smaller and smaller. They seemed to be generally happy, and I was happy for them. The bad part of this was that it was a cruel reminder to me of what time I had missed watching them make that transition from child to young adult and that time was gone forever. All I can say is that I did the best I could with the resources I had at the time. I do have some fond memories of those high school years with them though. I was blessed with "band geeks." Some may think that is a bad thing, but really it is not. The band kept all of them focused and their idle time filled. My oldest did so well as to even be the "director" of the High School band her last year or so. I couldn't have felt prouder watching her stand on that podium with the big ol' hat and baton with the entire band in front of her. I could not catch every event she directed, but I did get to see a few. A great perk to these visits was that they occurred right in the middle of a high school football game. I discovered in my old age that I loved watching Thursday and Friday night High School football. It was a great sport and brought back so many fond memories of my time on the gridiron. My next youngest daughter played with the flag crew in the band and sang in the choir. While my daughter was directing the band during her last year, my son had become involved with the percussion section in the band, so I got a "two for one" visit with them. When your time is limited you work to make it as efficient as can be and it gave all of us a chance to be together even if for a short while.

It seems the Good Lord was smiling at me a little bit because I would get a chance to at least watch some of my children grow up. In addition to my wife Michelle, I also inherited two little girls who were just toddlers when we married. Although we shared joint custody and visitation with their father, we both did get to spend a lot of time with them and watching them grow into the incredible young ladies they are today. It did make for some interesting comments and glances though when I would go to their elementary school counseling sessions. More than a few times I was asked "Are you their grandfather?" "Uh, no I'm their stepfather" it was pretty hilarious. Unfortunately, the smooth divorce transitions that I had gone through both times, for the sake of the kids, was not so smooth for Michelle and her ex-husband. He was bitter and angry that she had found love again, and about the idea that his kids had another man in their life. Despite the fact I knew exactly what he felt like and would never attempt to "replace" him, he made the entire joint custody experience miserable. At least Michelle and I were in a financial position to obtain the legal representation we would need in order to defend ourselves from his unending neurosis. Soon, my older kids were walking down the aisle of the auditorium to receive their High School diplomas. Three of them would now begin lives of their own. My daughter with Mary ended up being not only a band geek, but an athlete of sorts. She was into percussion like her idol her "big brother Jonny." She also ran the hurdles and short distance in track events. It was nice that her High

School was a lot closer than Reed City had been in the past. This made me able to attend more of her school extracurricular events. Mary would soon enough find love of her own and remarry as well. I was happy for her if she was happy. Life is too short to hate. It is said to harbor ill feeling against someone is like "drinking poison and expecting the other person to get sick." There is a lot of merit to this old proverb. Lisa too it seemed, had finally found the love of her life. He was a guy of my old acquaintance due to the fact we had attended elementary and junior high school together in Reed City and were friends. Much to Lisa's dismay every time we saw each other, Will and I always had a handshake and laugh. It seems Lisa still harbored a lot of hard feelings towards me. While I regretted that, I understood it and she had every right to hate me for the rest of her life if she chose too. I only wished she could let it go for her well-being, certainly not because I deserved any redemption from her.

In the years continued to work at Beaumont, my physical condition was deteriorating. It seems that having an amount of high explosive touched off in your close proximity is not particularly conducive to good health. Since I enjoyed my job, and being with my friends, I did not miss a lot of work despite how I was feeling physically. I was also struggling emotionally even if I would have denied it at the time. One wonderful thing about having a loving spouse is that they can be honest with you about yourself and see things about you that you cannot see in the mirror. Some of the situations she put up with in those early years when I returned from overseas defy description. One particularly troubling situation involved my driving. When I was in command of convoys in Iraq, I "owned" the highways. Simple, troublesome, little things like traffic, traffic signs (stop signs in particular) were all inconsequential to me and I just drove right through them. Not only is this frowned upon in the civilian world, but it is also a good way to either get killed. Or worse yet, kill someone else. After buzzing through 3 or 4 stop signs, and having my dear wife almost incur heart failure, we both decided that for the next few months she would do all the driving around town. I was also very intolerant of some people, mostly anyone who simply plodded through life haphazardly. Now I don't care how anyone goes about their day except when their day interacts with mine. Like fast food employees, or postal workers. If they did not give a shit about their job or moving any faster than the bare minimum required, that was their business, except for when it cost me time. I made no hesitation to uh... "mention" this to them, much to the embarrassment of my lovely wife. I was still operating on a military standard, that is to be assigned to a task, do it right, do it fast, do it efficiently, and complete it. I expected that the whole world should be operated the same way. Let's just say I was a disappointed more than a few times.

Civilian life was disappointing in other ways as well. In the military there is a camaraderie and a bond that underlies all else between servicemembers. This mostly does not exist in the "world." Your co-workers are your co-workers and at the end of the day, you went your way, and they went theirs. This took me a little getting used to. I was also beginning to have constant pain in my neck. When doctors would ask me to, "describe it." I would to equate it with having a screwdriver shoved between my shoulder blades 24/7. That pain, and the emotional issues I was experiencing, led me back down to the Veterans Administration health facility. Veterans Administration facilities have one great way to treat pretty much everything, and that is "Drugs". I had taken a Vicodin many years before, probably when it first came on the market as a revolutionary new pain reliever. This was when I had broken a bone in my foot in college. I remember it as being as wonderful an experience as you could expect from any medicine. My pain was gone, and I felt happy floating on cloud 9. Naturally, when a nice big bottle of these were given to me for my neck I was happy with my treatment and headed out the door. This was the beginning of my personal love affair with my "dragon." It didn't take long before the 1 or 2 every 4 to 6 hours became 2 or 3 tablets every 4 hours. In addition, I was placed on paroxetine to stabilize my ever-changing moods. I was having some difficulty sleeping as well. Because of the drugs I did not have any trouble falling asleep. It was staying asleep more than 3 or 4 hours at a time that became my problem. A lot of this was due to the "night life" I had experienced during my time in Iraq as well. I am certain the pills, which could still only mask so much discomfort and the numbness in my hands, was beginning to interfere with my duties at work. Considering that I worked with radioactive materials, needles and Patients, it was imperative that I have full, dexterous, function of both of my hands. After another visit and M.R.I at the V.A. it was determined that the only remedy to my neck problem was going to be surgical repair. I was approved to have surgery at a civilian facility as the V.A. did not readily have the neurosurgery expertise I required. This worked out great for me for two reasons. The first reason was that I could find the best neck surgeon in Midwest, and the second was that he had privileges to practice at my beloved Beaumont. The surgery went well, and I awoke feeling like Frankenstein complete with neck collar, laid flat on my back with my C.P.A.P strapped to my face. The most beautiful sight was my lovely wife's face when I first opened my eyes. Someone had pulled the screwdriver out of my back, and I had blessed relief at last. Somewhere around this time it was decided somewhere at the V.A. that my injuries were the result of my military service (of course they were), and that I would receive a "rating." A "rating" is a percentage of a complete disability you were decided to have. Once that was determined and confirmed you would receive a disability pension amount based on that rating. I was rated at 80%, which was a significant amount, and with the extra allowance given for being married with children, I was going to receive a decent payment each month for the rest of my life. Sitting down with my old friend from Detroit Diesel and having explained all this to him, he replied "you just hit the lotto buddy". I did not understand what he meant then, but I do now. Money, for the most part, would no longer be a challenge in my life. Although I was not by any means wealthy, I would be financially comfortable enough to retire if I chose to do so. The first thing I had to do was deal with this "monkey" on my back though. That was the drug abuse I was currently buried in. At one point during this period, I was taking the equivalent of 20 Vicodin per day. The bad part about Vicodin is that part of that preparation is acetaminophen (brand name: Tylenol) and that is extremely hard on your liver. Taking what amounted to 8-10 Tylenol per day for a couple of years is a good way to end up in the grave. This behavior pattern had to be stopped. Fortunately, at Beaumont, I did have access to substance abuse treatment and entered a 6-week outpatient recovery program. I successfully completed this much to the joy of my wife. Not only did discover I was wired to love opiates, but those people are just like alcoholics and are wired for their drug of choice. Not only was I going to be physically sick if I stopped taking the Vicodin, but with what pain I was still going to have the rest of my life, my chances of relapsing were also almost certain. That is when I was introduced to buprenorphine. This was a new, cutting-edge medication for folks just like me. It seems that regular opiates work on two sensors in the brain, the one that relieves pain, and the other that causes euphoria. Buprenorphine only works on the sensor that relieves pain, as well as preventing the user from going through opiate withdrawal. Although I had essentially traded one "dragon" for another, the one I had chosen would give me some pain relief, prevent me from getting sick, and not send me into liver failure and an early grave. I can say that it saved my life and I have taken it from that day forward.

Beaumont was going through some changes of its own at that time. In fact, health care was changing everywhere in the global economy. Insurance costs were soaring to astronomical levels without limit and there was no end in sight to this trend. Employers and people were rapidly becoming unable to afford health care insurance in any form. Something had to be done and the federal government began to come down hard on the industry to do some "belt tightening" and come up with strategies to bring health care costs under control. The health care industry became a lot less about "health care" and a whole lot more about "industry." Beaumont was no exception. Everything that made it such a wonderful place to work was no longer permitted in the department. Gone were our "Christmas on the 4th of July day" and "Hawaiian shirt day." Our Nuclear Medicine Technology certificate training program was also nixed in the name of cost savings. Perks such as department purchased and embroidered lab coats, Saturday breakfasts and anything else that could be cut to save a dime subsequently was. Moral in the department hit a new low. It was in this environment I was about to make one more major change in my life. A few years prior I had left the comfort of the Royal Oak P.E.T. department in order to build and start a P.E.T program at Beaumont's Troy and Grosse Pointe locations. This would be accomplished by Beaumont purchasing a mobile P.E.T. scanner and then having us spending certain days of the week at each of those locations. With my experience in P.E.T. and as a transportation officer I was a "shoe in" to be supervisor of this. I loved this position and was good at it. I never missed a quota and with my "handiness" with all things with wheels and machines, we never lost many imaging days due to down equipment. I was about to learn that "politics" plays a part in everything, not just the "field grade Officers" in the Army. A management restructuring was going to occur and despite my successes it was determined that another technologist would be my defacto supervisor and evaluator. You might normally think that anyone who is supposed to supervise and evaluate someone at their job performance should have a few qualifications. Qualifications like knowing what that job is and having more experience and seniority than the individual they are evaluating. My new "supervisor" would have none of these. In fact, she was one of my students who I helped teach when she came through our Nuclear Medicine Technology certificate program a few years earlier. It seems the leadership at the Beaumont Troy Nuclear Medicine Department was, and always had been, a giant "girls club' and I did not have the right "equipment" for the job. It was time for me to seek employment elsewhere. I applied for and accepted a supervisory position managing a large mobile cardiology department. I did want to give Beaumont one more chance to right what I felt I had been wronged. I then I filed a complaint with the new "Department Chief of Radiology." Soon my department supervisor and I were on route to their office to have a meeting to discuss it. After what was clearly a "snow job" I was getting it was clear to me, (just like it had been clear with the One-Star General in the guard so many years before) that I was getting fucked and there wasn't shit I could do about it. I always like to be prepared like the Boy Scouts so after hearing their decision I was prepared. The look on their faces when I slapped my pre-prepared resignation letter in front of their faces was priceless. They did not see this coming, but "Hey good luck with your new supervisor who knows nothing about mobile P.E.T." Just like thatI was off to start my new career, or so I thought. I had to do one small thing before I started my new job and that was take the pre-employment physical and drug screen. I was terrified that my buprenorphine would show up on my drug screen costing me this great new position, so I did what was probably the dumbest thing I have ever done in my life. And as you've read in the last few dozen pages I have done a lot of dumb things in my life. So ok, what I would do then is at least "top 5" material anyway. I figured I would cheat on my drug screen and just add a little water to my sample diluting my buprenorphine to an undetectable level. Drug screens obviously have come a long way since the days of ol' and my result came back "diluted specimen" so I was called back to repeat it. This time the collection would be UNDER SUPERVISION and the look of disgust by the technician when he saw the tube in my pants to cheat again was the ultimate in humiliation. I honestly now think that that moment was worse than the Chinese nurse for my first Army physical so many years before. He simply said "you're done" I pulled up my pants and slunked back to my car. I never heard back from that employer, I didn't have to, I knew exactly where I stood.

Now I seemed at another lowest point in my life and went from a great job, to probably a greater job, to NO job. I guess all things happen for a reason and just about that time my disability rating was raised to 100% as being unemployable since I had to have a second surgery on my neck. My first "fusion" was a complete failure and more drastic measures had to be taken. I had surgically what they called a "cage" put in, basically a wire cage completely wrapping my vertebra from around C-3 to the T-1 level. I would never work a regular job again and was officially "disabled/retired." It wasn't easy changing my mindset from one of "how many hours am I going to get in this week?", or "Am I going to have to work this weekend?" or put in requests for "time off" anytime I wanted to go fishing or hunting or spend time up North. My time was now my own and my income was sufficient and steady each month. People spend their whole lives waiting for that day, thinking it will never come. I was no different, yet my day seemed to arrive "just like that." Everyone also thinks that you will jump for joy and have a big party and just swiftly and effortlessly glide into this transition without even a glance in the mirror. I can tell you this is not the case. In my case, that emotion came in a month or so once I realized it wasn't a dream, and it wasn't a temporary change. I suppose it was probably due to the events that brought me to this point in the first place that caused this delay in happiness. Most working stiffs just put the "count down calendar" on their desks, plan their retirement party, get their gold watch and then it’s over. As you can read above, my “ending” was born of stress and turmoil.

CHAPTER 9: "A New Beginning"

This was going to be a new chapter in my life. It was strange to think about this technically being the "last" chapter in my life. A lot of people, and I know more than a few, once they retire they must just kick back in their lounge chairs and wait for death to arrive. I was determined that I was going to be different. For starters, I was just 52 years old and at least statistically I could have another 25% of life to go through. I didn't plan on doing it sitting on my ass.

Once I accepted the fact that I was not going to go back into the regular workforce it was time to consolidate my finances and see what I was going to have to work with. The largest financial responsibility, I refuse to call it a burden, was my child support had now ended. Although I never begrudged paying it, it was a VERY happy day when I received my first check without the mandatory $780 taken out of it. I did learn something else as well. Another perk to getting your 100% rating was that you were then considered to be "permanently and completely disabled." As such, you are entitled to apply for your Social Security benefits. That thought had never crossed my mind before. In fact, like many folks my age, I never, ever figured that that money would ever be there by the time I was old enough to apply for it. I did my homework and found that the best way to get through the mountain of red tape of the Social

Security "machine" was to hire an attorney who specialized in that. Their method of payment could not be more convenient. In a nutshell, if you are awarded your Social Security, like the V.A. benefits, you are retroactively paid from the date you first applied for it. Since nothing involved with the government moves quickly, it was safe to say a person would usually get at least 6 months back pay. These attorneys engage in a contract with you, the client, that you will allow them to take up to 1/3rd of any back amount you are due as payment in full. The bast part about this to me, and much less to the attorneys I am sure, is the fact that they are limited to a specific dollar amount by law. I was almost feeling a little down about having to draw on this, as I did not want to take advantage of an already "beaten" system. I asked my attorney "Did I contribute enough to pay my share on this?" He laughed and quickly replied, "Are you kidding? You worked from age 14 to age 52, you paid enough into the system for THREE people's benefits" I still received 4 digits on my back pay from Social Security even after my attorney took his "cut." In addition, I would receive a comfortable monthly amount due to my age, and the amount of my contributions over the years.

It also seems that after you work so many years for a major corporation you receive more than a final paycheck and kick in the ass. I had worked a combined 21 years at Beaumont Hospital and was fully vested in their retirement plans. A few months after my final punch out on the time clock I received a notice in the mail. I had to decide what to do with my share of that investment. Since I had a regular monthly allotment from Uncle Sam, I did not have to worry about that regular, steady income to pay my bills. I've always known if I ever won the lottery (unlikely since I really never play, the lottery is essentially a "poor people tax") I would take the "lump sum" payment and just have them write my name on that check. I had accrued a nice 5 figure amount through my years of hard work and did the same thing. "Yes, make that check out to John Roberts......" Now I had a healthy sum of cash and was finally able to do that one thing I had always dreamed of in the past. I wanted to buy some property. A piece of land I could call my own in the world. I found the most perfect 40 acres to be had, in my opinion, in all of Osceola County. This property had three unique things that made it perfect for me. It was located only one mile down the road from where I spent my teenage years at Pine River High School. The memories came pouring back every time I pulled into the small two-track that led to the field. I also had high school classmates both on the 40 acres next to me and the over 200 acres across the dirt road. I always felt how odd my life would have been if, like them, I had just stayed in the area. My dear old "brother-in-law" Ron, had stayed in the area once he got out of the Army in the mid 1980's. Unlike so many other folks that lived up there, he and his wife did very well for themselves. We had crossed paths a few times over the years, even after the times we were able to get together in the service. Our relationship had grown way past "brother-in-law" to "best friend." Now instead of hours apart we lived 10 miles apart. We would spend a lot of time catching up on the years gone by over a fishing pole and a few beers. It was great having him living close there, and more than a few times in the upcoming years would his knowledge of construction and expertise come in handy. The topographical highlights on the property were perfect as well. There was a tree line facing the dirt road, which blocked the view to the 12 acres of field which was the East side of the property. Behind the field was 18 acres of pristine hardwoods stand. I had these 18 beautiful acres of maple, oak, cherry and occasional beech trees. On the North boundary was a 150 acre stand of mature pine trees. These were very cool to see as were all telephone pole grade trees. On the East border was a deep swamp area, and no one was coming through that side onto my property. The South side was where my buddy from P.R.H.S. owned his 40-acre parcel with a beautiful home. The West boundary was the dirt, county road from which I had my "driveway". Across the road was my other friend owned 200 acres. A stream which had water year-round ran right down the center of the property from West to East. I honestly could not have found a more perfect place. From the moment I placed foot on that property, all thoughts of Colonels, Iraq, drug screens, and bumper to bumper traffic just went away. Michelle and I were going to build some of the fondest memories there we would carry for the rest of our lives. Our first "living quarters" here was a small pop-up camper I had purchased. I had to use a machete to hack through the sea of bracken ferns to make an area to set it up but when we went up there we would finally have a roof over our heads. In time I would add electricity, plumbing and sewer to transform this piece of heaven into a home. The only thing more fun than being in the country is being in the country with small children. I feel sorry for any children who must grow up without ever getting to spend any time in the country. The REAL country, not a park in the city. Not a field trip to a patch of woods, or a walk through Central Park, but real country. The real country is where the closest store is miles away. It's also defined as where you cannot see the house closest to you. And most importantly, by all "hillbillies" standard, the country is where you can just stand at your back door and take a piss (male or female) and not wonder (or care) if anyone is watching or can see you. This was a new experience for my wife too. She grew up entirely in an urban area. Even so, she has memories of the small, undeveloped area which was at the end of her road. She has mentioned playing in the field, seeing the animals and enjoying it. Of course, like all areas in proximity to the city, this spot would soon be paved over for the next subdivision and gone forever. Although my three oldest children were living their own lives by this time, my three youngest were still able to come and spend significant time with us up here. I'll never forget the looks on their faces and worry in their voices the one time when they came across a baby deer fawn just lying by itself in the field. "Is it abandoned?" "Will its mother come back for it?" "What do we do?" Of course, for me, I have encountered this situation many, many times in my distant past and knew exactly how it would play out. The fawn, lying by itself is a defense mechanism. Apparently deer have a unique feature helping to keep their young safe. The young are born "without scent" meaning that coyotes or other predators cannot use their most efficient sense, smell, to find and eat them. So, when mother and fawn (or fawns, deer frequently have twins) encounter a threat, the fawn just "drops" to the ground, the mother then works to gain the predators attention. The mother will then get the "dangerous predators" attention to then chase and follow her away from the fawn. That fawn then waits patiently, even sometimes to the point of being only inches away from the predator, until its mother returns to it. No matter how many times you see something like this, it never will cease to cause wonder in you. I also remember the time the kids found a rattlesnake on the property. I thought this was peculiar since Michigan is home to only one rattlesnake, the massasauga or "cottonmouth" which is not found in the fields or woods on my property. I figured I'd better investigate this "rattlesnake." Well, that ol' snake must have found him a great place to warm its bones because sure enough, when I arrived he (or she, I'm no herpetologist) was right where the girls said it was. And when it saw me it "reared up" flattened his head out like a cobra and gave me the most terrible hiss. I think the two girls jumped back three feet. This is where the knowledge of an old "hillbilly" comes in. I told the girls "Now watch this" that snake reared back to hiss again, and I yelled "hey" in a loud voice. The snake stopped, put its head down, and rolled into a coil entirely on to its back. It also barfed up a small frog and let its tongue hang out. My girls exclaimed "you killed it!." "No, I did not kill it" I said, but I did get to illustrate another great defense mechanism used in nature. You see, this was a common puffer snake. When first threatened, along with its questionable rattlesnake-like coloring, it rears up and puts on a most terrifying display. This alone is enough to deter most predators and the puffer snake is allowed to go on its merry way. If this tactic fails to chase the predator away (like I seemed to be to it now) it will then resort to "deterrent method #2" "Play dead." It does this almost effectively as it does the first method and now, hopefully, it has scared off anything that might like to eat a snake, alive or dead.

While we were loving every minute we got to spend on what was now affectionately referred to as "the 40", we still had to remain in proximity with the younger girl's father. He had taken a new job (about the 9th in as many years) and relocated to Brighton which was 35 miles further west from where we were in Farmington. As I was no longer held by employment to the metropolitan Detroit area, we would find us a new house and move closer to the girls as well. This led me back to my newly claimed "hometown" of Fowlerville. Despite how terrible my last experience ended in Fowlerville with Mary; I had come to love the town. It held that "small town" feeling like Reed City despite being only 45 miles from Detroit. Once I showed the town to Michelle, she felt the same way. The financial reasons that drove me to Fowlerville the first time were the same that took us back there now.

Although it was 20 miles away from the girls in Brighton, the property was still affordable unlike Brighton or the next closest town Howell. We found a beautiful, old, historic cape cod house built in 1906 as one of the original houses in the Village. This house would serve us for many years. It was not necessarily a "fix er' up" but we purchased it from a lady who, with her husband who recently passed away, had lived there for the last 50 years prior. During this time there had been no updates done on the house and the entire décor was circa "1975." That was perfectly fine with Michelle and I. This would give us the opportunity to redecorate it to make it our own. And that we did! It ended up being a perfect time to buy a house as well. The housing market was now in our favor with low costs and interest rates unlike the shellacking we took when we bought our first house in Farmington. Naturally, like small towns all over America, when you first move into a house there you become the new "focal" point for the rest of the townfolk. It would be at least 5 years until my house, after many updates, was no longer referred to by the locals as the "old Faultner house" The Faultner's, being the good folks they were, were the people who had lived there 50 years before us. After adding a fence, central air, gutters, concrete on both driveways, and a nice rear deck, it was now the "Roberts" house to all. Soon enough I was even running into my old friends from both the Village (from when I had lived there before), and my all my friends from the 1462nd based out of Howell. I truly felt at home here. Almost as much at home as I did on "the 40." It was a strange feeling though, it was like being in two different worlds for me, My world from the 1980's when I was a youth living by "the 40," and my current "world" in Fowlerville.

Time continued to march on, and nothing in anyone's life ever remains the same. I was 50 years old now, and like everyone at that age, began to reflect on where I was going to be for the "second half" of my life. Over the past 8 or 9 years we had done well at "the 40" It was no longer "vacant property" but a home. I had electricity installed, a well drilled for water, and a professional well and septic system installed. I had purchased a decent used mobile home to replace the "pop-up" camper and poured a nice cement slab to place it on. I had also, with my own two hands and some help from friends, constructed a large barn. I had even tried my luck at farming. Over the years I had raised chickens, ducks, rabbits and one year even raised three pigs from piglet to market. I cleared the fields of bracken ferns. That was no easy trick as those ferns had 300 million years of evolution on their side. The visits not only included my children over the years, but now my grandchildren also came to visit. It was a wonderful place. For Michelle and me though, its use was winding down and we had to decide what we were going to do. It was sadly a 6 hour round trip from our house in Fowlerville and the "40" was getting used less and less. As much as the kids loved the property when they were younger, like all teenagers, their thoughts were more on high school activities, boys and cars then spending a "boring" weekend in the country. Although I did have a good, regular income coming in every month, it was still a heavy financial burden paying essentially the bills on two houses. Some decisions had to be made.

Many years earlier, I was going on a vacation to Germany and was very excited to see all the places that I had been as a Soldier some 20 years earlier. My father said, "I think you're going to be disappointed." I could not even imagine that happening, so I asked him what he meant. He said, "You are expecting to find something that isn't there anymore, a place will never be the same as the memory you carry of it" I didn't understand at the time, and I pressed him no further. Then, a few weeks later, while standing in the parking lot of the housing complex that was once my "barracks": staring down at the faintly painted parking spot marked "Battalion Commander" I knew exactly what he meant. Every old Army place I went back to visit was now either completely gone or had been re-purposed into something else. My old "motor pool" where I had worked so many late nights, was now an outdoor market. Pretty much all the fine drinking establishments and all of the night clubs that I had frequented were also all gone. It seems that once all Uncle Sam's military cash stopped flowing from the Soldiers pockets into the local entertainment economy took a huge financial hit as well. It was certainly nice to see Germany, but my dad was right, it was most certainly not the same as it was in 1984 and never would be again. I bring this up because there had always been that same kind of lingering feeling on "the 40." It was great hanging and living next to two of my high school chums. It was nice having the two of my brothers that were always there, who were now close enough to spend some more time with. It was also nice to spend some quality time with my folks.

I did not realize that quality time with mom and dad was limited. I was still working at Beaumont when my father got the news he had lung cancer. It shouldn't have been a huge surprise considering the lifestyle my father lived. He had smoked cigarettes his whole life and most certainly a joint or two with some of his Vietnam Veteran friends. In the Navy his M.O.S. (the Navy does call it something different, but since you know what M.O.S is, I'll stick with that one, damn "Squiddies" anyway) was boiler tender. The job was just as it was described, as it was the era before nuclear power and all of Uncle Sam's vessels ran the same way. That was by coal-fired, steam powered turbines. All that steam was generated inside of immense boilers located on the vessel. The rest of the ship had to be protected from all the heat and steam generated by these boilers and the Navy accomplished that just like every other industry on the globe did at that time. Those boilers were lined with fire-resistant, asbestos laden bricks. Asbestos was (and still is for the record) the best heat insulation due to some very specific qualities it had. Not only was the boiler lined with those bricks but every "hot" pipe going everywhere on the vessel was wrapped with shredded and molded asbestos fibers. His job was to scrape the soot and other byproducts of combustion from the inside of the boiler as well as disassemble and reassemble any of those pipes that needed work. All this generated asbestos dust that he inhaled. Just when you might think poor guy might still get away with all that, he spent many years of his adult life later working in the "oil patch" sniffing hydrocarbon fumes. When you first start that work, the fumes almost take your breath away from time to time. Eventually you “get used to it.” That isn’t necessarily a good thing since that’s a person’s body telling you to “get the fuck out of here and get some fresh air”. At the end of the day, my dear father earned a living and kept us clothed and fed,, that was the limit to his financial wealth. All that hard work would eventually cost him his life. In February 2013 my father passed away quietly with all of us by his side. I know everybody refers to their fathers as their “heroes” but very few could actually name single events that earned them that title. I can think of so many reasons and specific events, I would have to write another book to list them all. The world lost and heaven gained a good man, and I lost an inspiration and hero. My mother lost the “love of her life” for the past 49 years. On that cold February day, thankfully the day AFTER Valentines Day, my mother lost her sole reason for living and the source of her happiness on this planet. She effectively died right there with his that morning; it would just take her 5 years to physically catch up with him.

Naturally, being married 49 years, my mother was exposed to pretty much the same carcinogens my father had been over the years. Also, like him, she smoked cigarettes to her dying breath. I was glad to still have ‘the 40” at that time, so I could go up and spend extensive periods of time with mom and coordinate her care when she got sick. Over the past 5 years all of us kids made every attempt to bring some measures of happiness back to my mother without avail. She did occasionally show a glimmer of joy when her grandchildren visited but that was about it. I was with her at the doctor’s office when she finally went to the emergency room for a sore hip she had been suffering with for some time. I could almost see something what wrong when the E.R. doc came into the room. He started with saying "No, your hip isn't fractured", and "No you don't have a sprain"; "I have some bad news for you Mary……" He then explained that hip pain was due to the metastatic cancer that was in her hip bone. That cancer was also in every other bone and organ in her body. My mother had C.O.P.D anyways so shortness of breath was no stranger to her. We then made an appointment with an oncologist, but I knew how that visit was going to end. Naturally my mother wanted no treatment besides palliative care to keep her comfortable. God Bless "Hospice." I can't say it enough, that organization is the only one who can make an impossible, unbearable situation, bearable. I stayed up on the 40 pretty much off and on for the entire 6 months my mother had left to live. My wife was not able to join me up there as often as she might have liked because we were still sharing custody of our two girls with their father daily. But bless her for having to endure another extended separation from her husband for reasons beyond her control. I drew the only strength I could muster simply by talking to her and knowing she was there even if only for emotional support for the time being. It was a cloudy August afternoon when my daughter came in and woke me from a nap to the words "she's gone." While the thought of losing my "yakking buddy" hurt a lot, it was hard to be too sorrowful knowing that now, finally, she was where she belonged in this universe. That was next to her husband of 49 years. I managed to get them both cremated as per their wishes and their ashes are now resting together side by side in the same cemetery. This happened to be in the same cemetery that I had started my working "career" so many years before. It wasn't a year later, roughly 60 days after reaching his goal of living 100 years, my grandfather "Sid" passed away. Again, although I was saddened, I did get to spend a lot of time with him in his last few years being up on "the 40" Although my dad (Sidney's son) had passed away, I still had 3 uncles and an aunt who would take care of whatever arrangements were necessary for their father. When it comes to "estate" affairs, a "son" always outranks a "grandson", and I was thankful for that in this case. I did have some "pull" with the military, being a 100% disabled, combat Veteran and I would use that "pull" to make sure my grandfather received the recognition he deserved from Uncle Sam. When his Nation called him, despite having a wife and two small children, he answered the call and served in the United States Navy in the Pacific in WWII some 80 years earlier. I knew who supervised mortuary services in the Army in the State of Michigan and discovered that the same office did all branches of the military. I had a copy of grandpappy's DD214 since a few years before I had gotten him all the medals he had earned in the 1940's as well. A few phone calls later and I spoke to a Lieuteantnt Commander from the Navy (That's O-4 Major for you Army folks) telling me that the Navy would take care of everything. The Navy did a beautiful, professional, breathtaking job playing taps, presenting the flag from the top of the casket, neatly folded, to my Aunt and lowered grandpappy down for his eternal rest.

I had relieved all the memories of my youth I could possibly relive up north, and now both my parents and grandfather were gone. All the reasons I had for keeping "the 40" were dwindling down. Staying up there was expensive, lonely, and in the Wintertime could be dangerous. Michelle never, ever rushed me or pressured me to sell that property. Being smart as she is, she knew that this was something I had to arrive at that decision of on my own. It was now an easy decision. Members of my family that never made a lot of visits when I lived in Fowlerville, never made any more visits when I lived closer. I looked around the property, and now there were more memories of death and days gone by there than dreams for a bright future. Michelle never had the past memories of the area that I had experienced, and it was getting that each subsequent stay up there was an exercise in boredom for her. If I had asked her to move up there with me permanently, she would have, but I know she would have been extremely unhappy. And considering how much she had endured during two extended combat tours I was not about to ask her to sacrifice anymore. I had a dear friend who lived just down the dirt road from me up there, who just so happened to be a realtor as well. I took his professional advice, priced it accordingly, and put it on the market. Even with the time and money I had spent on everything, if I received anything even close to my asking price we would receive a tidy profit. A few days later my buddy put the good, old "For Sale" sign on the property. It didn't take very long, and some offers started rolling in. Like any property for sale, you must endure the first few ridiculously low-ball offers, the crazy "Oh I can pay you so much per month" offers and so on and so forth. I was not in a financial position to accept any of those, nor would I have even if I was able. That property was the main accumulation of my life savings, and I wanted nothing less than a nice check with six figures on it. I guess it's said "ask and you shall receive" because in a couple of weeks I had a buyer for my property, a real buyer, with cash. I originally thought I would have some hesitation selling this property as I did have so many great memories there. If I did, the guy who was buying the property helped me alleviate them. He was a "good old boy," younger than I was, and an avid hunter and outdoorsman. He was originally a country boy who had fallen into a sum of cash, literally. He had a small accident while working on a barge as a stevedore on the Mississippi River, and because of this he had a wad of cash to chase his dreams with. His dream was to have a nice piece of property to call his own to hunt coyotes and other predators on. That property was the answer to his dreams just as it had been mine 10 years or so before. If I had any doubt about him being an old "hillbilly" at heart, those ended when he asked me if I had any preference to denomination of bills that I wanted him to bring to the closing. He thought he had to bring cash to a closing, all six figures of it! My realtor and I laughed, "Uh, NO cash, just go to a bank and get a cashier's check, or other certified funds and you'll be just fine." And on a rainy, summer afternoon, just like that, he had the property of his dreams, and I was over $100,000 richer than I had ever been in my life. I was scared to death holding all of that money at first because I knew it would be the last time I would ever have that large of a sum of cash in my life and I wanted to use it wisely. It would need to last me a long time. In the end, it was all good.

Chapter 10: "On the Road"

It was time to settle down now and truly relax in my life. My older children were all well into their lives and I had been blessed with 4 grandchildren. I had often reflected that when I was at age 18, I thought I would never live to see the age of 30. As I have spoken to many men that are now my age, many of them had thought the same way. That just seems peculiar to me why an entire generation would have such a glum prophecy about themselves. I still have no idea why that is, but simply that I had the same idea as well at the time. I would have never imagined then that I would ever reach my 50's, be married and have children and grandchildren of my own. Regardless of my prophecies and expectations,, here I was, and it was okay. Another curious reflection is the fact that as a child you never really see your parents as "people." They are your parents, they know everything, they are capable of anything, and are responsible for everything. It is not until you are truly an adult that you begin to think of them as not your "parents" but regular people like everyone else, and you. They are people who have their own aspirations and dreams, wishes, good days and bad. This revelation does not mean a lot to you until you arrive at the point that you, and everyone else must eventually face. That is the point when your parents are reaching the end of their mortal days. It is only then when you truly see them as "people", they speak to you as "people" and if you've done everything right over the years, they are also your friends. I have made this transition at both ends. I had the time to spend with my parents during their last days to share their feelings, hopes, dreams and reflections as they made their big "transition" I have to remember that my children are at the point where they are beginning to see me as a "person" as well. I think I must have done something right though because even with this fact, we all still get along and are able to have chats and laughs like friends.

All was progressing well, and Michelle and I were settling nicely in our home in Fowlerville. Everything seemed to be going the way it was supposed to for a guy now in "retirement." Our house was great, and we even began to have a little social life. She was never the most social person to begin with. That quality is the total opposite of how I am and probably one of the things that attracted us to each other. Finally, after over a decade together now, we started to "rub off" on each other a bit. My wife, once quiet and introverted, no longer has any trouble in conversation. She had made a few friends of her own along the way, and enjoyed the same friends that I had. I, on the other hand, learned not to wear my heart on my sleeve quite so much. In my older years, I finally took the extra time to choose my words more wisely. I also make a habit now of re-reading an e-mail before I just hit the "Send" button. There are a lot of benefits to being retired at an earlier age. I remembered talking with Ron just when I first retired and he had a word of "warning" for me.

He said, "This is great now, but you wait in two or three years you are going to be so bored." He was wrong then, and now 9 years later is still wrong. In fact, many, many, times I have thought to myself, "How did I ever get anything done when I was working 40 plus hours a week?" I think the part I enjoyed the most was getting to spend the extra time watching my two last girls grow up. It was finally looking like I was going to be in at least some of my children's lives from their start all the way into adulthood. It was surprising how much of the bullshit that I learned in High School, stuff that I was so certain I would NEVER use again, that would come back to haunt me. I was surprised how much of this I was able to regurgitate when it came time to help the girls with their homework. School kids these days have it so much easier than I did back when. If I had had the resources for learning that these kids have, my life would have been a lot easier. I asked the girls if they realized that they literally have the Library of Congress in their pockets to use for reference? I had to do my schoolwork the old-fashioned way, using books and microfiche machine. You know you're getting old when you must explain to your kids what a microfiche even is. The look on their faces, when you describe a television set which had no color screen, weighed a ton, and then only got 13 channels or less is priceless! To even watch those 13 or so channels "Rabbit Ears" and tin foil were usually required. Only gentle readers in my age bracket or older will have any idea of what I am referring to.

I was enjoying all the time with my other older kids as well as with "their" kids. It is a great feeling when they call you to ask you some parenting questions or your ideas. I have always believed that being a parent is truly the ticket to immortality. It is nothing physical you will leave on this planet that you will be remembered by, but the stories that are passed from generation to generation about you. I still fondly remember my great-grandfather sitting on the park bench in his back yard on Bittner Street so many years ago in Reed City. You knew he had done this hundreds of times because when he walked out the back door of the house you could see all the walnut trees surrounding the back yard start to shake with life. All the squirrels and chipmunks knew something that I did not know at first. In the satchel my great-grandfather carried were unsalted peanuts still in their shells. From the canopies of the trees, down the large trunks, and quickly across the lawn all creatures great and small would come. They would climb the sides of the bench, his shins and any other method they could, to be handed a peanut by "great-grandpappy." I could have sat and watched for hours at the dexterity those furry little creatures had to use to get at those peanuts. The only real danger involved in this activity was if you were a woman. That was because that one of these squirrels or chipmunks could get stuck in your purse as they would go in there looking for peanuts as well. This activity became well known to the other Reed City residents and eventually there was even an article written up about it with a photo in the local newspaper "The Osceola County Herald."

I found many ways to occupy my time from day to day and create my own memories. One nice thing about retirement is that it gives you the opportunity to rediscover passions that you may have had to give up due to work. It was time for me to find some of those as well. One of those was fishing. I always had loved fishing, but when I was in my “career” years, time for fishing was a luxury I rarely had. I always tried to take a few days off each April to spend the weekend camping up North with my friends for what we referred to as “Trout Camp”. What is “Trout Camp?” you may ask? Why it’s the same as “Deer Camp” sitting around swilling booze around a campfire with your friends awaiting midnight on the last Saturday of April instead of the 15th of November. That April day is the opening day for the regular trout fishing season in Michigan. Just exchange the fishing poles for deer rifles and change the calendar to the 15th of November. From a distance, an “outsider” would never know the difference. I no longer had to wait for anything but the season to do my fishing. Would have always said for years “I am a trout fisherman”, but that was all about to change. My buddy from the 1462nd in Howell had a nice house in Brighton which was on a lake. This lake would be the one that changed me from trout fisherman to bass fisherman. Trout are pretty simple creatures, if you can get something they eat in front of them, they take a bite and reel them in. Bass are a lot more finicky, their feeding patterns and diet changes with each season and to be successful you have to know what the “flavor of the month” is. In addition, trout you just yank right out of the river, at least anything 15-16” or less. Bass are solid muscle, swimming in a lake, and are nearly the top predators as far as fish are concerned. If you hook on to a 2-7# bass, there is no “yanking” it out of the lake. Trout are like the card game “poker”, you can only catch what fish the river and day may send your way. The bass species, with enough skill, knowledge and expertise can be MADE to bite virtually year-round. I loved the challenge and was successful at it. My buddy also had a pontoon boat for which to ply the bass on his lake, and it was a great morning when 3 or 4 of us “Veterans” (both fishing and military) could get together on that pontoon and spend the morning landing some bass. On especially good Saturdays our fishing mornings would end up around a backyard fire and more alcoholic beverages in the evening.

Another old passion I had a chance to revive was my love of coin collecting. I can't even remember what got me started back into that hobby, but some cool things had happened since I stopped collecting probably 40 years earlier. The first, and most important thing was that money needed for a collection wasn't anywhere near the hurdle to obtain now than it was when I was 12 years old. I did make a small attempt at going back into my numismatic hobby around 15 years ago when I was married to Mary. I did acquire some really nice specimens then as well. I remember a couple of them specifically. I had an 1803 Silver Dollar that was in fine condition. How could anyone hold a coin like that and wonder if it wasn't in Thomas Jeffersons pocket, or where it had been over the last 200 plus years? I picked one coin up simply because I remembered as a kid what it must be like to own a piece like that. The coin was a 1921 Saint Gaudens Double Eagle $20 gold piece. I know it felt great in your hand, was truly beautiful to behold, and was a good way to keep $400 or so tucked safely away. I would come to remember that $400 when I started collecting again. It just occurred to me, that in addition to a wife, the time with my daughter, my first house in Fowlerville, the feeling in my right hand, most of my hearing, a couple of vertebra in my neck, and the arthritis I now have that I can add this modest coin collection to the "Things 9/11 cost me." Mary sold my collection upon my first departure to Iraq. Not without my consent, I wanted to make sure she had no financial difficulties in my absence. Like everything else in my past, I put those memories where they belonged, in the past. I did start my collecting again and it didn't take long until I had accumulated far more specimens than I ever had before in my life. I was looking to gather complete sets of type coins and did a pretty good job, Finally, it was safe to say, I had complete sets of every quarter, dimes, nickels and pennies from the year 1900 on. I had every half dollar from 1964 to this very day and almost every silver dollar from 1878 until they stopped making the "real" ones in 1999. I never could bring myself to get interested in those Sacajawea dollars as they are just a damn ugly coin. I was able to do things as a coin collector that I could never do in the past. My limitations of time and finances were no longer the hindrances they had once been. I joined our local coin club, and soon enough ended up being the secretary. I was to learn more about coins with this group that I had in the past. I was also able to make an entirely new set of friends who shared this same passion as I. It was nice being able to hold specific coins, the 1909S-VDB Lincoln Cent for example, which earlier in my life were simply beyond my means. There is one "key date" coin that I never did get into any of my collections, the 1916D "Mercury Dime." For reasons beyond any of our understanding this one coins price had just gone through the proverbial roof and was staying right there. A specimen in "Almost good" condition (literally worm flat and barely legible) carried a value of around $1000. I could afford one, but one thing I prided myself on was that every specimen in my collection was pleasing to the eye. An "AG Almost Good" specimen is most certainly not pleasing to the eye. Not my discerning eye anyway.

Another thing my "time" now allowed me to do was a lot more travel. This was one of two things my lovely wife and I are passionate about. The other thing is motorcycling. It was a beautiful thing having two interests that go together like peanut butter and jelly! I could write an entire novel about my experiences on a motorcycle. Hell, I could write a novel about motorcycles themselves as I have owned so many different ones in my life. My friends referred to me as the "bike whore" since about every three to five years it was time to trade my current ride in on the newest mode. Unlike many motorcyclists, I was not by any standard, "brand loyal." My choice of brand, type, or style of, motorcycle was entirely determined by what caught my eye at the time. It is safe to say I have owned dozens of motorcycles over the years. I've had a lot of good times on all of them. There are some things I do remember as particular "highlights" to my motorcycling life. One of which was my first ride on a Harley Davidson. Of all the motorcycles I had previously owned, one that I had never was the good old Harley Davidson. They were simply, financially, beyond my reach. My father-in-law at the time, Mary's father, found himself in the middle of one of those man 'midlife crisis." One of his personal side effects of this syndrome was his desire to start riding a motorcycle again after decades. He was a man of wealth at the time and purchased him a beautiful, virtually new, forest green, metal flake, Harley Davidson "Road King." He did have enough sense to realize that after such a long pause from being on two wheels he may not want to drive the 60 miles from where he purchased it at to his home. Those 60 miles just so happened to be among the most heavily travelled roads in the entire state of Michigan. He proceeded to call me up for a favor. "Can you go down and pick this bike up for me and bring it to my house so I can practice on these side roads for a while?" Gee, let me think that over, YES. So, he picked me up and we went to where his lovely new motorcycle was waiting for me to "pop its cherry" for him. It was the most beautiful thing I had ever seen to date on two wheels. I climbed on, fired it up, and away I went. I soon discovered that everything I had heard about Harley Davidson (H.D.) regarding speed, torque and handling were all true. It really was a completely different ride from anything else I had ever been on. It truly was “love at first feel” (to quote AC/DC) and I had to have one. Within two weeks I purchased my own H.D. a barely used H.D. Electroglide. The Electroglide is basically the Road King with all the extra bags on it, nothing more. The dealership was in Thiensville Wisconsin, and I took the greyhound bus to get there. I drove that bike from Wisconsin to St Ignace Michigan along the Lake Michigan and Lake Superior shoreline. If you have never seen this area, much like the coast of California, it truly is one of the most beautiful places on earth. The only drawback to that lovely ride was the fact that it was Memorial Day weekend. To the rest of the civilized world, Memorial Day is the start of the summer season. That does not apply to the U.P. During my 14-hour trip the temperature was between 31 degrees and 52 degrees. When you add the 50-70 MPH windchill onto that since I was on a motorcycle, you get the picture. I still loved every freezing moment of that trip. I've had so many fabulous rides over the years it would be impossible to write them all, but a couple really are worth mentioning. Another incredible ride was across the Chesapeake Bay Bridge between Maryland and Delaware. While I was stationed at Ft. Eustis Virginia, I wanted to take a weekend and visit my cousins who lived in Dover. To get there you must cross the bridge. Now the word “bridge” does not really do this stretch of road justice. I want to say it is a 5- or 6-mile stretch of intermittent bridges and tunnels which cross the Chesapeake Bay and take you to the Delaware state line. The first mile or two wasn't bad, the bridge was solid, and I could use the right lane which was paved all the way across and not heavy grate like the left lane. The first tunnel wasn't bad either, maybe only a couple of hundred yards long. Well, the bridges got longer and completely covered with grate, the tunnels got longer as did the slope of the road going into and coming out of the tunnels. In addition, traffic was picking up significantly and doesn't slow down for shit. About a third of the way across this thing, I began to see very dark clouds and lightning strikes over on the Delaware side. One thing about driving on a span like this, whether in a car or motorcycle, is that once you are on it, you are committed to get all the way across. By the time I was 3/4ths of the way across the rain started and by the time I hit Delaware I was caught in an absolute deluge. Although I was VERY happy to have solid ground underneath my wheels, it was raining so hard that I could not see, and water began flooding the street. Now I have ridden in pretty much every type of weather you can imagine, but even I have my limits. It was time for me to pull the bike over for a little while. No sooner had I pulled the bike under the cover of an overpass, (along with 20 other motorcyclists who felt the same way about riding in that type of environment) than the storm blew over, the sun came out, and the temperature went back into the mid 80's.

For most of the years Michelle and I were together, she rode on the back of my bike as my trusted "co-pilot." One year, in the continuing search for her perfect Christmas present, I decided to ask her if she thought she might like to drive a motorcycle. I was very surprised when she said that she may be interested in giving it a try. I purchased the H.D. "riders academy" training course and for the following 4 days Michelle went on a motorcycle. A couple of great things about these courses, firstly, you ride THEIR motorcycles, so the inevitable dings and scratches are not happening to your motorcycle. Secondly, the infinite patience that is required to teach someone how to drive any machine with essentially a "standard" transmission. I simply do not possess that kind of patience and why let a little thing like that cause ripples in your marital "pool of harmony?" She passed the course with flying colors and was riding like a pro in no time. Well naturally, now that she was an official driver, we wanted to get her own bike. We found her a beautiful Indian "Scout" and it was a perfect match to the Indian "Chief" I was driving at the time. It was neat to see someone new into motorcycling being as excited about it as I was many years ago after my first few rides. More than a few nights she would come home and say, "I had a shitty day, I'm just going to go for a ride." She gets it and understands that "in the wind" feeling I've always had now. From that moment forward we were two bikers instead of one! Motorcyclists are a close-knit group and always have been. It is an unwritten rule that when you pass another cyclist on the road, you just naturally wave at them. Every group of people who share a common passion just naturally will flock together and great social events occur. Motorcyclists are no different and now that Michelle was officially a biker, these social events took a new meaning for her. One of the annual social events we used to enjoy each time was the Sturgis toy run. Sturgis Michigan that is, not the Sturgis of motorcycling pilgrimage fame in South Dakota. Usually around the 3rd week of July every year the Boys and Girls club of Southern Michigan hosts this event. It was an entire weekend of riding, camping, drinking, naked, biker fun! The very first time Michelle pulled into the farmers field with me, the same field where the event was always held, to find our parking spot she got her first clue as to what kind of weekend it would be. Attached to a motorcycle next to us was a small trailer with a patch of astroturf on it, complete with a vertical stripper pole. Sure enough, in a few hours there was a line of scooter tramps waiting to impress the crowds with their dancing prowess. Or more accurately lack thereof, but everyone loves a good excuse to strip their clothes off in public I guess. Although this was the first year that Michelle attended this event, I had attended for quite a few years before that and made some of the locals as friends. It was nice to have friends in "low places" I suppose, and it was the one chance each year I got to catch up with them. The schedule was always the same. Friday nights were set up, drink, stay up until the band stops playing at 11 pm, then head back to your campsite and keep partying until you passed out or daylight arrived. Saturday started with everyone making a forage for breakfast, maybe a few beers, and then every biker in the place lines up for the "toy run." All 3 or 4 thousand "bikers" would then embark on a 50 or so mile trip through the beautiful St Joseph River valley area for a couple hours. Once everyone returned safely to the campground the real party began. This was because the event also provided free beer! Saturday night ended up much like Friday night did, and suddenly Sunday morning was upon you. Early Sunday morning, bleary eyed and hungover, everyone packed their tents and bags and headed back to their homes and reality. For 362 days everyone had to be doctors, lawyers, mechanics and janitors, but for 3 days each year you could live the "biker lifestyle" and proverbially "let it all hang out." I honestly could not think of better therapy for anyone. We did attend a lot of these types of events but honestly, despite a different band and venue, the events were very similar. There is one exception to this rule though. I mentioned the location of Sturgis South Dakota as it is just such a pilgrimage for bikers. Much like Christians flock to Jerusalem, or Muslims to Mecca, for one hot August week each year, thousands of motorcyclists descend on this small town in the Black Hills region named Sturgis. It would almost be a travesty if I had never gone to this event at least once. So, in 2013 my honey and I threw the bike on the back of a U-Haul trailer I rented and headed west. Now there is always a small group of bikers that will say "unless you ride your motorcycle to Sturgis it doesn't count." Fuck them, we passed through some of the fiercest thunderstorms, hail and all, a couple of times we were on the way there. We just grinned as we watched those poor bastards get hammered by the weather on the highways. No regrets whatsoever as to us trailering the bike. Once we arrived there we discovered that it really did live up to the hype I had heard about it. We had rented a "tent site" at Glencoe resort for the week. A few things you quickly discover at Sturgis. The first will most certainly be that if there is a way they can reach into your wallet legally, they are doing it. Nothing is free or inexpensive. I think our "tent site" was almost $500 for the week and this is for a campsite with no electricity, water or sewer. You might also think that renting that campsite would allow you to come and go into the campground to get to your tent. You would be thinking wrong; each tent site must also be purchased with a 'Wristband" that has to be worn by each person coming into the campground. Those cost $175 each additionally as well. Long story short, that little campsite for my two-man pup tent and Michelle and I was almost $1000. It was something to do if only once though. I imagine Jerusalem and Mecca are the much same during their pilgrimage weeks. We had a great week though as we saw and did many things that we will probably never get to do again. The motorcycle riding in the Black

Hills area is breathtaking and there are tons of historical things to see. The old, wild west towns of Deadwood and Lead are close by, and the "Badlands loop" off I-90 is a must see. Also, if you managed to drive the 400 miles across South Dakota passing by 75 or so billboards that say "Only xxx miles to Wall Drug" you are a better person than I. For what it is worth, the scenery, history and block wide strip mall that composes "Wall Drug" is worth the stop. Many times, I reflected upon how fortunate I was and how everything was progressing just the way it should have. I should have realized that those are the times when things can only go one way, bad.

Bad was going to be the understatement of my life. One of my favorite holidays used to be Halloween. I loved Halloween even more as an adult as I did as a child I think. I never was that much of a candy lover, and walking around in the dark during what was usually shitty weather night was never my idea of fun. As a grownup it was great. Some of my best adult Halloween nights were from the years before when I lived in Fowlerville. Mary would take our daughter around trick-or-treating, and it was then my responsibility to entertain the kids that came to our door. I was passionate about that as well. Nothing I have always hated more were the "grown-ups" who would make the extra effort to turn all their lights off and close their blinds on Halloween night rather than hand candy out to the kids. I wonder how they would have felt as children if everyone in the neighborhood they grew up in did that to them. I tried to tell myself that "maybe they just don't have the money for candy" or truly are "away for the evening" even though in most cases I realized I was fooling myself. Apparently I was fooling myself on one key issue in my life as well. That issue was the fact that my son Jonathan was healthy and well. Jonathan always marched to a different tune than you might say. When he was young and a boy and boys liked to do things like go hunting, or exploring, camping his idea of entertainment was different. He was an artist as much as anything, he made it perfectly clear rather than go out ice fishing; "Hmmm sit on the ice, in freezing weather, to cut a hole in the lake hoping I can catch a fish, OR sitting here in the cabin relaxing to music looking out the window over a hot cup of coffee, let me think that over" he would rather stay in. It had nothing to do with laziness either, he could be described as many things but never lazy. He was the quite the opposite, always driven to be successful. His only flaw was that he always associated success with money. From an early age he had decided that he wanted to be "rich.". Even though I have never had a lot of money, I personally have always known I was "wealthy." A harsh reality in life that he simply refused to accept was that unless you are born into money, it is rare that you will ever legally earn enough to be financially wealthy. I tried explaining this to him numerous times, but he refused to accept it. And it wasn't as though he went without life's basic needs either. And I had no problem helping him out financially if he was in a pinch from time to time. As he grew older, he tried numerous schemes, plans, and ideas to "hit the jackpot" but never found the success and money he was always in search for. To this very day I do not understand his obsession with being "rich." No one in my family was financially wealthy, nor did we put much stock in the pursuit of wealth. He did have some other health problems growing up. He was plagued with dental problems like his mother, and poor guy had a toothache more times than I care to remember. The government seems to think dental care, like optical, is simply an unnecessary luxury because no one on any kind of government health insurance program has any coverage in either of these. On more than a few occasions I brought him down to stay with me and paid for emergency dental work for the poor guy just to give him some relief. As a teenager he began to have headaches and upon doing an x-ray, it was discovered that he had a mass in the back of his head. This was diagnosed as histiocytoma X, a fairly rare but risky type of tumor that needed to be removed. So, Jon underwent brain surgery and had a 2" x 2" chunk of his skull removed with the mass that was situated in the dura of his brain. A ceramic plate was installed, and 4 screws held that in place. As the mass was attached to the dura lining it was felt that he should have some radiation therapy to the area to further reduce any risk of recurrence. He seemed to get through that fine and had no further issues. Jonathan was also a homosexual.

A lot of folks in my inner circle always seemed, for reasons unknown to me, that this would cause a huge rift between me and my son. It reality it was just the opposite. The only thing I wanted for my son was the same thing that every parent wants for their child. That is for them to just be happy. With the Good Lord as my witness, I never judged or criticized him over his sexual orientation. I have always worked to try to be as good a Christian in my life as I can be. Yes, it does say in the Bible that the Lord abhors such behavior, it also says that no one should work on Sunday or eat creatures that crawl along the bottom of the sea. I know that a lot of so called "righteous and mighty" religious people sure like to poke fingers and think, "those people are condemned to burn." I remember a couple of passages myself in the Bible as well. One phrase comes to mind specifically in regard to those folks "Judge not, lest thee be judged." Another verse I remember well is "All sin is created equal in the eye of the Lord." Jonathan was also a person of faith and at one time in his early teens he also briefly looked into attending the seminary after he graduated high school in order to become a Catholic priest. That dream of his just went by the wayside like so many dreams before and after it. Even if the dream of being a priest passed him by, his faith in the Lord and wanting to do right by him never did. A lot of uneducated folks have a lot of opinions about homosexuality. Their opinions can only be as fact based as any opinion of mine could be on speaking of what it is like to be a black man. Since I am not one, I will never truly understand what it is like to be one. Same goes for homosexuality. Nothing on earth makes me angrier than to hear one of these idiots spout off with "Oh it's a matter of choice, they can choose NOT to be gay." That makes no more sense than asking THEM to NOT be heterosexual, I also know that if it were in fact a choice, my son would have chosen not to be gay. I believe when he looked in the mirror he hated what he saw and believed the Lord did too. I always tried the best I could to give him any extra love and support I could in this regard. It truly did not make any difference to me; I just wanted him to be happy.

We did have a good, open relationship as he grew into adulthood. Now he was my friend as well as my only son. He dated and went through a few "significant others," but finally found a nice guy and they shared a life together for over seven years. A lot of people would tell me that he was struggling emotionally, but as a father what could I do? I made a point of staying in touch with him as best I could and try to always get together for some laughs and a meal. He and his husband moved down to

Ypsilanti Michigan, and he enrolled at Eastern Michigan University. They found a small apartment and he was hired as the building manager, so he could earn his rent. He really seemed to enjoy this and worked hard to try to get through school. I don't think he ever really did well as far as academically. He did get involved with the EMU theater group though and it was as happy as I ever saw him. For reasons unknown to me, school just did not work out for him, and he and my son-in-law moved back up North to be closer to their families. I don't believe he liked it that much up North, but he was closer to his mother and grandmother. He did manage to land a good job at Reed City Glass with his sister. As the years rolled on. I knew that he was using marijuana and drank some beer but I guess I didn't know to what extent. I did find out later that he was a chronic marijuana user and alcoholic by most standards.

If you would have asked anyone in America what the greatest crisis we ever faced as a Nation at that time, certainly "9/11" would have been their reply. 9/11 would not hold a candle to the bullshit that was just about to roll down the proverbial pipe. We began to see little blurbs on the news about people becoming sick and dying in China. This wasn't necessarily a new development since virtually every shitty flu in history began in China. What was a new development was how many body bags were being filled over there. It was also a new development when they started showing pictures on CNN (Communist News Network in my book) where China was quarantining entire provinces. The videos of sprawling suburban areas completely devoid of traffic and people reminded me of some bad zombie movies. It didn't take long until the pathogenic organism was discovered and it was most certainly not the flu. A new term was about to be burned into the American lexicon, "Covid-19." That was short from Coronavirus 2019. Now Coronaviruses are nothing new, in fact they are the little bastards responsible for what we have always called the "common cold." There was nothing common about this one though. It was causing deaths like the S.A.R.S virus before it, and some very peculiar symptoms like frontal headaches and the loss of the senses of taste and smell for weeks on end. This virus was a "political football" even before it hit the shores of the United States. President Donald Trump, wanted to completely (albeit temporarily) seal the border between the United States and China. The Democratic legislators had a fit over that, not so much because it may or may not have been prudent to do so, but simply because the idea came from the G.O.P (Grand Old Party, nickname for the Republican Party). It wasn't long and the daily, infected people numbers being reported on the news were not only coming from provinces in China, but cities along the west coast of America as well. Covid 19 had made its way to America. As far as I am concerned America died the day that covid hit the shore. Everything that I fought for in the military, principles like freedom, life, liberty and the pursuit of happiness, went right out the window in the name of "national emergency." I discovered, much to my dismay, establishments like the A.D.A. (Americans with Disabilities Act), and H.I.P.P.A. (Health Information Protection and Privacy Act) had clauses written into them stating that "If the governor of a state determines there is a health or statewide emergency, this emergency will take precedence over these acts." And every governor rushed to declare a "Statewide Emergency" essentially sidelining their entire legislative body giving them complete autonomy to do whatever they wished in the name of "public safety." Despite the many, many warnings great American thinkers like Thomas Jefferson, Benjamin Franklin and the like wrote to warn us about throwing our cherished institutions, like freedom of choice ,out the window for any reason, public paranoia overrode them as well. It became a battle as to what politician could claim to be the quarantine "champion" in the U.S. At first the "Nazi" who was warming the governors' seat in Michigan ordered people to remain in their homes except for emergencies like groceries and the like. Mask wearing, regardless of ability or health risks to individuals with C.O.P.D or vocal cord damage like me, was mandated. All businesses were ordered to close, and even the ones that sold essentials were mandated as to what they could or could not sell. It was ludicrous, stores were told they could not sell seeds for their gardens, but the new marijuana dispensaries were allowed to remain open. At first all the public access sites to Michigan's great outdoors were all closed. Then they were re-opened to boats, but no boats equipped with motors. Childrens playgrounds had things like the swing sets, slides and other play equipment wrapped with yellow police "Caution" tape so as to prevent the kids from using the playground. The stupidity just grew exponentially as the public grew more and more afraid.

This was the social environment on Halloween night in 2020. I was pretty upbeat to begin with as I had put a sign out in my front yard first thing on Halloween morning that my house WILL be open for trick or treating that evening. I began to see other people setting up the holiday evening for the kids as well. The evening started off very well and we were getting a lot of kids at my door in Fowlerville in their costumes. This never fails to make me smile. The numbers of kids may have been down a little bit that year, but surprisingly not too much. As the crowds wound down, I called my buddy on the phone just to shoot the shit and see how many trick-or-treaters had shown up at his door that evening. In hindsight, as many of us have probably thought, I would have loved to have had a crystal ball at that very moment. At least by 10 pm or so that Halloween night when I went to bed, it was with a smile on my face and a hopeful feeling that everything may end up and be ok after all. That feeling would last only a few hours and be torn from me in the most horrible means I can even describe.

My dogs started barking like hell in the middle of the night. Now they do bark on occasion, but only for a minute or two as they think they hear some "hoojoo boogieman" (more likely rabbit or cat) in the backyard. This time was different, their barking not only continued, but increased in volume until my eyes started to flicker. I also then heard the frantic knocking on my front door. Just like anyone else, my first thought was "What in the fuck is going on at 2:30 in the morning?" I threw my robe on and went to the front door. I turned the porch light on and saw my oldest daughter sobbing furiously with her husband. If I wasn't wondering "What in the fuck" before, I certainly was now. I opened the door and asked her "What's the matter honey?" It was then after a moment's hesitation she uttered a sentence no parent ever should have to hear. "Jonathan hung himself last night." I am lost now trying to figure out how to write what my emotions were at that very moment. I know I wanted to say "Where is he at? Is he alright?" Your brain does not immediately register that the phrase "Hung himself" automatically implies, he is most certainly NOT alright. It takes a few moments before it slowly starts to occur to you that he is actually dead. Then the questions want to start flowing out, "How?" "Why?" "Where?" "Accident?" but nothing will come out of your mouth. Especially when you realize that none of those questions really matter anymore anyway. I learned that another of life's rumors turned out to be true at that moment. Just like the time I fractured my head on the oil rigs and truly saw "stars" flying around my head, this time I felt the physical "punch in the gut" So there I stood, mind spinning, stomach hurting and feeling truly lost. Surprisingly, no tears immediately came. It's not like they weren't there, it was just a long emotional inventory that was going to be required before I could let them go.

Until that point in my life, I truly had thought I had experienced the worst things life could throw at a person. I have been in combat, had seen shattered bodies lying on roadsides, brains and guts sprayed on inside of blasted vehicles. Nothing, nothing compared to the feelings I had as the realization that my son had taken his own life began to soak in. Just like anyone else passing, that time feels like a whirlwind as there are arrangements that must be made. His body was sent to the Pruitt-Livingston Funeral Home in Reed City. This place was where virtually every one of his family members that had proceeded him had gone. Considering it wasn't even two years earlier my friend and undertaker there, Faron, had helped our family with the arrangements for my mother. He was almost like family in that strange sort of way and at least I felt like someone I knew was taking care of my boy. By all reports his death was clearly a suicide and the state would not require an autopsy. At the time, none of us particularly wanted to order one either. I think we all felt like life had violated him enough by this point and could not bring ourselves to think of him being carved up on the cold, steel table. In hindsight, it may have brought the comfort of some answers if we would could found out, like maybe his brain tumor had returned causing him to react in that way. At the end of the day, it really didn't matter as nothing was going to bring him back to us. Starting with Faron himself, no one really knows what to say to you when your loved one commits suicide. You hear plenty of the compulsory "I'm sorry for your loss" but can always see the caution in people's faces when they say it. It was one of many times I was very thankful for my military friends. My daughter and her husband were not able to stay with us in Fowlerville that All Saints Day, but it was only a couple hours after they left when two of my "battle buddies" were at my door. How they had heard what happened was beyond me, but I was very happy to see them. They immediately made sure I was as okay as I could be and assured me that I would have nothing to worry about in Fowlerville at my house while I spent what time was necessary up North. Their appearance and support meant (and still always means) more to me than they will ever know. And although they were there for me, as well and including my "brother from another mother" Ron who would always have an open door for me. Even with all of them there by my side, I truly do not think I would have survived if it weren't for my wife Michelle. Poor girl, I know not only was she heartbroken; Jonathan had been in her life for the 14 years we had been married, but she felt so bad for me and simply did not know what to do to make my pain go away. There was nothing she could do, and she knew it. With every rotten thing that had happened to me in my life I always turned it around and tried to make something good come of it. Like the 30 days I spent in jail, I used that experience as the impetus to turn my life around and go to college. After 9/11 I rejoined the Army and was part of getting America a little "payback." Even after everything good that was America died from Covid-19, I tried to be a beacon for freedom even if my protests and lessons mostly fell on deaf ears. But this, this "rotten thing", I could not twist any good whatsoever from it. There was maybe one thing. Although I could not turn back the hands of time and take back all the horrible shit I had done to Lisa in the years we had been married so long ago, this did give me a proper opportunity to apologize correctly to her. And while sobbing away, I did let her know how truly sorry I was for the way I acted and treated her and that she deserved so much better. For the first time in over 30 years, I like to think it gave her some comfort to know that I recognized what an asshole I had been and suffered myself because of it. I can only hope it would give her some comfort in the years to come, especially in the circumstance of just having lost her only son as well. According to Jon's husband, one thing he always specified that he did not want to happen and that was to be cremated should something happen to him. This placed his husband in a particular predicament. Of course, like all suicides, he did not obviously think of all of us who would have to take care of these arrangements. He died, like so many in my family did, virtually broke. This left the burden of expense to his husband, and it was important to him (his husband) that his last wish to be buried was honored. Of course, we wanted to help him achieve this as best we could to maybe give him some tiny bit of comfort. Unfortunately, this was going to cost approximately $10,000 of which he had none. We were forced to have his husband solicit for funds via the new trend of a "Go Fund Me" account. And although no one in our immediate family could be called "people of means" we were not penniless. Monetarily, between what we could gather together, as well as that "Go Fund Me" account, we were able to give Jon the kind of funeral service that he had indicated he wanted. My only son was laid to rest on a cold, windy, but sunny November day in the same cemetery that 6 generations of his family before him were laid to rest in. Just like I told Jonathan before he was lowered in the ground, I knew we would have to part someday, but never, NEVER like this. And just like that, my son was gone. The one thing that wasn't gone, and will never be gone, just like every suicide, are the unanswered questions. Well those and the dozens of broken hearts never to be mended, and the piece of a father's heart never to be replaced. His oldest sister purchased him a beautiful marker; he would be very happy to see it. I have been to the cemetery and his grave only once, to say my final goodbye. As far as I am concerned, just like my parents and grandparents, there is nothing remaining of them up there in the ground anyway. Just like in the movie "Forrest Gump" "That is all I have to say about that."

The years continued to move on and life in Fowlerville was as nice as any small-town life could be. My kids all grew and graduated and had families of their own. The youngest two girls had finally graduated high school themselves and were moving on with their lives. I had fallen into a decent routine of fishing, golfing and partying with my friends in the area. Although my heartache was still there, it was easier to deal with this routine and of course time. While all the kids now went their separate ways and chased their hopes and dreams, life was winding down for Michelle and I. Michelle started to get bored and she felt like life was passing us by. The visits to and from the kids and grandkids became fewer and fewer as they grew, and their schedules filled. Although we were financially secure, Michelle took a job simply for "something to do." The extra money was a godsend though as we were paying half of the tuition for the two youngest girls community college tuition. While Michelle worked, I took pride in being the best "house husband" I could be. While she went to work and drew a paycheck, as far as I was concerned, she deserved to come home to a clean house and hot meal. I did my best to make sure my end of the "deal" was kept. Another of the hobbies I began to look forward to eagerly was ice fishing each year. It was the only thing I could do to beat the doldrums of the days, weeks and months of Michigan's brutally cold Winters. It took a lot more effort than it ever had to try to keep a positive outlook on life, and freezing assed, grey weather lasting for weeks on end did not help. I have always heard the secret to keeping your sanity in places that have four seasons is to find something you like to do specifically in each of the seasons. That meant in Michigan for 4 months you had better enjoy things like skiing, snowmobiling, cross-country skiing, ice fishing and so on. Of all these things now, the only one I could even stand or really physically even do was ice fish. As I recall, even as a kid I did not like a lot of that shit. Had a few good times on a snowmobile. Went skiing a few times, Went cross country skiing more than a few times. Even then, I did those activities simply because there was nothing else to do rather than really liking them. I guess I just can't stand to feel cold. I never minded the heat so much. Even in Iraq, when it would approach 120 degrees, I would rather ten-fold been in that temperature and environment than in 40 below zero. It was during one of these particularly cold weekends I decided to go up North with Ron and the "guys" and spend a weekend on the lake ice fishing. We went to a lake

I had never been to before called Portage Lake in the upper Northwest corner of the lower peninsula. My friend and classmate from P.R.H.S. had a home an hour or so south of there so we always had a warm place to lay our heads. The fellowship, for me, was more important and entertaining than fishing ever was on these adventures. I've always thought it was peculiar how no matter how many years and miles had gone by since our P.R.H.S. days, when we all got a chance to get together it seemed just like yesterday. Memories I had long since filed in the 'cold case" area in my head always came right back to the surface. I guess that is a common thing with all people though. Another of those "déjà vu" moments always occurred when I would go to parent teacher conferences at the girls' schools. Something about stepping into an elementary school classroom just makes the senses reel, and the fond memories come back as well. This particular fishing weekend, the weather was extremely poor and the fishing turned out to be poor as well. At least in my older years I was now able to afford some of the basic comforts which made ice fishing at least tolerable. When we were kids we would all go ice fishing armed with the bare necessities to catch some fish. One of those was a large metal pole referred to as a "spud." To catch fish through the ice you must punch a hole through the ice. This is what the "spud" was for, it was a large, heavy iron rod 4-6' tall with a chunk of flat steel welded to the bottom of it. This chunk of flat steel was honed to a sharp edge and smart people even attached a rope to a hole drilled through the top of the spud. More than a few "spuds" lie at the bottom of Michigan lakes because of the not so smart people who did not attach a rope only to have the spud slip out of their hands when they finally burst through the ice to the water below. Once your hole is created, you simply drop your fishing line with bait into the hole and wait for the fish. You could upend the bucket you carried your equipment out on to the ice with for a "seat" and there you would sit. It really doesn't matter how much clothing you put on, when you're sitting on a bucket, in the elements, on a block of ice, you are going to get cold. We did not have to do this anymore though. We came equipped with an auger for drilling holes instead of spudding and an ice shanty to sit inside of. When you take a two-person tent and place it on the top of a frozen lake over a hole in the ice it is no longer referred to as a tent but an "ice shanty." Ice shanties have a lot of benefits that go beyond simple shelter and warmth. One was that you could actually talk to the person beside you and not have to scream over the howling wind. You also had a nice place to put your drinks and equipment without having to worry about everything being blown across the ice with the first gust of wind. If you are wondering why I am going into detail about ice fishing, like anybody gives a fuck, it is because it was in this environment that the epiphany that would change my life was about to occur. I was sitting having a few cocktails with my buddy Daryl inside the shanty watching our poles for the fish to bite. I put a small "spoon" on the end of my line just to try something different and see if I would have any luck. The best part about Portage Lake was that, due to the fact it was essentially a bay to Lake Michigan, the water was crystal clear and you could easily see to a depth of 20 or 30 feet into the lake. Suddenly my ice fishing pole bent way over and I had a fish on the line. A very large fish that is. Now being a bay of Lake Michigan the species of what could be on the other end of my line varied widely. There were bluegills, perch, pike, bass and lake trout all in this lake for the taking and I had one of those larger species on the end of my line. The drawback of being in an ice shanty is the fact that you are in close quarters with everything and the space for which you have to fight a large fish is extremely limited. Also, an ice fishing pole is small and rigged with a very light strength line as most of the fish caught are under 12-14' or so. Despite all of this, I fully intended to land my "sea monster" as it was the most excitement I had in hours. This fish was pulling like hell on my fishing line, and I went to loosen the drag on my reel in order to let this thing run a little bit to tire it out some before I started to attempt to reel it in. In the process of trying to release some drag, I lowered the tip of the ice fishing pole through the hole in the ice rather than have the fish snap my pole in two. Then, for reasons unclear to me to this very day, I simply let go of the pole. Remember the crystal-clear water I referred to earlier? This made it very easy for me to watch my pole go "swimming" away into the depths, fish, pole, spoon and all. Daryl looked at me, giggling away, and said "Did I really just see you let your pole go into the lake?" I was speechless. The pole wasn't outrageously expensive, and my ego was bruised far more than my wallet was. It was about time for all of us to go back to the cabin anyway. We took all our equipment down and proceeded to head back across lake towards the pickup truck. I somehow lost my footing on the ice and proceeded to do a back flip on the ice landing squarely on my back and the back of my head. Nothing seemed to be broken and we went back to the cabin. No fish were harmed during that excursion but as I was lying in bed later, still thawing out, I knew I was going to have a surprise for my wife when I got home.

In the 14 plus years I had been married to my wife, she had always hinted about how a dream of hers was to travel the United States and see some of it while she was still young enough to do so. I was not as excited about this as she was. That was only natural I suppose considering the miles I had put underneath my heels at that point. In addition, I loved my new Fowlerville house and had reconnected with all my friends and neighbors that I had associated with so many years before. It was also frightening to me the thought of being "homeless" or the feeling of not having that one place I could call "home" It's human nature to always think of one thing while traveling, "How much longer is it until we get home?" Is there really any better sensation than that feeling when you first walk back in the door of your house after a long trip? If you do not have a house, how do you ever feel at home? And worse yet, I wasn't getting any younger and what would happen if I really got sick or injured or something and was unable to perform the rigors of "living on the road?" Michelle had said many times in the past, "What happens if one of us gets injured or sick? Are we going to wish we had done this before for the rest of our lives?" I thought about that a lot, and it finally made sense to me. Home is wherever you are and as far as a house, once my house is sold and my VA mortgage paid off, we could always buy another house. And that house would not be in Michigan. Any state where a majority feels that their lives are worth more than individual liberty and freedom is no state I will ever be a permanent resident in. So, when I walked in the door, after that weekend on the ice, the first words out of my mouth to Michelle were "Call a realtor." You could have heard a pin drop and the look on her face was priceless. Of course, her first response was "Are you serious?" "Yes I am, were doing it!" She was so happy I thought she was going to break out in dance! I, on the other hand, was starting to feel the twinges of terror setting in. I always get like that when I'm about to plunge into something that there is really no plunging back out of. The sort of things like selling your house, everything you own, saying goodbye to everyone you know and hitting the highway.

One thing my lovely wife has always had though, is a soothing effect on me. It was safe to say that she knows me better than anyone else on the planet and I do believe she knew exactly how I was feeling at that moment. She said all the right things and once the proverbial "ball started rolling" with the realtor sign in the yard my apprehension started easing a little bit. Michelle had been thinking about this lifestyle change for quite a while and had done her homework. Her unwavering confidence in this certainly eased my fears tremendously. I thought at first it would be very hard to sell all the material things that I had spent a lifetime accumulating. I have always been a nostalgic kind of guy and many of the physical things that I owned also had a tremendous amount of sentimental value as well. I would have to adjust though due to the simple law of physics. That law is that you cannot put 2300 square feet of shit into a space of only 600 square feet. Pretty simple. The first thing you must do in a situation like this is to perform an inventory. Not necessarily an inventory of numbers, but of numbers, usefulness, sentimental value and so on. So, you pick an item up and ask yourself, "Do I or will I need this on the road?", then "Am I going to be heartbroken if I sell it?" or (more times than I care to recall) "How many of these do I have" Once I had determined that it was something that I could part with, it went to "the boss" (my wife naturally) to be plastered up on the Facebook marketplace page for sale. I had braced myself since the very beginning to the fact that I was probably going to lose my ass financially on these household items. It was truly a shock to discover that not only was I not “losing my ass” but I was getting almost as much in resale as I had paid for the items new. I must tell you, that took the “sting” out of selling all of this shit a great deal. Hard to be too brokenhearted when you’re standing there with a fist full of good hard cash. I was very surprised how quickly all this stuff sold. In the span of 30 days virtually everything I owned was sold. We had pared down all this household stuff down to the bare minimums of what we thought we could use in a 5th wheel. The biggest question was going to be the house. We had put a lot of time and equity from the 40 acres into that house and needed to recoup this in order to pursue this new dream. We still had a terrible heartache in regard to the financial shellacking we took on the house we sold in Farmington. The housing market was now completely opposite of the situation when we sold before. Unlike being the buyers at the “Top” of the market value, we were now the “sellers”. Not only was the market value at the extreme high end, but there was a tremendous shortage of properties available for sale anywhere. Our house went on the market late on a Thursday afternoon and by Saturday evening, we had entertained 11 shows and 3 offers, one of which we accepted. We did have another ten shows scheduled for that Sunday, but we already had an honest offer, which was $8000 over our asking price and honestly we were tired of the hassle of showing the house. In the space of 31 days, start to finish, everything we owned had been sold. We now had to decide on what type of unit we were going to live in on the road. This was another time Michelle’s research was a lifesaver. She knew all about “Class A” Class B” and “Class C”. types of motorhomes and trailers. One of my original concerns was feeling claustrophobic when all of this was done. I grew up in an overcrowded, stifling hot mobile home as a kid and had no intentions of living like that ever again. Now each class of motorhome has its own benefits and limitations. We had a couple of requirements that had to be met which would help narrow down our choices. The main requirement was to how to transport our motorcycles in addition to our home from point A to point B. One of the reasons we decided to do this was because of those motorcycles. Michelle and I both enjoy riding, and it just always seemed stupid to be living geographically in a place where you must keep your motorcycle in storage for around 6 months every year because of the weather. Another consideration for us was our pets. We had 2 dogs and 2 cats when we began this adventure and had to consider their welfare in all our plans. Then the question anyone contemplating this lifestyle must ask themselves "once we settle our home down how are we then going to get from Point A to Point B"? Now if you have a class A motorhome, you can either pull a car behind you (affectionately referred to as a "toad") or try to drive your 35' Winnebago into the McDonalds drive-through. We could have trailered our motorcycles behind a class A and maybe got by with one exception. If one of our pets got sick how would we get them to the veterinarian? We would also be limited to buying an amount of groceries as to what we could carry on motorcycles. Neither seemed like a great choices. Class C is the smaller motorhome type usually on a truck chassis. Most are under 30' and size alone would be prohibitive to us. Class B's are now the latest rage. These are the "zombie apocalypse" vans that are all self-contained. Naturally anything that is popular comes with a price tag to match. These fancy Class C's were no exception. Despite their size, the technology incorporated into them drove many of them into a price range of 6 figures. For us these were way too small anyways, and they cannot pull motorcycles behind them. This narrowed our choices down to either a standard pull-behind trailer or a 5th wheel. This made our choice easier yet. A pull-behind trailer generally will not come with a garage, and you cannot pull a second trailer behind a trailer in most states. Our perfect home would be in a 40' 5th wheel. We also would have to find one of those that had a garage in the back of it. With this kind of arraignment, we would have everything we needed!. We then purchased an awesome 3500 RAM with my old friend from my mechanic days a Cummings diesel in it. This would have plenty of power to spare with which to pull all this stuff with. Then, once we were set up on our location, we would have our bikes for fun, our 5th wheel to live in, and the pickup for the driving the pets, getting groceries and travelling during inclement weather. We quickly found our dream house in a lovely 2012 40' Keystone Fusion "Toy Hauler." The name was more than accurate. On Easter weekend 2022, leaving everything that held us solid down to the earth behind we were on our way!

Chapter 11 “Where does it end?”

I was immediately thankful that I had some experience as a truck driver in my past. Whizzing down the road with the better part of 9 tons behind you is not for the faint of heart. And of course, in good old Michigan style, we no sooner got 40 miles down the road and then a Spring blizzard was upon us. Now what most people do not realize is that getting 9 tons rolling along at 60 to 70 miles an hour is no big trick. Getting all that weight to stop when you need it to; now that can be tricky!. Technology, I have since discovered is not all bad. This is particularly where automotive technology is concerned. This was particularly evident when I flipped that cool assed button on my new Dodge Ram called the “Engine Brake.” Why slowing this beast may not be all as bad as I thought it would be. I guess one way or the other I would be finding out in a few short hours. We were now a few more hours down the road and hallelujah, the blizzard ended. We even got some sunny skies and things were looking up. Then came the city of Chicago, all 40 or 50 square miles of orange barrels, traffic, lanes under construction and fucking crazy people behind the wheel. Now 9 feet wide will seem like plenty of side-to-side room, that is if your ass is driving a Prius. When you’re in bumper-to-bumper traffic in a construction zone with your 9 ton, 10 feet wide, 52-foot-long vehicle sharing what amounts to only 3/4ths of a lane with a bleary eyed, sleep deprived truck driving psycho at 65 miles an hour it doesn't seem like all that much room. In addition to this, unbeknownst to my wife, I was having flashbacks like a bitch of driving in packed highways in Iraq maneuvering this monster through town. Of course, just having my life viciously re-arranged probably didn't help either but it was all good. A couple of hours, deep breaths, and white knuckles later, we were through the big city and headed out into the countryside. My wife had found us a beautiful spot in what was called "Bluff Country" in the fine state of Minnesota.

"Workkamping" was another relatively new term in the American lexicon. Although the word was new, the premise actually had been around since the great depression in the 1930's. A person, or family, would exchange a place to park their "home" and hook ups to water and electricity (after the year 1995 to be sure) in exchange for a certain number of hours performing a particular job. Michelle found us an especially nice arrangement in a place called "Hidden Bluff's" in Spring Grove, Minnesota. She had everything set up before we arrived, which was a great relief to me. My greatest, "new" fear was to arrive somewhere and have nothing waiting for us. One thing that the "dad" in me has always felt was important was being able to provide for my family in every regard. That meant keeping a roof over their heads, food to eat, having heat, air conditioning and so on. One great, unwritten, rule of Workkamping was that your "start date" was essentially when you arrived. This meant I did not have to be in any hurry to get anywhere. Most adults spend their entire working lives making sure, in one regard or another, that they are "on time." My greatest new discovery about retirement? The term "On time" now meant exactly when I arrived. I did not have to be in any hurry to get anywhere. If we were tired, we stopped. We could spend the night in any truck stop, or rest area or anywhere weary travelers could safely park their vehicles. Michelle and I had the extra bonus of not being financially strapped so when we were tired for the night we could afford to stay in a motel. Now a lot of people may wonder why we would rent a motel when we had a house attached to the back of our truck. It was simple, in a 5th wheel unless you extend all the slide outs and awnings and such it was virtually impossible to move around in. And one thing truck stops, rest areas and the like abhorred was people with 5th wheels and campers that set up "shop" in places that are supposed to be temporary halts. So, we would be on the lookout for Motel 6 locations or another favorite, Super 8. We chose these particular places because they were clean, they were cheap, they were everywhere, and they accepted pets. No matter how many miles in each "leg" of the journey we would take, there was nothing more relaxing than putting our rig back in the "trucker lot" getting all settled into a room, letting our doggies out and having a good shower in an air-conditioned room. A few short days, and long miles, later we had arrived at "Hidden Bluffs" for our first engagement as "Workcampers." The park was nice and most definitely in the country. We were about 10 miles from the nearest town of Spring Grove and almost 25 from any real place considered "civilization." It wasn't that Spring Grove was necessarily a bad place, just small. It had a gas station, a hardware store and an IGA grocery store. It has the distinct privilege of being the first Norwegian settlement west of the Mississippi river in America. They were all very proud of their

Norwegian heritage and had the museum to prove it. It was a wonderful museum, and the town was full of friendly folk. Three unique things Spring Grove did have was a brewery, distillery, and soda pop factory like no other. The distillery was one of the few totally organic and local bourbon distilleries in the country. The name of the distillery was the Rockfilter distillery, and their logo was "Very Independent Spirits." Now I have never been one of those tree hugger types of people and figured that so much of all that "organic" bullshit was just another method to reach into your wallet. Despite my thoughts, I must admit that this distillery had the best bourbon I have ever tasted in my life Their proprietary brand "Giants of the Earth" a title taken from a Norwegian folklore, is especially tasty. My wife, not being much of a liquor drinker, even enjoyed this establishment. They could turn these heavenly bourbons into what I like to call "floo floo drinks" to fit anyone's taste. I know that this place does ship their products across the country and know that I must order some here sooner than later. That's the bad part about moving every season, if you find a particular product, food, activity or location that you truly love you only have a limited amount of time to indulge your love affair. Another little establishment in Spring Grove I will always miss is a little brewery and diner called "Fat Pat's." The name was fitting because in addition to some incredible micro-brew made right on the premises, they had a barbecue sandwich and restaurant that was second to none. Surprisingly enough, this place was only open for food on Thursday and Friday evenings. Each of these evenings they could count on being packed full. We made a point to be there for our "goodies" at 4 pm sharp when they opened the door to make sure we could get our BBQ in a timely manner. If you arrived 30 or 40 minutes early it was ok too as they did start serving beer around 3 pm. Their fruit ales were especially wonderful. The other hidden taste gem in Spring Grove was the little shop that manufactured “Spring Grove Soda.” It was the best black cherry soda I have ever had. They also made this concoction called “Rhuberry” which was a mix of strawberry and rhubarb. Considering this has always been my favorite flavor of pie, being able to drink it out of a bottle was just as well. One thing you always had to remember about Spring Grove, like every small town in America, there is no such thing as “nightlife.” On weekdays everything closes around 6 pm, and on the weekends, the “late night” hotspot, the distillery, was only open until 11 pm. If you wanted more than that for entertainment you would have to drive the 25 miles or so to either Decorah Iowa or LaCrosse Wisconsin. Both were bigger towns with all the amenities you would expect. Now I have heard my whole life about how the south, or Texas was the “home of barbecue.” This my friends may be true as to the “home” but if you want the “best,” make a trip to that little corner where Minnesota, Iowa and Wisconsin come together. Go to “Bluff Country” it is worth the trip.

Now one thing Michelle and I always planned to get accomplished during this adventure was to see the sights and tourist attractions in each location we stopped in. Despite being in the “Land of 10,000 Lakes” Hidden Bluff’s doesn’t have a real bass lake within 30 miles of the damn place much to my dismay. What it did have was a river that went all the way around the campground which had the best trout fishing ever. I never left that river empty handed during the entire 6 months we spent there. Just put a small spinner on your line, cast across the river a few times and you could count on landing some brown trout between 7 and 14” long.

Not trophies to be sure, but the best on a dinner plate you could ask for. In addition, the drive anywhere was completely scenic and beautiful. It is called bluff country because it is in the Mississippi river valley. All the cliffs on either side of the mighty Mississippi river are beautiful. It reminded me a lot of the Black Hills area in South Dakota. While we were there, we went to the "Mall of America," down to the Mississippi river in LaCrosse and took one of their river cruises. We were always regulars at the best barbecue joints in all three states. When we left at the end of September we felt pretty good that we had experienced the best the area had to offer.

I must admit I have the best navigator, planner, and "Friend with benefits" a guy could ever ask for. That is my wife. She landed us a gig for that Winter in Southern Arizona. All Workkamping gigs are different in their arrangements from location to location. About the only common denominator for all of them is that you get to set your R.V. (Recreational Vehicle, or "home" in our case now) up free of charge. All other amenities besides that are negotiable. I guess that "hookup" is negotiable as well, as the number of hours and whether one or both of you would be required to work in exchange for the rent varies as well. it's important to note that the term "hookup" or F.H.U (full hook up) in my text refers to the lot, water, sewer and electricity for your R.V. It most certainly does NOT mean "casual sex" as the younger generation frequently uses that term for now. Now that I've cleared that up I can continue. In Minnesota we got a full hookup in exchange for one person, Michelle, working at least 20 hours per week. In addition, they also paid her a small salary for each hour worked as well. The internet service was free, as was the water and sewer. The electricity was not free, but we are given $120 per month credit towards any electric costs. We never even came close to using that much in Minnesota. In Arizona the arrangement was a little different. They have no paid positions for workkampers at the R.V. resort we stayed at except for the general manager and maintenance supervisor. That was still ok by us as we did not really require any more compensation to survive except for the free rent. Since they did not offer paid Workkamping, they required less hours in exchange for the F.H.U. Since these were also "volunteer" positions I was able to join Michelle at work. The water and sewer were free, and we were allowed $150 per month towards any electric costs. They did offer free internet, but the service was terrible, so we decided to spend the $30 per month for the premium service in order to "stream" our televisions. We only came close to using the electrical stipend the last month that we were there due to us needing to run some electric heaters. Despite being only around 40 miles north of the Mexican border, Southern Arizona had the coldest Winter on record for decades that winter we were there. I have pictures of 4 inches of snow on our motorcycles one cold morning. I even had to invest in an insulated water hose to prevent our water supply from freezing. Regardless of the weather, the positions Michelle and I held were wonderful. This R.V. resort was just that, a "resort" rather than simply a campground like Hidden Bluffs was. It had a great swimming pool, hot tub, recreation room complete with pool table, and an awesome banquet room to host "activities" in. Michelle and were part of that "activities" crew. We planned and helped set up for holiday parties for the major holidays, hosted bingo (for money, big sport in the "old folks" community) on Monday evenings, a monthly breakfast and a monthly celebration for everyone who had a birthday or anniversary during that month. Michelle was right up her alley, and was always great doing things like this! In addition to the variety of campers you meet along the way, the variety of workkampers and personalities of the folks you will work with can be broad as well. In Minnesota, we worked with a younger, diverse group of folks somewhat reminiscent of a carnival crew. Here in Arizona, despite there being no written age requirement, you did have the feeling that you were working in an "over 55" community. Everyone we worked there with was older, like me I guess you could say, but were in a lot different socioeconomic place in their lives than the crew in Minnesota. At Hidden Bluffs, most of the workers were younger and were trying to earn a living by Workkamping. There in Arizona, pretty much everyone was retirees like we were and had already earned their money in their careers. You could feel it in the general atmosphere there as it felt much more like "fun" and a lot less like "work."

Another huge difference in Arizona was that we were basically in the middle of the town of Benson. No longer did we have to embark on a two-hour adventure to go to the grocery store or civilization. We could simply walk out the gate and down the half block to the Safeway grocery on the corner. Better yet, right across the street from Safeway was a "Jack in the Box" restaurant. Now I had never been to one of these before, as they are not currently operating in Michigan, but I'll just say it's one more reason I'll never move back to Michigan. The food is great, and their breakfast burritos are to die for.

When we weren't doing our required 10 or so hours a week volunteering to pay for our keep, we could flop into the pool or hot tub and relax. We met some great folks there and made some long-term friends. An additional benefit was the wealth of knowledge these folks had regarding "living on the road" full-time. Unlike Minnesota where everyone just kind of came and went, these folks in Arizona were professional R.V.er's also commonly referred to as "full-timers" in the Workkamping community. I don't think that anyone that worked with us there really required an income to survive anyway. All of them were retired professionals who had their monthly pensions coming in, or as my friend used to refer to as "Mailbox money." This creates a completely different dynamic in a group of people. For starters, there is no real official starting time. People start their tasks when they wake up. That time varies widely depending on what the previous evenings social calendar had on it. I always thought I drank a lot, but there were folks in that group that I was not even in the same league of. To say the booze ran freely was an understatement, but despite that fact there were never any problems or arguments between anyone. I guess when everyone is in a place where they are happy and realize how blessed they are, there isn't too much to bitch about. Of course, there was some "cackling" between a few folks but all of it was harmless. There was a lot of things to see outside of Benson as well. One of the requirements that I personally had for each new location we went to was that we would be able to ride our motorcycles year-round. Now Benson Arizona is geographically located in what is referred to as the "high desert.' I believe Benson was at an elevation of just under 4000 feet and more than a few places we visited, and rode went over 8000 feet. One place close by we enjoyed was the Mount Lemmon recreational area. Mount Lemmon was at an elevation of almost 9000 feet up and it required taking a 20 mile, winding, curved, 20 mph road all the way to get to the top. It is worth the trip; the scenery and vistas are breathtaking. Pretty much every direction you looked in Benson you were surrounded by mountains. I will never forget the sunrises or sunsets there. We were also geographically in the middle of where the American "Wild West" events happened a hundred or so years ago. The original city of Tombstone was only 25 miles away and is a beautiful motorcycle ride from Benson. Naturally it has now been completely turned into a tourist trap, but it is still cool to go and experience it and listen to the stories. The best stories from the era were told to us by the operator of the horse-drawn carriage ride we took through the town. What trip to Arizona would be complete without a visit to the Grand Canyon? We were lucky enough to have our youngest daughter visiting with us, so it was a good time for a road trip. Driving on the way to the Grand Canyon we made a stop at a place probably everyone who has watched television in the last 20 years had seen. They may not be able to but tell you what or where it was, but would recognize it nonetheless. This place was officially called Meteor Crater. Fifty thousand years or so ago, a meteor the size of a house had slammed into the earth leaving a hole in the ground a couple of miles across and a mile or so deep. One thing I have discovered in all my travels was that most of these great and phenomenal locations are much less impressive in person than they are on the big screen. Mount Rushmore in the South Dakota hills is a prime example of this. Every photograph taken of it is taken at just the right angle to make it appear completely majestic and larger than life. Most people, like me, will think "That is it?" Meteor Crater is no exception upon first glance. Once you pay for your ticket, get through the great museum, and step outside onto the rim of the crater, your brain grapples with the thought, "Why this isn't so big." The people who designed the museum and location must have thought about this happening and came up with the perfect cure for that perceived disappointment. You see, Meteor Crater is not hyped up to appear bigger than it is, it is just simply that it is so large your mind cannot immediately grasp how big it really is. This is cured with installation of the small, free to use, field telescope that is mounted on top of the fence surrounding the crater. If you go to the scope, you'll notice a small sign next to it. The sign simply says "At the bottom of this crater there is a 6-foot mannequin dressed up as an astronaut, and it is holding a 3 foot by 5-foot American flag. You, at first, look down into the bottom and think "Oh bullshit, I don't see anything", but when you put your face up to the telescope and look down, then you can see that astronaut. It is at that very moment your mind reels and you start to grasp the true size of the crater. There is no such mystery at the Grand Canyon. It is huge, it looks huge, it feels huge and is every bit as majestic as every picture ever taken of it. We had the good fortune of visiting the canyon during the off-season and there were very few people there. Additionally, since the town of Williams Arizona we stayed in the night before is at an elevation of just under 8,000 feet, the temperature when we arrived at the Grand Canyon was only 14 degrees. This kept a lot of the masses of tourist humanity far away as well. Driving back from the canyon to our little homestead in Benson, I noticed a sign on the highway showing that the city of Winslow Arizona was only 22 miles away. Michelle thought I was crazy when I turned us around and headed towards it. The one thing I knew that Michelle did not, was the fact the town of Winslow Arizona had been made famous by the band "The Eagles" and their song "Take it Easy" 40 years or so earlier.

She had never even heard of the song, let alone the location of Winslow which is mentioned in it. It was one of the few times that the 13-year age difference between us was apparent. Upon arrival in Winslow, standing right on the corner (just like the song says) of the main street and Route-66 was a large bronze statue of Glenn Frey of "The Eagles" leaning against a post. There was also a great mural of the "Girl in the flatbed Ford slowing down....." on the wall behind it and a real 55 Ford Flatbed pickup truck parked at the curb. I've got great pictures of me with all of it, and naturally once we left to head home I knew there was one more, small thing that I had to do. I had to find that song on Sirius XM radio so Michelle could finally hear it and make the association. It was a great day, and just a few hours later we were tucked into our own bed again. Another thing I was excited about, while preparing for our Winter in Arizona, was the fact that I would finally be able to do some bass fishing. Yes, trout fishing was great in Minnesota, but never quite like the action casting your jig or "wacky rig" against the rocks or bank only to watch the fishing line start swimming away from you. Then, with a giant tug to set the hook, the fight is on. We had read in the brochures about Benson, while researching it as a potential winter homestead site, was that it was only 7 miles away from Willow Lake. Willow Lake, according to the Arizona Fish and Game department, was a small, shallow lake with great fishing action while catching sunfish, bluegills, small and largemouth bass. This was going to be wonderful. It was only about a week after our arrival that I figured it was time to go out and get some REAL fishing action going. With great excitement and fervor, I loaded my pole and tackle box into my truck and headed out towards the mountains and Willow Lake. I found it curious that there were not any signs in the area telling me where this lake might be. My curiosity turned to heartbreak as I discovered the one thing that the brochure failed to mention. This was the simple fact that the lake was completely privately owned. There were no public access locations on any single square inch of that shoreline. All I found in the location of the lake were all the private roads that I could only assume lead to the lake. On the intersections of each of these roads were the rows of mailboxes of the fortunate bastards who managed to own lakefront property in Arizona. It was looking like another season of having a lonely, lonely tackle box. A month or so later I did finally get to feel some vindication for the heartbreak I had suffered. While standing in line at Safeway, discussing this very issue with the teller, the lady standing me in the teller line behind me informed us that not only was Willow Lake all private, it was also all dried up. Those "lucky bastards" with their beautiful waterfront homes, all in my imagination of course, were currently living next to a 15-acre mud flat. I did finally get to do a couple hours of bass fishing at a reservoir near the Mexican border only 45 minutes or so away from our resort. I never got a bite, but it was still nice making the effort and standing on a lake. Although our resort did not have bass fishing, it did have one unique activity to participate in. This one thing the resort had, unlike any other resort in America to my knowledge, was its professional observatory set up. With the help of the two "Space Geeks" who volunteered to work on the equipment and host viewings each night, we were ready for a special treat. We got a chance to see Jupiter (and a couple of moons), Saturn (and the rings), a comet, a nebula, and a couple of stars close and personal. It was, for me in my life, another first as well as accomplishing something I had always wanted to do. The one thing that you can count on when you're staying busy is how fast the time goes by. It seemed like a flash and it was already April and the temperature was rising. This was our sign that another season had in fact ended and our time in Arizona was growing short. A few weeks later we "wrapped up" our home and had it latched back on the back of the truck.

Michelle did a fine job as she always does, finding us suitable locations for the next season. It is always a stressful time for me as it is the one time in my otherwise simple existence that a lot can go wrong. Vehicle breakdowns, traffic accidents, things getting broken in transit, and most of all, the thought of not having a place to "call home" All of that was quickly alleviated once we arrived at our new gig for the Summer the Snug Harbor resort. Snug Harbor resort is located in central California almost equidistant between San Francisco and Sacramento. Of course, when letting all my friends know we were going to be spending the Summer in California their opinions and advice came pouring out. One anecdote I have always remembered is "Opinions are like assholes, everybody has one" and that is a truly a fact. The funny part is that an overwhelming majority of these "helpful hints" were from folks who have never even been to California. Their entire understanding of California was based on what they had seen broadcast on the news over the years. As you can imagine, their opinions and the reality of life here vary widely.

We still could not figure out by looking at the map how a mere 700 or so mile trip could require 17 hours to get there. Hell, even with a fifth wheel attached I can go faster than 30 miles an hour. Didn't take long down the road to figure that out. Snug Harbor resort is smack dab in the middle of what is referred to here as the 'Delta Region" of California. It is called that because it is the river delta of the Sacramento River. This delta is the main water supply to the NAPA and Imperial Valley regions of California. These regions grow a tremendous percentage of the nation's vegetables, and virtually all the grapes for the wines produced in America. Normally, having been around the world, there isn't much in terms of things that I have never heard of, but here I began to discover a lot of them. The first of those things is a levee road. The delta is as much dredged waterways called sloughs (never heard of these before either) which are freshwater "rivers" bringing all the water from the mountains down into the valley while flowing on their way to the Pacific Ocean at San Fransisco Bay. Our resort is a small spur of land on the side of an island with the Steamboat Slough on one side, and a small dead-end estuary on the other side. Our "home" is backed right up to the estuary side and if I dropped our patio down off the back end, I would be sitting over the water. This place could not be more beautiful and the variety of wildlife I have seen here I have never had the opportunity to see before. There are two ways to get on this (Ryer) island, and only one if your pulling a 5th wheel. The first way is to take the levee roads. The only way I can describe this is to call them a "paved dirt road." They do have posted speed limits of up to 50 mph, but on any of them if you are going faster than 40 you are taking your life in your hands. If you are pulling a trailer, you will probably not go faster than 25 mpg. The 17 hours estimated arrival time was now making perfect sense. If you are not pulling a trailer, AND are lucky enough to have them be operating, there are two ferries that will shuttle traffic across Steamboat Slough. This little boat ride shaves a minimum of 40 minutes of driving on those levee roads. There is so much to see at this location there is no way we will catch all the sights here. We have gotten through both of our prior locations with the satisfaction that we did visit at least the biggest attractions. We're going to try our very best to see all of the tourist attractions and natural beauty here though. Our 2nd youngest daughter came out to spend a week with us and we did a little of that sightseeing. Before she arrived we did check out the biggest tourist attraction on my wife's list and made a trip to San Francisco and the newly opened Alcatraz prison. I'm glad that it reopened so we could visit. It had been closed for a couple of decades and after a small "takeover" by a local Native American Tribe, it was finally acquired by the United States Park Service. The U.S. Park Service then turned the historical site into a National Park. While our daughter was here we took a two-day road trip and went to see the cities of Carmel by the Sea, and Big Sur. Both these locations, as well as the famous Route 1 used to get there, are regarded as being some of the most beautiful places on earth. Another perk of this trip was the beach located at Carmel by the Sea. On the south end of that beach is the famous golf course Pebble beach, and on the north are some of the most expensive houses on the planet. When we are not sightseeing, Michelle is working full-time and making some good extra money. I am currently spending my days taking care of our home, Michelle, and volunteering around the park. And much to my happiness, lots of fishing. The bass fishing has been great! Although there are largemouth, smallmouth and striped bass here, the vast majority of what I have been catching is striped bass. These are great, they get huge, fight hard and give me that good old bass excitement. Now I could ramble on for pages regarding my current location but then brevity has never been one of my strong suits. I am 58 years old and here I am for the foreseeable future. Despite my experiences, life is good, and I am blessed more than I deserve to be. So that's this "Soldier's Story" so far.

Yes, war and conflict made a huge impact on my life, but that experience is still just a side note to a much greater story. Unlike so many other servicemembers all over the globe, I refuse to let my experiences as a Soldier be the complete definition of my life.

EPILOGUE:

Well, as I've always said it's been a hell of a run. I still have my days and my moods as I guess everyone does. As much as everyone likes to think they are so different and unique, in reality all people are pretty much the same. The only really thing different about me, the reason I felt I was unique enough to write a book anyway, was the myriad of experiences I have had the good fortune to enjoy. My buddy Ron told me the first week or so after I "retired" that "You wait a year or two, you'll be bored stiff." That has not been the case at all. In fact, I wonder how I had time to get anything done all those years I was punching the clock. I am fortunate enough to have a great relationship with my other kids and they are a great source of inspiration and joy to me. We lean on each other quite a bit and it comes in handy. I was having one of my moods and decided to lean on my oldest daughter a little bit to shake the doldrums. After unloading that emotional burden and hoping the gloom would pass somehow she simply told me, "Dad, you've been through some fucked up shit, you are entitled to have a bad day or two." That alone gave me a completely renewed sense of balance, a smile, and suddenly the blues didn't quite seem to blue.

Another thing I have always told anyone who was interested, "If the good Lord struck me dead this moment, I could go through the gates with no regrets, I have squeezed every ounce that life has to offer in the 58 years I have been blessed with so far." Don't get me wrong, I am by no means finished and ready to throw in the proverbial "towel", but my